To Sushil
and family
with affection

New Delhi
13 November, 2000

Restructuring South Asian Security

Restructuring South Asian Security

Major General Vinod Saighal

Manas Publications
New Delhi-110 002 (India)

MANAS PUBLICATIONS
(Publishers, Distributors & Exporters)
4819/XI, Varun House, Mathur Lane,
24, Ansari Road, Darya Ganj,
New Delhi - 110 002 (INDIA)
Ph.: 3260783, 3265523, 3984388
Fax: 011 - 3272766
E-mail: manaspublications@vsnl.com

©Major General Vinod Saighal

First Published 2000

ISBN 81-7049-121-5

No part of this publication can be reproduced, photocopied, translated, etc. in any form whatsoever, without prior written permission of the publisher.

The views expressed in this book are those of the author and not necessarily of the publisher. The publisher is not responsible for the views of the author and authenticity of the data, in any way whatsoever.

Typeset at
Manas Publications

Printed in India at
R.K. Offset, Delhi
and Published by Mrs. Suman Lata for
Manas Publications, 4819/XI, Varun House,
Mathur Lane, 24, Ansari Road, Daryaganj
New Delhi 110002 (INDIA)

Dedication

The Book is dedicated to the India of my dreams.

Preface

Old soldiers don't die. They simply fade away. After nearly four decades of active military service the temptation to get away from it all was becoming too great to resist. Except that while I was pondering over the matter my mind kept going back to the time, not long after Independence, when I opted for a career in the Army. I was very young when I made the decision, the Republic of India even younger. What I do recall from those days was that the famous words about "India keeping its tryst with destiny", spoken from the ramparts of the Red Fort a few years earlier, still redounded in our young ears.

As I hung up my spurs I failed to detect even the faintest echo of that stirring oration amongst the political elite of the country – the leaders who would take India into the next millennium. Our dreams lay shattered. Strife was everywhere. Poverty and hunger stalked the land. The *sadhus* and *fakirs* had also forsaken religion and joined the fray. The land of Buddha, Mahavira and the Mahatma could rejoice to Ram *or* Rahim but not to Ram & Rahim.

I was deeply troubled by the sight of what I beheld.

What follows is a compilation of thoughts, talks, articles and essays from an old warrior who decided to soldier on.

Major General Vinod Saighal

Editors Note

The issues covered in the book span a remarkably wide spectrum of disciplines from the strategic issues facing the subcontinent (& the world) to demography. Many of these chapters have been original formulations and have had an appreciable impact on policy making within this country (and elsewhere). However, the final result on the ground, which is mired in the negative spiral of politics, corruption and criminalisation and not in the positive spiral of good governance, hope and destiny fulfilled, is not yet discernible.

The sections within the book are arranged in strictly chronological sequence. Besides the articles, each section includes at least one talk delivered by the author. The original nature of the talk has been preserved in order to retain the immediacy of the issues.

Mudita Mehta and Monish Verma (M&M)

List of Acronyms

ASEAN	Association of South East Asian Nations
BIMARU	Bihar, Madhya Pradesh, Rajasthan, Uttar Pradesh (Indian provinces)
CAR	Central Asian Republics
CBI	Central Bureau of Investigation
CEO	Chief Executive Officer
CTBT	Comprehensive Test Ban Treaty
ECM	Electronic Counter Measures
FDI	Foreign Direct Investment
ICJ	International Court of Justice
IIPS	International Institute of Population Sciences
LNG	Liquified Natural Gas
MAD	Mutually Assured Destruction
MDT	Modified Disarmament Treaty
NAM	Non Aligned Movement
NATO	North Atlantic Treaty Organisation
NCC	National Cadet Corps (India)
NFHS	National Family Health Survey (India)
NGO	Non Governmental Organisation
NPT	(Nuclear) Non-Proliferation Treaty
NTF	National Task Force
ONGC	Oil & Natural Gas Commission (India)

PRC	Peoples' Republic of China
R&D	Research & Development
SAARC	South Asian Association for Regional Cooperation
SOFA	Status of Forces Act
TNC	Trans National Corporation
UNCTAD	United Nations Conference on Trade and Development
USSR	Union of Soviet Socialist Republics
WTO	World Trade Organisation

Contents

Preface 7
List of Acronyms 9

Section-I
International Affairs

1. Taiwan Straits Stand Off: The Aftermath 16
2. A Blow for the World 20
3. Looking Beyond CTBT to a MDT 24
4. Eastward Expansion of NATO 30
5. From Economic Intelligence to Strategic Intelligence 34
6. Dealing with China in the Twenty-First Century 57

Section-II
Subcontinental Affairs

Introduction
7. A Farewell to Arms 81
8. Leadership in the Army 85
9. National Security: The Dangerous Drift Must Stop 89

10. Force Multiplication at the Intermediate and Lower Ends of the Technology Spectrum	94
11. India's Security Imperative	103
12. Restructuring the Armed Forces	107
13. Subcontinental Realities at the Turn of the Century	124
14. Strategic Challenges for India in the Third Millennium	143
15. Remoulding the Subcontinent	154

Section-III
Ecology

Introduction	
16. Ending the Menace of Poaching	177
17. Ecotone Restoration	180
18. Ecological Revival of the Planet	184
19. Revitalised Ganga Action Plan	196
20. Demilitarisation of the Himalayas	199

Section-IV
Demography

Introduction	
21. Population Problem in India	206
22. Doomsday Clock Ticks Away	222
23. Defusing the Population Bomb	227
24. For Operation Population	231

Section-V
Constitutional Reforms

Introduction
25. Model for the Restoration of Good Governance — 236
26. Proliferation of the Bihar Model of Governance — 244
27. Ghettoisation of the Political Elite — 250
28. Revitalisation of Indian Democracy: Transitional Modes — 255
29. Marginalisation of the Indian Voter — 271
30. Appeal to the Parliamentarians of the 13th Lok Sabha — 274

Section-VI
Trauma and Critical Care

Introduction
31. Global Perspectives of Trauma and Disaster – 21st Century — 279
32. Understanding the Nature of the New Societal Traumas — 284
33. Traffic Accidents: Driven to Disaster — 291

Index — *297*

Section-I
International Affairs

1. Taiwan Straits Stand Off: The Aftermath
2. A Blow for the World
3. Looking Beyond CTBT to a MDT
4. Eastward Expansion of NATO
5. From Economic Intelligence to Strategic Intelligence
6. Dealing with China in the Twenty-First Century

Taiwan Straits Stand Off: The Aftermath

The Chinese do not have a penchant for adventurism. Whatever they undertake is generally well thought out and fits into their long-term plans. Hence they must not have been unaware of their relative military capabilities vis-a-vis Taiwan and the United States of America. The post-Deng succession struggles notwithstanding, there is an essential continuity in Chinese policy. To many observers around the world the Chinese military demonstrations would seem to have had an opposite effect-that of stiffening the Taiwanese resolve. It would certainly lead to increased military spending on the part of Taiwan and several Asian neighbours; increases of a type that would ensure unacceptable retaliatory damage on the Chinese mainland. Have the Chinese miscalculated?

Maybe not. Maybe their action in the Taiwan Straits has a deeper meaning, There could perhaps be a hidden agenda. At a later stage trade-offs between the superpowers might be in the offing. However cynical that might sound, the world should have shed all illusions after the Gulf War. Whatever its motivation China has thought fit to announce, in as dramatic a fashion as possible, that it has arrived; and that it is not content to wait till the next century to be counted as a superpower, possibly at par with the USA. It wants the world at large to take note of, and Asia in particular to comprehend, the new reality.

Taiwan Straits Stand Off: The Aftermath

There is no tentativeness in the manner of China's announcement. Irrespective of the final outcome of the confrontation the ground reality stands irrevocably altered, not only for China's Asian neighbours but for the world at large. It really does not matter as to who blinked first or whether there was a need for anybody to have blinked. New power equations are already taking shape. These require to be looked at more closely.

To begin with, ASEAN will have to re-evaluate an entire range of options, both military and economic. Japan's role could possibly get diminished in Asia and the world. By continuing to put itself exclusively under the US military umbrella, well after it could afford to look after its own defence, it prospectively abridged its freedom of manoeuvre. No doubt it became an economic superpower but even economic superpowers have to face military realities. In fact, the economic surge of several other Asian tigers has already taken the lustre off Japan's unique economic position of yesteryear. The Pacific Rim nations will be forced to hasten decisions that they hoped could be pushed to the opening decades of the next century. Australia has already started making fresh economic overtures to India. Much closer cooperation between the navies of the two countries might well be in the offing. Indonesia, Malaysia and Singapore too would consider closer ties with India in the economic and military spheres. These moves will be dictated by the need for abundant caution. Regional threat perceptions, based on physical insecurity, are quite distinct from global economic linkages. No non-Asian power will henceforth care to get mired in an Asian conflict of the Korean or Vietnamese type.

India too will have to take note of the altered military reality. Taking pains to arrive at sensible accommodations with its giant neighbour is one thing. Allowing military disparity of a nature that will mortgage the future of coming generations to develop is quite another thing. The first aspect bespeaks statesmanship of a high order. The second betokens an unpardonable lapse on the part of the country's defence planners. It has nothing to do with lack of resources for defence. It has everything to do with 'wrong' equipment priorities and an "unrealistic" appraisal of the military realties. (The military capability being developed by China is awesome enough for even USA, Russia and Japan to view with disquiet.) It is still not too late for India to attempt to make up for decades of neglect in this vital field. An "independent" National Security Council has to be set up immediately to review the entire gamut of security options; and for recommending steps for immediate narrowing – closure will now be impossible for a long time to come – of the (security) vulnerability gap. The emphasis will have to be on self-reliance. Leaning over backwards to further US interests will add to, and not diminish India's insecurity. India must assess its own interests independently. Irrespective of China's actions in the Taiwan Straits, India should not allow itself to become a party to US containment of China.

What has been considered so far are regional issues which, although affecting the world at large, have a greater import for China's neighbours. There are many other issues resulting from the confrontation in the Taiwan Straits that call for urgent deliberations at international fora. An immediate fall-out in the latter category relates to the CTBT. It would seem to have been overtaken by events. Linked to the reported transfer of nuclear technology by China to Pakistan the bottom would seem to have been knocked out of the foundation on which the US proposal rested. Whatever the perceptions of individual countries the tenor of the debate would change considerably.

The most important lesson to emerge from the Taiwan Straits happenings is the irrelevance of the Security Council in confrontations between superpowers, between nuclear weapon states, or any confrontation which the major powers embark upon. Flare-ups of a similar nature on the part of other countries would have invited strong denunciations, charges of irresponsible behaviour or the wrath of the Security Council. In the present case there was a relative hush. This quietude, resulting from a trepidation at the mere thought of a clash amongst the titans, presents an ideal opportunity to take a fresh look at the make-up of the Security Council. This august body needs to be re-cast for meeting the needs of the world as a whole rather than the compulsions of nuclear monopolists. Once again, it becomes starkly clear that in almost every situation where the world is really threatened with potential catastrophe "on a global scale" the Security Council has no role to play.

Strange as it may sound the ultimate outcome of a potentially world-sized crisis might, in the final analysis, be decided by the election compulsions of individuals rather than any rational thinking on the part of world leaders. The Taiwan Straits crisis has given the world an opportunity to look dispassionately at a host of issues which have been brushed under the carpet due to coercive diplomacy. What a strange way of moving into the next millennium.

2

A Blow For The World

India's unequivocal rejection of the CTBT in its present form is not only on behalf of the people of India, but also on behalf of the billions of ordinary human beings around the world who might not even have heard of fission or fusion – the silent majority who find no representation at a conference that would condemn the world to a perpetual vertical spiral, way beyond the MAD madness of the cold war years.

In declining to once again succumb to coercive diplomacy India's lone appeal is an appeal to reason. It is an appeal for sanity. Shorn of the scientific and diplomatic doublespeak which has appeared in learned tomes on the subject, the essence of the CTBT that is sought to be locked in place in accordance with the worldview of Washington can be simply stated as follows: "the most powerful nation in the world, which is light years ahead of all other nations in military, scientific and technological might, does not wish to consider any form of disarmament reduction proposals for making the world a slightly safer place." The logic is perverse, it is irrational.

It is the irrationality of its position that has led the most militarily secure nation in the world to single-handedly snuff out the faint glimmer of a nuclear-free world in the next century. Is this really the outcome that the proponents of the Treaty (in its present form),are looking for? Will it not have just the opposite effect? Unless there is a common goal towards which humanity is perceptibly headed, it is only a matter of time before secret laboratories mushroom all over the world. Perverseness creates its own warped logic. If the strongest power that the world has ever known continues to put its might and money into more terrifying forms of global destruction, no treaty in the world can prevent the rest of the world from following the leader. This is where reason has taken a back seat. Unless the dialogue is brought back to a more rational plane, the world can never become a safer place. The only thing that a treaty without a tangible disarmament schedule will lock into place, till well into the next century, will be the mad experimental urge for the next set of global military competitors experimenting with destructive systems that defy analysis; systems that have no danger of being replicated by any so-called rogue state or terrorist organisation, "unless the genie is first released from the bottle in the super laboratories of the super proliferators."

It is still tempting to speculate on all that could have been achieved if the US, at this defining moment in world history, had produced a leader of Lincolnesque stature and vision. Had that been the case, America would by now have worked out a comprehensive blueprint for universal nuclear disarmament; and shepherded the world in that direction using and not abusing the intellect and vigour of a great nation. Nearer our time, even a Roosevelt would have used the unique opportunity provided at the end of the cold war to show the world a completely different way, the direction in which the world was instinctively headed till the military industrial complex of just two or three nations, representing a miniscule portion of the ruling elite of those countries, pushed the world back in the direction of the abyss from which, at last, it seemed to have found its way back. Sadly for the world, the leaders of USA today are in the mould of neither Lincoln nor Roosevelt. This is certainly not the road to salvation that the nations should be following as they march into a new millennium.

This new post-cold war madness has not yet taken hold of all segments of the societies of nations with the most advanced destructive military systems. The hysteria has not yet again been whipped up to a crescendo to drown the voice of sane elements. These elements must come to the fore and push aside the handful of people who are misleading the world at large; as well as their own people. A simple test, conducted right in the heart of America can be used to decide the outcome. Let 20 or 30 Nobel Prize winners (those whose credentials as true-blooded Americans are impeccable) be given unhindered access to all the secret weapons research being undertaken in the USA. After that, let the Pentagon, the state department and the national security agencies give them the full measure of their (justificatory) dose – of the type reserved for the Senate while soliciting funds or for new Presidents when they come to the Oval office. After that, let the Nobel laureates express their opinion.

The scope for the reasonableness of this other world view can be tested further to cover the entire spectrum of the nuclear haves. The future of the next generation is being decided, almost-exclusively by governing military hierarchies, whose top decision-makers would invariably be well past their prime. How many younger people, or even people in their thirties or forties, would be involved in the decisions regarding the survival of the next generation. Here we come to the next test, a more universal test.

Let us take ten universities at random in any of the states possessing nuclear weapons. Let a panel of experts in each of these countries prepare a resume of the arguments being put forward by their representatives at Geneva against incorporating a clause for reduction of nuclear weapons in a time bound manner. The lone country holding out (India) would send another panel to present the rationale for its stand at Geneva. At the end of the presentations, let the student bodies and the teaching faculties in the selected universities give their vote in the presence of neutral observers. Does anyone have any doubt as to the outcome?

This would expose objections of the treaty negotiators at Geneva to India's plea for incorporating a clause for a time bound elimination of nuclear weapons.

India does not have to go on the defensive for holding out for the future safety of well over 99.9 per cent of humanity. "India is not isolated at Geneva. It is the handful of negotiators of a handful of nuclear weapons states holding on to an indefensible agenda who stand isolated."

No matter what the inducements or threats, India owes it to the world to veto a CTBT which comes without reckonable disarmament clauses, in definable time frames. The matter is so vital for the future of the human race that even in the case of India being offered a permanent seat in the Security Council and access to the latest missile and nuclear technology, the answer would still have to be a ringing 'No' to any private trade-offs.

Looking Beyond CTBT to a Modified Disarmament Treaty(MDT)

The Indian stand at Geneva in the second half of June 1996 has effectively helped to bury CTBT in its present form. It is a reprieve for the world. It gives humanity a vital second chance to go in for "meaningful" nuclear disarmament in this century itself. Now that the artificially-engendered frenzy of a deadline is over, the whole world, irrespective of earlier positions, can examine afresh whether the CTBT was being propelled in the right direction.

It is indeed sad that one of the most important lessons of history was being ignored by the framers of the Treaty. History tells us that unequal treaties, even between victor and vanquished, are doomed to failure as they carry within themselves the seeds of future discord. Here we are not talking of victor and vanquished but of sovereign nations mortgaging of their own volition their future security, in perpetuity, to a handful of Nuclear Weapon States (NWS) without any tangible concessions from the latter: to eschew research into deadlier forms of global destruction and a timetable for phased reduction. The irrationality displayed is on the part of one hundred and eighty sovereign nuclear have-nots (for countenancing such a lopsided treaty) and not on the part of the five NWS who hold the world to ransom.

The first aspect to be considered is whether the nuclear have-nots are negotiating from a position of strength or weakness. Should they go to the NWS with a timid plea for a return to sanity or should they "demand" of them, in the name of humanity, that they listen to the voice of reason. Conceivably, the have-nots have yet to recognise their strength: perhaps for the first time in the history of the race there is a global consensus – a universal abhorrence of the nuclear monster.

A careful study of the power structures in the more important Capitals would reveal that in the world there are not more than a few thousand people who "actively" fuel the arms race. Even if this figure were to be multiplied by a factor of ten or one hundred, it would still not give an answer to the question as to how nearly five thousand million human beings were allowing such an infinitesimally small number to lead them towards a future which should cause grave concern to all inhabitants of the planet. Such a state of haplessness is an insult to the intelligence of every individual. It is a "negation of the collective will of mankind".

At the next meeting of the Conference on Disarmament the NWS have to be given notice that there can be no Treaty unless they are ready to start the dismantling process in a time bound programme; that the citizens of the world "demand" that no fresh research be undertaken for the production of nuclear weapons. Whatever else be the aims of the Conference, it should give a call for the mobilising of all universities in the world to launch an universal "satyagraha" to rid the world of the monster that threatens their children's tomorrow.

Fortuitously for the world an impasse was reached at Geneva at the end of June 96. A fresh look at the way in which this most important nuclear disarmament conference was being conducted has highlighted a glaring omission. While individual countries are represented at disarmament conferences there is no representation for the Planet Earth or mankind as a whole (a few hundred disparate NGOs hanging around do not fit the bill). It is folly to believe that individual nations are capable of looking beyond their noses. Not only are they not capable of looking after the interest of the globe they often end up sacrificing their own national interest to the election compulsions of individuals or the stranglehold of global "patrons".

The setting up of a permanent World Nuclear Council (WNC) then becomes the first order of business. Such a Council would comprise fifteen respected world citizens from all walks of life who stand out for their commitment to humanity – way beyond narrower national or regional interests. The WNC members would be nominated for a single six year term, except for the first Council members whose term would vary between six to ten years, depending upon the replacement pattern. One-third of them would be replaced by fresh members every two years after the first Council has completed its initial tenure. Since the composition of the WNC could prove to be contentious several methodologies allowing for global participation could be thought of for preparing the panel for the first WNC. One way could be to nominate two of the most respected universities from each of the UN member states. In the case of countries with extremely small populations only one university would be selected by the UN Secretary General. The next step would be for the heads of these universities, in consultation with their academic faculties, to suggest three names of people considered the most suitable in the world to be nominated as members of the first WNC. The panel of approximately five hundred names thus obtained would be reviewed by the General Assembly of the UN for final selection of 15 WNC members. There are several alternatives for further refining or fine tuning the selection process. Thereafter, the WNC itself, in consultation with the UN Secretary General, would decide on the replacement members every two years. It would be noticed that the Security Council has no special role to play in this democratic process which involves the whole world.

The charter of WNC would include, inter alia:

* To act as an independent watchdog and moderator on behalf of the UN General Assembly at all disarmament negotiations involving more than two parties.

* In case of an impasse to present independent proposals.

* To publish independent data representing the WNC viewpoint for dissemination to governments, global media and universities throughout the world.

* To prepare blueprints for one to one accession to model disarmament treaties between individual nations and the UN. Conditionalities for automatic accession at some future date in the event of certain specified happenings could also be appended.

* To evolve modalities for neutral monitoring by personnel whose credentials would be considered impeccable by all parties.

* To evolve mechanisms for assumption of residual nuclear stockpiles in the interim between the initial accord to the Modified Disarmament Treaty (see below) and final disarmament. Since the time between the initial accord and complete nuclear disarmament could take years or even decades, modalities for Standstill Agreements to cater for the concerns of current super NWS to maintain their "qualitative" force advantage against several million strong conventional armies that could be mobilised

by the emerging powers of the next century will have to be taken into account for a period varying from ten to twenty five years. During this period contingencies for release of limited nuclear weapons to aggrieved parties (NWS) for restoring unacceptable imbalances, *in extremis*, purely as a defensive measure, could be built into the MDT.

In as far as it relates to the re-drafted text of the CTBT the non nuclear weapon states should issue a statement from their respective capitals that they would hereafter be a party to CTBT only if it incorporates the simple provisions of the MDT as follows: (a) categorical assurances from the NWS for the immediate cessation of all further laboratory testing of nuclear weapons technologies; (b) time frames for total disarmament; (c) consequent upon these stipulations being met by the NWS the three threshold nuclear weapon states would agree to immediate Standstill Agreements as a prelude to complete nuclear disarmament; (d) all remainder non-nuclear states would automatically accede to the Treaty thereafter. Any contentious issues relating to inspections, monitoring and the like which remain unresolved would be submitted to the WNC for final arbitration. Once accord has been reached on the basic principles outlined in the MDT there should be no question of the Treaty being held up on account of minor differences on the footnotes.

No treaty concluded between sovereign nations, which aims to prevent the imperilment of the planet, should contain any "opting-out-of-the-treaty" clause on grounds of supreme national interest. As it goes into the next century the world cannot allow the special interest of an handful of people or any one set of people to jeopardise the future of mankind as a whole. When relating to globally destructive systems (or activities) the plea of "supreme national interest" becomes untenable. If there has to be a (temporary) exception to this caveat it should apply to the weakest nations on the globe. It cannot apply to nations who have the wherewithal to devastate the globe.

This is as good a time as any to go into the manner in which globally applicable treaties are negotiated, especially in areas where the future of mankind is at stake. It is seen that statesmanship and diplomacy have declined to a level where they no longer command respect. Coercive diplomacy and duplicity must now yield their place to sober and straightforward negotiations that restore goodwill and harmony between nations. A just treaty which is "genuinely" perceived to be fair will be respected by the vast majority of nations and peoples of the world. Such a treaty has every chance of holding till appropriate governance models which cater to the looming global crises of the next century are established. A treaty which is *ab initio* suspect, even amongst its most vocal proponents, will founder on the reef of global disenchantment.

Eastward Expansion of NATO: The Third Climactic of the Twentieth Century?

A great paradox comes to mind when one thinks of Western Europe in the new world order. of the twenty-first century. The question that surfaces, first and foremost, is whether the core nations, the prime movers as well as the prime intellectual shapers of the concept of a great European Community, will be able to retain their individual identities once the larger grouping is fully in place.

Not many people in Europe, or elsewhere for that matter, question the ineluctable need for a United Europe. The European Union might even be an economic and geopolitical necessity in the next century – both for itself and in the interest of a more balanced world order.

It would hardly be an exaggeration to state that without the core nation's initiatives, and even persistence, the process of European unification may not have started in the twentieth century, now coming to a close. The dream of a United Europe had fired the imagination of European thinkers, statesmen and military leaders well before the coalescence actually began to take shape after the Second World War. The difference being that earlier attempts were predicated on unification by military force.

Although the establishment of the European Community came about by voluntary action on the part of the states of Western Europe there is an exquisite irony in the manner in which the union was forged: an irony that would make the spirit of that military genius Napoleon Bonaparte shake with mirth. It would perhaps induce a *frisson* in the pale ghosts of Stalin and his successors at the thought that whatever anyone might say at this stage, the European Community, was founded to a large extent on military pacts and because of military pacts. This requires elaboration.

Supposing that at the end of the World War in 1945 there was no military threat from the Soviet Union, would the NATO military alliance still have come about? It can be argued that the impetus for the European Union which was, and still is, a "Western" European Union came initially from the limited economic grouping already in place at the core as well as the military coalition that had been established. Not unsurprisingly, the pattern is being repeated in the final years of the twentieth century. The Eastward expansion of the European Community is still being "piggy backed" on the Eastward expansion of NATO. The question that needs to be addressed by all Europeans is whether the military dimension is submerging the other dimensions that enrich the cultural identity of nations and societies.

The dismembered entities of the Soviet Union can hardly pose a military threat to Western Europe in the conventional sense of that threat as it was understood when the military power of the Soviet Union was at its height. Russia still has the nuclear capability to take on the West or anyone else for that matter and destroy the world. While it can devastate the globe with nuclear weapons, conventionally it cannot even tackle Chechnya, leave alone Europe, now or in the foreseeable future. Therefore, it becomes necessary for the democracies of Western Europe as distinct from the military hierarchies of NATO, to sit back and take stock of the situation. By giving greater weightage and overriding priority to the military expansion in Central Europe "prior to" an economic union these same military hierarchies could again be endangering lasting peace and stability in Europe. France, Germany, Belgium the Netherlands and Italy should realise this better than anyone else.

The forces that have come to the fore in Europe are perhaps (and not so inadvertently either) forcing the military machine in Russia to regain its primacy. Surely another arms race would be the last thing that the people of Western Europe desire. And yet, the present policies of their leaders, possibly under intense pressure from the other side of the Atlantic, are leading exactly to a situation similar to the one that obtained in Europe after the First and Second World Wars. Apparently they have not learned any lesson from the ravages caused by those earlier wars. Did not their people suffer enough? One begins to wonder whether the intellectuals of Europe have opted out. Do they still exist?

It is tempting to speculate as to what the shape of Europe, perhaps the whole world, would have been if the end of the Second World War had not signalled the division of Europe into military blocs; which in turn led to the 'bloc-isation' of the whole world, i.e. the Western bloc, the Communist bloc, and the Non Aligned bloc. Having barely got out of one military confrontation (the War itself) the leaders of the victorious powers rushed headlong into another formidable military confrontation. Had there been, at that time, a greater intellectual ferment, pushing for a more liberal, interactive and humanistic approach to the configuration of the new world order for the second half of the twentieth century, the world could have been going into the twenty-first century with greater hope for the future of mankind. This obviously did not happen. Such liberal interaction did not take place. The intellectual ferment on both sides of the divide was quelled with unmitigated ferocity. Even the middle ground was usurped by governing hierarchies that simply could not get out of the military confrontation mind-set.

This mind-set continues to prevail in the post Cold War era.

Thrice in this century, the statesmen of the great powers, who had it in their grasp to shape the destiny of the world, failed to rise to the occasion. The first time was after the First World War; the second time the opportunity arose after the Second World War; the most recent opportunity was when the Berlin wall came tumbling down. Leaders who could have been great players ended up by becoming bit-players. They either lacked stature or vision, or both.

We have to consider another possibility. The possibility can be worded in the form of a hypothesis which states that the continued ascendance of the military industrial complex in Europe over several decades which in human terms translates into a three generation continuum, has led to an intellectual stagnation in Europe; that when successive generations of Europeans (and Europe in its true sense stretches from the Atlantic to the Urals) rose phoenix-like from the ashes of the two great climactics of the first half of this century, they thoughtlessly traded the weapons of the intellect for weapons that could annihilate mankind all over the world.

The eastward expansion of NATO is a global concern. It could conceivably trigger off a fresh arms race. At the very least it would exacerbate tensions. Fissures that could have been papered over could again congeal into permanent divides. Mutual suspicion could bring back the era of hidden hatreds barely disguised under surface civilities. Another historical opportunity at global harmonisation is being missed in the lifetime of the twentieth century – our century. As at the turn of the last century the global decision-makers are primarily the leaders of the Western world, this could turn out to be, their last chance in world history to usher in an harmonious world order. Can they measure up to the challenge – and the opportunity?

From Economic Intelligence To Strategic Intelligence

While the subject of this article would appear to be relatively new for India and the developing countries, the dominant society in the Western World learned its intricacies long ago. It would hardly be an exaggeration to state that a clear grasp of the progression from economic intelligence to strategic intelligence to world dominance was a linchpin in the march of the leading Western powers to global ascendancy in the half-century that followed the end of the Second World War. As an example, the concerned US agencies spent almost as much effort in estimating annual Soviet grain production in some years as on the adversary's military might. In this day and age the importance of this co-relation could be at par with the two super components of global dominance: military might and economic might.

It is not as if well-informed people in India and the developing world are entirely unaware of these linkages. Many economic experts of Indian origin are reckoned amongst the best economists in the world. The same applies to the leading scientists and data analysts in several disciplines. What is generally lacking is the ability to assimilate the vast array of inputs and indicators into a cohesive policy planning tool for developing strategic options in the years ahead; or for taking timely action to ward off potential threats before these actually engulf a country or a region. This becomes doubly important for a country like India, which has taken a major step towards charting an independent course of action in the global power play of the twenty first century.

Modern day students of the (emerging) theories of power shifts would not have failed to notice the grand reversal that has taken place in the *inter se* importance between military might and economic might. Throughout recorded history the great civilisations that created wealth became prey to hardier marauders from outlying regions, after they became effete. The latter overturned empires and plundered the wealth of settled communities. This is perhaps no longer the case. There are several reasons for this reversal. Their elaboration is not part of this article. The readers would do well, nevertheless, to keep the pithy statement at the back of their mind for the presentation which follows.

India's nuclear explosions are only the first step on the long and arduous journey for securing a more equitable global order in the next millennium – for itself and the developing world. India is part of Asia. The Third World is its milieu. India should not – even if the others were to countenance it – join the exclusive rich man's club, the nuclear club, or seek a permanent seat in the Security Council the way it is presently constituted. India should not abandon the Third World as many others have done. India should endeavour, in the first instance, to get the G-15, G-77 and NAM to pass resolutions to the effect that the use of nuclear weapons is a crime against humanity – and the planet. It should not forget its historic mission and get bogged down in CTBT and NPT. Unless the concept of supreme national interest yields place to the concept of supreme planetary interest treaties would remain infirm wherever they include a clause for opting out in the supreme national interest. In that case, no one could be sure as to when a country might suddenly decide to opt out and disturb a carefully constructed global equilibrium. By the same token, the declaration of "no first use" becomes meaningless unless such a declaration was deemed to be "irrevocable".

Should Indian leaders at the helm of affairs today forget the larger global issues in order to get out of temporary difficulties – by compromising with the global stalwarts for limited gains – the whole exercise would have been in vain. If India is able to stay the course then it will become a natural leader for ushering in progressive global harmonisation in the twenty first century. "To stay the course" does not mean running around for largesse from the Western world. It means instead putting one's economic house in order and grasping the essentials of the linkages between economic intelligence and strategic intelligence; linkages that will play an increasingly important role in the years ahead.

Defining National Security

There is a distinct need to define or, re-define, the term "national security". Over the years the term has been stretched in many directions, both objectively and subjectively. In the latter case, to make it fit into the context in which it was being used. Wrong emphasis can be misleading, often hopelessly misleading. Till about the Second World War and possibly in the earlier decades of the Cold War national security was mainly centered around military security, and by extension, military might. Later, when the economic revival of the war-ravaged economies of Germany and Japan started impacting strongly on the world economic plane, many defence analysts started including economic might as an essential component of national security. The pendulum kept swinging in this direction till the time that a very sane proposition became overused to a ridiculous extreme. This could have serious repercussions in the long run.

The examples of Germany and Japan could be misleading. Both these countries were anchored firmly in some of the strongest military pacts that the world has seen. As a hypothesis, just for one moment, lift Germany out of its NATO anchor and Japan from under its US umbrella and position these countries, one each, in Africa or the Middle East. In these new locations, especially during the periods of turmoil of the last half-century, could anyone really say that they would not have had to give almost equal weightage independently to their military security.

The point to be noted then is that the factors relating to national security become variables: in relation to space (geographical location); time (whether there was stability in the region during that period); the attitude of the super powers towards the countries concerned; the hostility of the neighbours (or otherwise); the internal security situation; economic vulnerability; social equilibrium and a host of other factors. The diagrams which follow would perhaps explain this relationship more clearly. The first diagram relates to the national security perception model for developing nations as obtaining in the early stages of the Cold War. The second diagram relates to perceptions of national security as obtaining today. The percentages would vary for different countries. They could also vary as a function of time. In short, according to the models, they can seldom be constant for any length of time.

"Perception" of National Security in the early Cold War Period (1960).

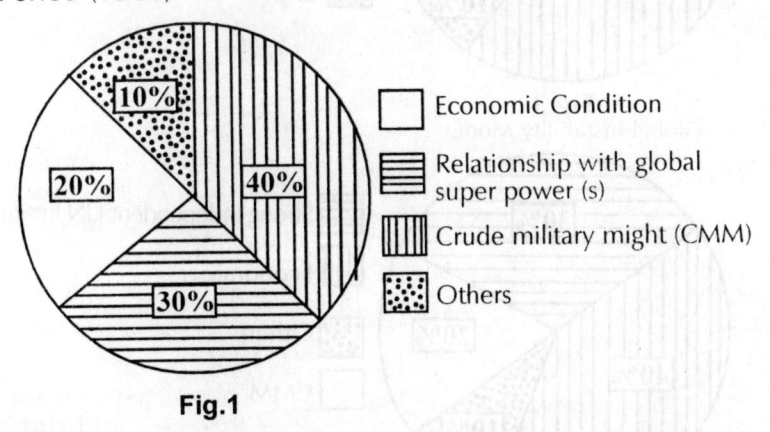

- Economic Condition
- Relationship with global super power (s)
- Crude military might (CMM)
- Others

Fig.1

"Perception" of National Securty obtaining today (1998).

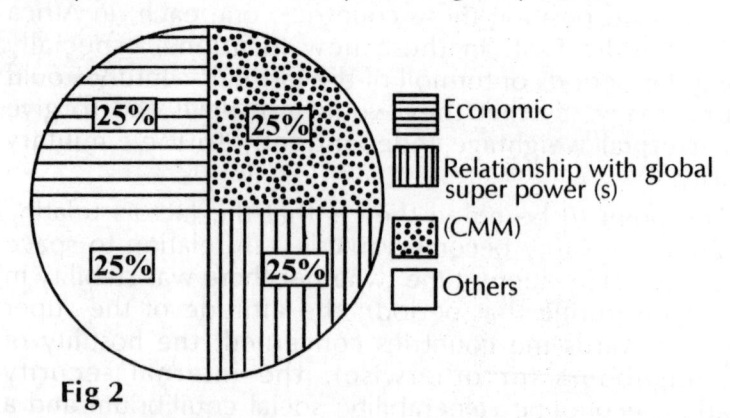

- Economic — 25%
- Relationship with global super power(s) — 25%
- (CMM) — 25%
- Others — 25%

Fig 2

"Perception" of National Security likely to obtain around Year 2050.

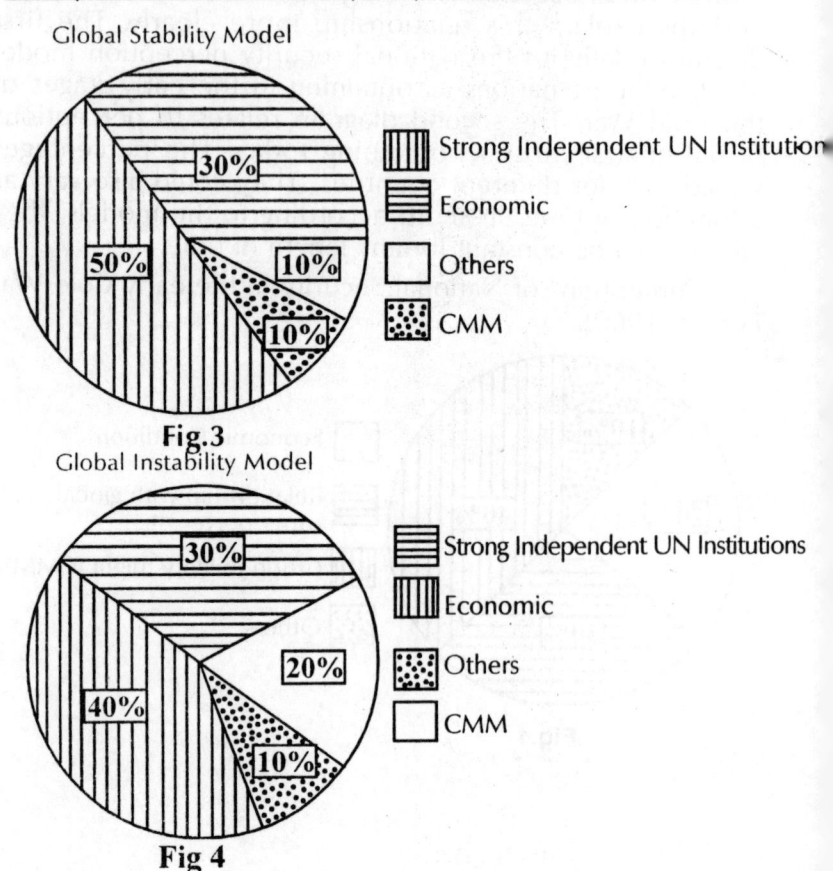

Global Stability Model

- Strong Independent UN Institutions — 50%
- Economic — 30%
- Others — 10%
- CMM — 10%

Fig.3

Global Instability Model

- Strong Independent UN Institutions — 30%
- Economic — 40%
- Others — 10%
- CMM — 20%

Fig 4

It was important to spend time on the national security models because people in different countries have to now consciously decide as nations, as national entities, as to which direction they wish to take and the direction that they would like other nations to take. Having arrived at a consensus on this basic issue they would then have to tailor their policies accordingly. Taking care always to retain flexibility so that they are not caught on the wrong foot in the coming decades; a period which could be leading towards global stability or, in worst case scenarios, global instability. It is thus seen that the principal factors remain variables, based on the internal situation in a country and several externalities, often beyond the control of developing nations. What does stand out irrefutably is that with the strengthening of the UN system in its true non-discriminatory meaning the military expenditure could automatically fall dramatically worldwide over the fifty years period, which is the range covered by the global stability model 2050. (See Fig3). Should, however, the UN continue to function in its current mode the military expenditure of nation states would hardly ever come down. The five permanent members of the Security Council will see to it that the world does not benefit from any peace dividend, now or later.

So far the discussion related to national security. Its ingredients were discussed at some length. Now it is intended to analyse this aspect from an entirely different perspective. A national "insecurity" model is projected below.

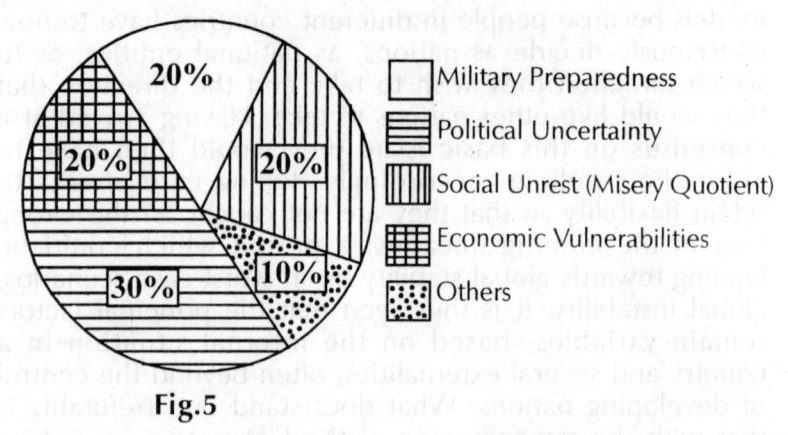

National Insecurity Model for Developing Nations

- Military Preparedness: 20%
- Political Uncertainty: 20%
- Social Unrest (Misery Quotient): 30%
- Economic Vulnerabilities: 20%
- Others: 10%

Fig.5

The model just seen (Fig 5) is not the reverse of the other models of national security that preceded it. In fact, this model is more applicable to many African countries still in a stage of transition. Several Central and South American countries have passed this stage in the last decade or so. The model fits perfectly a country like Pakistan. In that country, which is in a state of terminal decline, national insecurity has resulted directly from the pattern of governance over the last fifty years. The State of Pakistan, with or without the backing of USA and China, does not face any major external threats *per se*. Future threats that might emerge would be the direct outcome of the policies pursued by the Pakistan establishment. Apparently Pakistan can no longer be governed except through brute military force. This is the legacy of fifty years of military rule and misrule. No amount of funds or military hardware poured into the country can save it from itself.

India, to a somewhat lesser degree, is also tending towards the national insecurity model state. Today a large number of people, both at the Centre and in the provinces, have come to regard the political hierarchy as the biggest menace to the security and cohesion of the country. The fact that only a miniscule percentage of terminally corrupt elements, enjoying political power or patronage, are holding the vast majority of their countrymen to ransom does not lessen the gravity of the danger that lies ahead if the country continues along this path. At the close of the twentieth century Indian insecurity stems more from a fractured polity and social and economic disparities than from external military threats. India might yet escape a fate similar to that of some other countries that have gone into an economic tailspin because of its size, diversity and the resilience of its people. Juxtaposed to a near total ethical and moral decline in the governing hierarchy there are signs of resurgence in many other sectors. The latter will strengthen national cohesion and security in the long run. This assessment becomes important because when one talks about intelligence – be it economic or strategic – it implies *ipso facto* an augmentation or diminishment in national security, taken in its holistic sense.

The national insecurity models do not apply to stable Western European states or for that matter, Japan. Now, or in the foreseeable future. It could, however, start applying to the United States of America unless that country dramatically changes course. Referring to the dominant superpower of the century in this fashion may appear strange when demonstrably the USA is at the zenith of its power, both economically and militarily. Countries like India must prepare themselves for the economic *tsunami* that will hit all parts of the world should a situation of the nature highlighted above come about.

The Decline of US Power

Why is a statement of such overarching global import being made when all economic indicators – on the face of it – point in the other direction. The reasons can be briefly stated as follows:
* There are no overt military threats to the USA. But when a mighty nation, blinded with its economic and military might, starts defining the whole world

as its sphere of influence and talks of "full spectrum domination" in every region of the world, the end of such dominance is at hand. It is against the laws of physics. It is contrary to the grain of history. It is a challenge to the spirit of freedom at the end of the second millennium.

* The US stock market capitalisation is artificially high. It is way above its intrinsic worth. The Chairman of the US Federal Reserve has already started issuing cautious warnings. They are not being heeded.
* The US economy has developed great vulnerabilities and potential infirmities.
* Demographic changes in the USA will end the Anglo-Saxon domination of the USA and the world in less than twenty or thirty years.
* Heightened income disparities will destroy whatever social cohesion that still exists.
* A gradual rise in planetary consciousness.
* The concept of supreme planetary interest superimposing itself on the concept of supreme national interest.
* The pig-headedness of the US leadership in opposing, almost single handedly, global consensus in several areas.
* Although the US had a head-start, globalisation is a two-way traffic
* US arms sales around the world will, hereafter, show appreciable decline. (The world has to prepare itself for the reaction of the US military establishment when that happens. Likely outcomes: abrogation of existing treaties i.e. forcing another arms race upon the world by progressing research in anti-satellite, anti-submarine and ABM weapons; the second outcome could be the augmentation of Pakistan's capability to wage war against India).

Several statistics could be adduced to support the belief that the US power could decline far more rapidly than imagined at this point in time. (One example, taken from an article on derivatives appearing in an issue of Time magazine is given below).That is unless a different leadership emerges to change course. It is also possible that the traditional allies of the USA in the Continent of Europe, as distinct from the Anglo-Saxon world, might start setting out on an independent course. Such veering off would not necessarily weaken the Western alliance. If it acts as a moderating influence on the USA, it might actually save the Alliance.

Chase Manhattan	$7,615	$82.00	482%
Morgan Guaranty	$6,143	$116.30	1114%
Citibank	$3,024	$51.00	297%
Bankers Trust	$2,128	$38.50	642%
Nations Bank	$1,695	$10.40	58%
Bank of America	$1,593	$21.80	116%
First National Bank,	$1,249	$12.40	275%
Republic National	$271	$6.00	183%
Bank of New York	$5	$2.50	50%
Chicago Bank of Boston	$146	$1.50	34%

(Source: TIME, May 25, 1998)

Energy and Oil

At the beginning of the year, this speaker had occasion to deliver a keynote address to scientists and participants at a workshop "Technology Vision ". One of the key recommendations that were made at that time related to the establishment, at the highest priority, of an inter-regional energy consortium. A sort of Project Manhattan to ward off one of the most serious threats to India's future security. Need has been felt to revert back to it today because the issue of energy security is still not being tackled with the vigour that it deserves. Since shortfalls in India's future energy needs could seriously undermine the nation's security it is important for everyone to pay greater heed to it rather than leave it to just the concerned ministry; many of whose incumbents in the past have not always furthered the national interest.

A few economic indicators with strategic ramifications, way beyond just the day to day fluctuations in the price of a barrel of oil, are reproduced below. These have been picked out from various national dailies in the past few weeks.

* Western dependence on Persian Gulf oil is reducing just as Asia is beginning to source more of its energy requirements from the region.
* Intra-Asian competition for assured supplies has already begun and is set to intensify in the coming decades. China, Japan, Taiwan, Malaysia and South Korea have made investments in the West Asian oil sector usually in deals which provide for "assured" supplies over the long term. Kuwait and Saudi Arabia have made investments in the other direction, including projects in India. The current economic crisis in East Asia, according to some experts, could spur the integration between West and East Asian oil markets rather than curb it.

* A list of the East Asian investments in the West Asian oil sector makes for useful reference. Japan has the widest spread in the West Asian oil sector. Its Arabian Oil Company has been operating in the neutral zone between Saudi Arabia and Kuwait for sometime now and it also has upstream operations in Oman. Japan's investments and off-takes are key to the natural gas projects Oman and Qatar are developing, following discoveries of huge reserves. The Japan Indonesia Petroleum Company has also got a 25 per cent stake in the Al Bukhoosh oil field in Abu Dhabi. South Korea has a 5 per cent stake in the Omani and Qatari gas projects and a 50 per cent stake in Oman's Bhkha oil field.

* One East Asian investment which attracted notice recently was that of the Malaysian Petronas's 30 per cent share in Iran's Sirri oil field. Petronas is a part of the consortium along with the French Total and Russia's Gazprom in the $2 billion project to develop this field. It was feared that the US would squeeze off credit lines and/or punish the three companies by way of enforcing the Libya/Iran Sanctions Act but the US administration has recently indicated that it will not impose sanctions against the three companies on this account. Petronas also has a 30 per cent stake in the project to develop the South Pars oil field.

* Compared to the three countries named above China has been a slow mover on West Asian investments. It has signed a $1.2 billion production sharing deal with Iraq to develop the Al Ahdab field. However, China has been much more active in attracting West Asian investments into its own oil sector. Saudi Aramco (which) has a 25 per cent stake in the planned expansion of the Fujian refinery in China, has offered to build a 200.000 barrels per day refinery in Qingdao and expressed

an interest in a project to expand the Moming refinery. Kuwait Oil Company has a 14 per cent stake in China's Yacheng 13.1 oil field and is trying for a role in the expansion of the Qilu refinery. China's stakes in the West and Central Asian oil sector is expected to increase substantially. It became a net importer of petroleum products in 1993 and it is estimated that West Asia already supplies half of China's crude imports. West Asia's share in China's crude oil imports is expected to reach the 70-80 per cent mark in the next ten years or so. (The US Central Command bestrides the region. China would be aware of the further US expansionist designs).

* India has recently become open to the idea of foreign investment in the energy sector and among the West Asian countries Oman, Saudi Arabia and Kuwait are at various stages of exploring investments. However, the traditional reluctance to make upstream investments in West Asia has not dissipated. India has an opportunity to invest in Qatar since it is offering a 5 per cent stake in upstream investments in its Rasgas project if a natural gas deal comes through. Rasgas is one of seven international companies vying to be suppliers for the Petronet LNG venture.

The strategic implications of the economic indicators given above would be obvious. Economic growth being heavily dependent upon energy consumption, the first aspect that stands out from the figures is the relative inability of India to match the investments being made by major energy consumers in Asia to secure their future supplies. China and Japan have strong reserves reckoned in hundreds of billions of dollars and not a pitiful twenty billion dollars plus. Hence, India's options are likely to remain limited unless ruthless streamlining takes place immediately in the energy sector within the country.

Continuing with the energy sector the ramifications of two separate events that are almost on the verge of taking place should be appreciated. The first relates to Afghanistan and the second to Iraq. Taking Afghanistan first, it will be recalled that the strategy for pushing the Taliban into Afghanistan was predicated upon opening of the oil route through pipelines via Afghanistan, Pakistan and on to the Arabian Sea. Extremely heavy outlays by Saudi Arabia and several US oil majors (with the tacit support of the US government) helped to buy out local warlords with exorbitant sums; thus helping the ragtag band in overcoming resistance in large areas of Afghanistan. This strategy was conceived to undermine Iran's pipelines from the Central Asian Region (CAR). The strategy may have to be modified by its principal backer, the USA even if the Taliban succeed in overcoming the Northern Alliance.

The reason is that the laying of the pipelines was a race against time. The pipelines are already being laid elsewhere. Iran, Russia and China have apparently moved in faster than expected. European consortia have joined hands with the Russians. Some of them might even take a stake in Gazprom. Even if Russia and Iran are unable to keep the Northern Alliance from being pushed out from most of the areas still held by that Alliance the chances are that heightened guerilla activities stretching all the way to Peshawar might make the laying of pipelines across Afghanistan an unviable proposition.

Since the rapid conquest of Afghanistan was carried out more through financial than military might the last might still not be heard of that doughty warrior, Ahmed Shah Masood. Taking a leaf out of the Afghan book it may not sound too improbable that Pakistan troops in the North West and Baluchistan change sides in a similar fashion when a strong Taliban government starts coveting parts of Pakistan. The former have recently laid claims to some Momand areas. US interests might themselves again follow this course when they dig down in Baluchistan, which could well become another Diego Garcia for the USA.

Several activities undertaken by the USA over the last two decades – including economic activities – when taken together point in this direction. A similar plan was afoot in the Bay of Bengal. An erstwhile Bangladesh regime might have gone through with the Status of Forces Act (SOFA), regardless of consequences for the entire region.

It would not be out of place to deal here with the Taliban bogey in as far as it relates to Kashmir. People have been expressing alarm at the prospect of the Taliban turning towards Kashmir after consolidating in Afghanistan. While such an eventuality needs to be prepared for and the situation closely monitored it must be clearly stated that the Indian Army is more than capable of dealing with an eventuality of this nature. The Taliban mostly "bought" their way through Afghanistan. They did not "fight" their way through Afghanistan. Regardless of their religious zeal or fanaticism neither they nor their backers can hope to match the fighting ability of the Indian Army in difficult, inhospitable terrain. What does need to be kept in mind, however, is that the talk of reducing the strength of the Indian Army will remain premature for a long time to come.

Coming next to Iraq, that country's oil exports have been severely curtailed under the embargoes mandated by the UN Security Council. The world, at large, has become alive to the impossible strain that the embargo is placing on the common Iraqi people, especially the children. But for the obduracy of the Anglo-Saxon lobbies – for example, Australia is benefiting handsomely from the wheat for oil exchange – the rest of the world would have lifted the embargo long ago. It is well on the cards that the objections of the Anglo-Saxon lobbies will be set aside, with or without their consent, sooner rather than later. When that happens, and Iraq starts pumping oil at full capacity, it could severely undermine the cohesion of OPEC. From this point onwards several positive and negative scenarios could develop for India in the near future. These need to be analysed in great detail by multidiscipline teams, both in the Government and Industry, so that certain advantages can be quickly pressed home and negative reactions anticipated and parried.

South East Asian Meltdown

Since the meltdown was first perceived in Thailand almost a year ago the devastating economic gyrations of many of those countries have dominated the headlines continuously to the extent of engendering a certain weariness. One has to be careful. The effects of the South East Asian economic turmoil will be around for quite a while. Much has been said on the subject by donor agencies, aid agencies and a host of others. Without repeating what has been oft repeated it would still be worthwhile to recapitulate a few of the salient facts that are relevant to this discussion.

* In the past IMF rescue efforts have pushed national governments into devaluing currencies as a means to export-led growth. But this is not working any longer. The worst affected South East Asian countries have seen the value of their currencies fall between 35 and 70 per cent against the US dollar in the past one-year. Most countries have had to cut government budgets and raise interest rates.

* The drastic fall in the value of most currencies should normally have given these countries a comparative export edge. This hope has generally been belied. Exports from Indonesia, Malaysia, Philippines, Singapore and Thailand have actually fallen marginally in dollar terms since August last. Overall exports have actually declined 5 per cent in the first quarter of calendar 1998. This suggests that the crisis is worsening and not improving. (Which means that the older economic theories linked to devaluation are not working any more. Perhaps

they were ill-suited to economic crises of such magnitudes).

* South East Asian nations have another predicament; large intra-regional trade. The result is that the collapse of one economy is pulling down the others. Japan seems to be doing no better. In fact, the fall of the Yen promises to increase Japanese exports to Europe and America over that from the ASEAN region.

* A leading financial publication in SE Asia (Business Times) estimated that the economic crisis wiped out $ 35.5 billions from the stock exchange i.e. 35% of its capitalisation in the first half of 1998.

* "Over the space of a few short months the possibility of major (Asian) Airlines exiting the market has become a real one" – Aviation industry expert Peter Harbison.

The long-term effects of the South East Asian meltdown need to be gone into thoroughly by India. To date, most of the inputs have come through Western sources, including the World Bank and IMF. Even if they were to be taken at face value it has to be realised that the perspective is one that would be seen from a telescope mounted in the West looking Eastwards. The view reflects Western anxieties, vulnerabilities (in the form of unsecured loans and overexposure) and opportunities. The same telescope looking Eastwards from India would give a vastly altered perspective. This exercise has to be undertaken now. The questions that the government, defence analysts, economic experts and industry in India should be posing could possibly be along the lines tabulated below:

* Rising unemployment in SE Asia linked to the demographic shifts. Its effect on India.

* Spillover effects of Indonesia's growing hunger and anger.
* Who will benefit from the fissiparous tendencies that are supposedly emerging in Indonesia. Are these being encouraged from the outside?
* The South East Asian countries will no longer be able to afford sophisticated armaments from the West. Does this offer opportunities for India? (Not necessarily armaments sales but more positive initiatives for regional stability).
* What will be the effect on India of changed patterns of ownership of vital economic assets which are being picked up at throw away prices by cash surplus US and Western enterprises?

India has to anticipate these changes of which only a handful have been listed. Concomitantly, it has to be remembered that it was the devaluation of the *renminbi*, the Chinese currency in 1994 which, by hindsight, seems to have been one of the agents, according to some economists, that started the process of the South East Asian meltdown. A further devaluation of the *renminbi* cannot be altogether ruled out. This writer is of the view that the South East Asian meltdown was inevitable. The speed at which the American economic growth model was superimposed in itself contained the seeds for the debacle which followed. There are lessons in it for India and the developing world. If India plans ahead and improves the management of its economy the country could actually emerge as a global economic giant sooner than would otherwise have been the case.

China

The visit of a domestically beleaguered American President to China is long over. The short term, quick analyses of the visit hogged media headlines around the world for several weeks, before and after the event. There would have been US game plans for China and the world and Chinese game plans for the US and the world. We are too close to the event to fully appreciate the long-term repercussion of all that took place during the visit. America's closest allies would most likely remain in the dark of the secret understandings arrived at between the two greatest powers of the final decade of the twentieth century. Even Americans – who should be in the know – may never know as to what was finally conceded by the First Power to the Second Power, or the real compulsions for giving a boost to the elevation of the latter to bring it closer to the former, at least in terms of international standing.

Most analysts and opponents of the beleaguered White House incumbent have felt that the US President gave away too much. Those who believed that may be underestimating the US President's intellectual grasp of world affairs. May be there is a hidden agenda behind the far reaching concessions made to China. On the other hand the proposition has also to be looked at in reverse. The word "beleaguered" has been brought in twice in the last few sentences. Most people would presumably link it to the unfolding sexual scandal. It could, however, turn out that the other scandal relating to campaign funds might reveal itself to be the more serious issue. The US Justice department is reportedly investigating payments of sums from Chinese sources amounting to little over half a million dollars. In the USA today, where individual wealth has reached stratospheric proportions, the amount is so insignificant, especially in a city like Washington, that it would hardly amount to pin money for the really wealthy. So, the possibility can never really be ruled out that sums running into hundreds of millions of dollars might have been pledged for future use even if the money never actually changed hands.

What does become clear, however, is that major geo-strategic shifts have taken place in the wake of the Sino-American entente of July 1998. Japan, Taiwan, Western Europe, Russia, West Asia, India, South East Asia, amongst others, will have to take a fresh look at their own positions and the re-alignments – economic as well as geo-strategic – that would surely follow in the years ahead. The scope of this article precludes further elaboration.

Pakistan – End of an Era

India has got the upper hand in the proxy war that Pakistan has been waging against India, in one form or another, for a number of years. India could have done much better in this regard and possibly at lesser cost if it had understood the real nature of the proxy war. The true proxy war being waged against India (through Pakistan) started right after the partition of the two countries. The real wagers of this war were the Anglo-Saxon elite. They have waged proxy wars not only against India but against many countries of the world, not excluding China. The rest of the Western world and Japan supported this effort, directly, or tacitly, for nearly fifty years. That support may soon be at an end. Both Continental Europe and Canada, realising the folly of going along with the Anglo-Saxon domination of the UN after the end of the Cold War have started charting independent policies in several spheres indicating a desire for a more rational world order. In the case of Japan a major shift might be taking place in the public opinion of that country as distinct from the rigid stance of the government.

The outlying provinces of Pakistan do not really support the policies being followed by the establishment in the Province of West Punjab. Pakistan is in very dire straits indeed. No amount of armaments or money pumped in by the Anglo-Saxon brigade can save that state in its terminal decline. In a very short while the question of Kashmir, over which it has made so much noise, will cease to be relevant to Pakistan as it sinks deeper into the mire. India has certainly been the enemy number one for half a century. The ruling hierarchy of that country has made it the cornerstone of the policy for the survival of Pakistan and themselves. When chaos finally engulfs that country its people could very well first turn on their own masters and then on their supposed benefactors, China and the USA. The missiles and the handful of mini nukes will be turned on China via Xinjiang and on US assets in West Asia.

The world will soon witness, if it is not already witnessing, the first acts of nuclear blackmail – or state-sponsored nuclear terrorism. In reality it is an act of brinkmanship on the part of the Pakistan establishment, which is saying to the world: "yield to our demands, or else?" The trading of nuclear weapons for cash could become a bustling enterprise which would harm Western democracies – who have cornered much of the world's wealth – far more than India, unless Pakistan's bluff is called and that country's backers come to their senses.

Continental Europe has far more to lose than USA. The crude nuclear devices will be sold not so much for use against Israel as to terrorists on the Southern shores of the Mediterranean and the Balkan states from where even peashooter missiles could target most cities across the Mediterranean. Europe's Anglo-Saxon allies are not much concerned on this score, being further away. In the case of USA they are well ensconced behind the Atlantic and Pacific Oceans. Unless that is, some crude devices reach the drug syndicates and other elements inimical to the USA in Latin America. The Taliban too may demand their share of the crude weapons.

China and the Anglo-Saxon elites have been playing with fire in their blinkered fixity of purpose while setting up Pakistan against India. In the process they have disregarded the larger threat – to themselves, and their vitals, not vital interests. The terror bombings in Kenya should serve as a grim reminder.

India will not be the target of Pak missiles and nuclear weapons in the next century. There will be no military threat – conventional or nuclear – for India from a rump Pakistan – the Provinces would have separated and directly linked themselves to a subcontinental economic union. The threat to India will be demographic. India has to plan now for the economic threat that could materialise from a human influx that might result from the economic collapse of Pakistan. The tolerance levels for refugees from war, want or persecution – will be far less in the twenty first century. Few advanced countries will accept them as was the case in the second half of the twentieth century. Therefore, each region of the world will have to find its own methodologies for tackling the human or possibly sub-human surplus of the countries that comprise that region. Refugees from war and want.

Recommendations

Several important countries in the region whose economic strategies or options in the years ahead could have a major strategic impact on India's well-being have been left out. These include Japan, Russia, China, CAR and West Asia. Analyses in respect of these countries or groupings along the lines indicated earlier, with suitable refinements, should be undertaken more comprehensively in order to develop policy options for the government as well as for different segments of the economy that could be either benefited or hurt by unforeseen developments.

As a consequence of what has been stated above a few recommendations for consideration are tabulated below:

* Separate studies by the National Security Council, private sector and the like. of possible scenarios (in five to ten year segments) of: (a) Afghanistan; (b) Iran; (c) Indonesia; (d) Myanmar; (e) SE Asia as a whole.
* Re-orientation of the *inter se* importance being given to the study of foreign languages at the different government institutions at the official level, by giving incentives, if required. Greater emphasis to be laid now upon Chinese, Japanese, Vietnamese, in that order. The European languages will continue to attract students in the private sector in any case.

* Better integration between ministries for a finer understanding of the holistic nature of strategic intelligence in the twenty first century. For a start defence services officers should be laterally co-opted for given tenures in the Ministries of Home, Defence, Foreign Affairs and the Ministry of Finance.

* India along with the G-77 countries to set up a parallel and independent sovereign rating agency like Moody or Standard & Poor. China, Japan and several Western experts could be co-opted.

Conclusion

To conclude it needs to be reiterated that having taken the plunge India has no choice but to go the full distance. Having come thus far, should the political leadership of the country make compromises – to ease the country's immediate difficulties in the short term – then the whole exercise would have been, in a sense, futile. Nobody makes space for anyone willingly in today's world. India has to stand firm to safeguard its own interest and those of the region to which it belongs. In the world, as constituted at the turn of the twentieth century, there is no such thing as a level playing field. The analogy is a contradiction in terms.

6

Dealing with China in the Twenty First Century

"It is in India's interest to see China strong enough to provide 'credible' bi-polarity in the interregnum during which the world moves towards the establishment of a globally respected United Nations system; one which would be capable of enforcing its mandate 'equitably' in all parts of the world without let or hindrance. At the same time it is 'vital' to India's interest to NEVER underestimate China's threat potential". (It is reasonable to assume that an intermediate stage could be a multi-polar world).

The rest of the paper will expatiate on this statement and address the seeming contradiction between the first part of the statement and the second. Beginning at the beginning, both countries represent two of the earliest civilisations that have been able to continuously hold on to their older traditions since the dawn of history. Historically, China has had a tradition of world dominance through power projections (i.e. the Middle Kingdom ideation). India, on the other hand, has never aspired to military or economic dominance. In ancient times when India was a powerful country the only influence it sought to project was one of peace and harmony. Today, at the close of the second millennium after Christ – and the fifth or sixth millennium dating from the ancient civilisations that flourished along the banks of the Indus, the Nile, the Euphrates and the Yangste – both countries have only recently emerged from the long night of foreign domination.

Having cast a quick glance at that earlier period it is time to look at the growth patterns adopted by the two countries since regaining their freedom after the Second World War. China fought its way to freedom. India, having taken recourse to Gandhian pacifism, had freedom delivered to it in a relatively peaceful manner. There was an enormous price tag attached to the pacific route to freedom – the violent partition of the country. After establishment of Chinese unity through the bloody route the Chinese leaders understood, more comprehensively than anyone else, that power, in the ultimate analysis, *did* flow from the barrel of a gun. They never had illusions on this score. Having understood the currency of power they went on to occupy Tibet before India was able to consolidate after the trauma of partition.

Indian leaders, on the other hand, never having learned from history – in spite of writing magnificent books on it – were not able to grasp the global reality of that period. They tried to re-build India on the platform of idealism; an idealism more relevant to the days of Emperor Ashoka and possibly the coming millennium rather than to twentieth century reality. They made way for the Chinese in Tibet. They have been making way for the Chinese ever since – and for the rest of the world. A humiliating military defeat never really taught them any lessons. India paid a price for its lack of realism and will continue to pay the price – with graver consequences in the next century.

With this resume, albeit sketchy, it is time to leave the twentieth century behind and look forward to the twenty-first; not forgetting, however, that India moves into the next century with the same mindset that dominated the thinking of its leaders in the past. It is worth pausing awhile, to move away from the region, and look at the two countries, China and India, from the other capitals of the world. How do they perceive these countries developing in·the next century, say in the years 2010, 2025 and 2050.

	India	China
2010	Nowhere	Well on the way to becoming the second super power of the world.
2025	Possibly a middle ranking power	Definitely the second 'super power
2050	Dominant power within South Asia. And?	Able to exercise global influence at par with USA and an independently assertive European Union.

(The projections relating to India could dramatically change (in the positive direction) from about the second decade of the century should India be able to stabilize its population and if professionalism in governance were to become the order of the day).

Models of China's Pursuit for Power

For the purposes of this discussion three models have been taken to examine China's probable development in the next century: to whit, Steady Expansion Model; Explosive Expansion Model; and Implosion Model. Diagrammatically these are represented in the following manner:

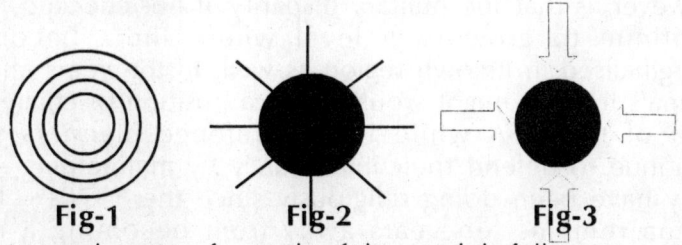

Fig-1   Fig-2   Fig-3

An explanation for each of the models follows.

Steady State Expansion Model (Figure 1)

According to this model – denoted by concentric circles – China expands its influence in the next century in ever expanding circles. Going outwards from the core, the first circle denotes the spread of Chinese *influence* to regions contiguous to China i.e. the Asia-Pacific region, North and South Korea, Taiwan, Japan, the Islands under dispute (notably Spratly Islands), Mongolia, Russia, South East Asia, South Asia and West Asia. The second circle denotes the spread of China's geo-political *power* to the whole of Asia and Australia. The outer and last circle represents the spread of Chinese geo-political *influence* to include the whole world minus North and South America.

The words, influence and power, have been put in parenthesis. The difference between the two needs to be understood in the context in which they are used here. Influence means that China's sensibilities would weigh heavily in any major foreign policy decision taken by its neighbours in Asia; whereas power implies that China would have developed the military capability to project that power in the region regardless of any intimidation on that score by USA. Russia would, in all probability, remain outside the ambit of such projections because of its retaliatory nuclear might.

India may not be able to challenge China, even in South Asia, if India's military disparity with its bigger neighbour in the conventional as well as the nuclear field remains vastly inferior, as at present. The tragic part, however, is that the military disparity, if not checked, will continue to grow to a level where India becomes marginalised in its own region as well. In the years ahead China's military might would be in a position to challenge that of the USA while Indian defence planners will continue to defend their inadequacy by maintaining – as they have been doing religiously since the 1970s – that China remains ten years away from becoming a real military threat to this country.

Dynamic Expansion (Explosive) Model (Figure 2)

This model depicts uncontrolled or runaway growth as distinct from the steady state expansion depicted in the previous model. It could in some ways be compared to what happened in Indonesia. The point at which the country explodes, in the Indonesian fashion, would be difficult to determine. It could happen in twenty years or after fifty years. There are several factors, which could propel the country in the direction indicated in the model. Some of the factors are tabulated below:

* The extent of consolidation of power by Jiang Zemin; and his longevity.
* Flowing from the first point the smoothness, or otherwise, of the succession to President Jiang Zemin when he leaves the world stage. It would be worth recalling here that had Deng Xiaoping not succeeded the great leader Mao and the so-called Gang of Four gained ascendancy in the post-Mao struggle the history of China, and just possibly the world, would have been different. It would also not be out of place to recall here the manner of fall of Mikhail Gorbatchev and the breakup of USSR.
* American attempts to force the pace of change of modernisation and democratisation in China; a pace that prevents the Chinese leaders from being able to control the fallout from such rapid change. It would arguably be the quest of American geo-political strategy to engineer the breakup of China (and India as well) so that no credible challenge would remain to American dominance of the globe in the twenty-first century, and beyond. And should America succeed in its endeavour then the turn of the European Union would assuredly come thereafter.
* The great economic disparity that already exists between China's provinces on the South Western coast (and now Hong Kong) and remainder China, notably the interior regions.

* Incomes disparities and growing unemployment due to the rapid changes in economic policy.
* The emergence of 'sleaze' as an increasingly effective weapon of war – both internally and externally. (Grand reversal of economic warfare patterns by China. China now uses this weapon subtly, and not so subtly, to influence economic policies towards China in the West, especially USA. In contrast India appears diffident, tentative, mostly unprepared and invariably subservient; regardless of the bombast for home consumption).

Implosion Model (Figure 3)

The Implosion Model differs from the earlier model in Fig. 2 in that under this model China collapses under the weight of its own size. Such a collapse, in the case of China, would be built up from growing internal unrest as well as pressure from outside tending to compress the nation from all directions. At this juncture, it is difficult to visualise such compression – the other term for it being containment – taking place with the collapse of the old USSR and the relative military insignificance of India. Additionally, China has reached a stage of military and economic growth that allows it to be capable of resisting American pressure. (Ambivalent attitude of Hong Kong's population should be kept in mind. Only surface integration of distinctly pro-Chinese elements has taken place. It is not inconceivable that in the run up to the handing back of the Crown Colony the British would have created a strong anti-Chinese bureaucracy that would resist change after the departure of the colonial power i.e. the pattern perfected on the subcontinent).

Increasing Disparity in the Military Capabilities between China and India.

At the very outset it must be stated that when the military capabilities of the two larger than life Asian countries are compared the ultimate power projection aims of the two countries are taken into account. It is fully appreciated that each country tailors its military might to match its geo-political aims. In the case of China it is avowedly well on the path to becoming a global military super-power. On the other hand India has no such ambitions – now, or in the foreseeable future. All sensible military planners and India's well-wishers – if any remain in the world besides Russia – would concede that at the very least India must possess the military wherewithal to ensure the security of South Asia and safeguard its limited interests in the Bay of Bengal and the Indian Ocean. Therefore, in the presentation this differential in the geo-political ambitions of the two countries is never lost sight of.

A number of defence reviews have appeared in the recent past highlighting the burning pace of China's military growth. Without going into comparative figures India must take serious note at the following military developments:

Rapid Increase in China's Military Capability.

* China's military expenditure growing at ten percent per year as per Western estimates.
* China's official defence budget excludes nuclear weapons development, R&D and soldier's pensions. Nor does it include sale proceeds from armaments. These were estimated at five billion dollars between 1991 to 1995. They would have increased since then.
* China's rapid reaction force which stood at fifteen thousand in 1988 has expanded to more than two hundred thousand in the last ten years.
* To give an example of the naval buildup, in 1994, 35 additional warships were under construction. Additional acquisitions planned were 46 warships. This was after the 4 destroyers, 5 frigates and 9 fast attack missile boats launched since 1991.

* The acquisition of SU-27s and other aerial platforms has been well documented and is not being listed.
* China has been building a rail link from southwestern Yunnan Province through Myanmar to the Bay of Bengal.
* Road networks coming into Nepal have also been developed at an accelerated pace.

In addition to what has been tabulated above India and SE Asia, if not the world, should take serious note of the aspects enumerated below:

* Without any conceivable threat to its territory – now, or in the foreseeable future, China's military expenditure is increasing exponentially. It goes beyond the needs of a military operation across its borders by another country or for any confrontation with its southern neighbours – individually, or collectively.
* China will soon project power by its sheer size well beyond the Continent of Asia. (USA, Russia, the European Union, the Koreas, Japan, South East Asia, West Asia and even Australia are learning to take into account Chinese sensibilities in their foreign policy projections. Hardly anybody takes note of Indian sensibilities beyond SAARC, if at all).
* The Chinese often go to great lengths to underplay their capabilities. They keep saying at every opportunity, "we will never seek hegemony". This has to be seen in the light of Sun Tzu's famous saying "never let out your real intentions. Lull your adversaries by all possible means. Hide your capabilities". Then again "we must conceal our abilities and bide our time" – statement reportedly made by Lt. Gen. Mi Zhenyu of the Chinese army. Indian defence planners must pay heed. Disaster

overtook the country in 1962. Should Chinese troops cross the border in strength in future they might not be inclined to pull back. Nor would anybody be likely to come to India's aid, the second time around.

* China was not powerful militarily in the 1970s. Yet, it did not hesitate to launch a massive invasion of its (then) fraternal comrade Vietnam. "Just to teach it a lesson", they said. It is recommended that members of the armed forces make it a point to read the book "Brother Enemy" by Nayan Chanda, an author and journalist who has won international acclaim.
* NORINCO, the Chinese ordnance company that supplies the PLA with most of its weapons has (it is suspected) approximately ten subsidiary companies spread around the USA.
* China's export advantage ratio with USA is said to be around 4:1. China has a sophisticated export "strategy" in place (e.g. underselling etc). Where the Chinese are unable to get straight-forward technology transfers of sensitive technology they follow a sophisticated pattern of identifying the firms supplying various components to the main supplier manufacturer of the equipment exported from the West and induce the sub-component supplying companies to set up manufacturing units in China. They know how to achieve their ends – by fair means or foul.
* Seizure of "Mischief Reef" from the friendly South East Asian country Philippines in 1995 has given it a forward perch in that region.
* Myanmar and Cambodia are firmly under Chinese influence. China has exploitation rights over sixty percent of Kazakhstan's oil reserves, edging out US oil companies, Amoco and Texaco.

Preparations in Tibet.

* All but 13 of 6,254 monasteries in Tibet have been closed.
* The new incarnation of the Panchen Lama chosen by Tibetan monks and the Dalai Lama – 6 year old boy Gendum Choeki Nyima – was made to disappear along with his parents. There is no trace of any of them.

Effect of South East Asian Meltdown on Geo-Politics in the Region

India must take note that the very concept of ASEAN has undergone a sea change from what it was just two to three years ago. A grouping that showed promise of becoming a force to be reckoned with now remains a shell of its former self. Because of the decline in the economies of the countries of the region – in some cases a catastrophic decline – few people take it seriously these days. Economic debilitation has brought in other types of ills. Firstly, ASEAN has lost its independent decision-making ability because many of its industries and economic assets have been taken over by cash rich foreigners who were the prime movers in engineering the crash. Most of the ASEAN countries will have to keep conforming to the dictates of Western banking consortia and the IMF for a long time to come. Secondly, deep fissures have developed within these countries; exacerbated by the personal animus between the leaders. It is not easy to visualise how the situation will improve if the personalities concerned do not alter their perceptions of each other. Last, but not least, there is very real danger of break up of the largest and most populous country of the group, Indonesia.

There is decidedly a vacuum developing in India's neighbourhood to the East. It will pose major foreign policy challenges for the bigger Asian countries of the region i.e. China, India and Japan. Should these countries act in concert to prevent the turmoil in the region from becoming endemic it would benefit the region as a whole. From present indications each country seems to be following its own agenda. Japan could end up as the worst affected as over eighty percent of its oil requirement flows through this region.

The Taiwan Question and its Effect on Global Geopolitics of the 21st Century

On the face of it there are only three countries of the world directly involved in the China-Taiwan standoff i.e. China, USA and Taiwan itself. Delving deeper one realises that any sudden absorption of Taiwan by China would be a cataclysmic event whose import might not have been appreciated to the same extent in India as it would have been in USA and Japan. The countries most affected by the ramifications of a sudden change would prefer the transition to be a gradual one, spread over several decades; even a century or beyond. Hence, the importance being given to the Taiwan question. The aspect will be looked at in several dimensions.

China's Military Capability to Physically Overrun Taiwan at the Present Time.

Should China decide to militarily subjugate Taiwan any time in the near future USA would almost certainly intervene. It would assist in the destruction of the Chinese armada, taking care not touch the Chinese mainland at any stage. Thereby not giving China any excuse to hit Continental USA with nuclear-tipped missiles. The Chinese are realists. Regardless of pronouncements they would not be foolish enough to start a nuclear exchange with USA. The adverse ratio against China in any exchange with USA – whatever the nature of the exchange – is simply too large. Japan would tacitly provide much more than logistics backup to USA. Therefore, one takes it that were China to mount a physical invasion of Taiwan the US response would be limited to naval and air support from aircraft based in Japan. Going by current estimates of China's amphibious capability, this level of support would be sufficient to put paid to China's invasion ambitions.

The next scenario to be considered would be to gauge the chances of success of a physical invasion of Taiwan from mainland China without any outside interference. The chances of success of the invasion are still rated low. There are several reasons for this. A tabulation follows:

* The weather in the South China Sea is highly unpredictable. Very strong winds or typhoon like conditions prevail in the Formosa Straits for nearly two hundred days in a year.

* Taiwan has been preparing for the eventuality for nearly half a century since the Communists took power on the mainland. They would be quite capable of neutralising the Chinese naval armada irrespective of any preparatory bombardment carried out by China. The (residual) force actually making a landing would be quickly destroyed by Taiwanese counterattack elements.

* A small nation fighting with its back to the wall does have a few aces up its sleeve as in the case of Israel. Therefore, it would not be too far-fetched to assume that Taiwan may have created a small nuclear stockpile to take care of its minimum deterrence needs. The Chinese themselves being great proliferators should know that if one side does not respect mutually agreed upon restraints the other party – the more vulnerable person – would be foolhardy not to cater for adequate safeguards. Hence, in a do or die situation, the back-to-the-wall Taiwanese would ensure that they take out Shanghai and a few other industrial hubs by whatever means. (It is very likely that Japan too would be just a screw driver turn away from a minimum nuclear deterrent of its own).

In view of what has been said above one reaches the conclusion that it would be in the best interests of all concerned to preserve the status quo while respecting China's claims for an eventual reunification of Taiwan with PRC. Taiwan would, in turn, have to ensure that it does not make a unilateral declaration of independence, thereby pushing China towards the extreme step. China would have, or should have, calculated that the physical destruction that would accompany a military invasion of Taiwan – even if eventually successful – would be so great as to push back by twenty, thirty or fifty years China's dream of global greatness at par with USA.

Global Effects of a Sudden Merger with Taiwan

Before leaving the question of Taiwan and going on to other matters it would be worth looking at, *en passant,* the effects of a peaceful merger between China and Taiwan in the near future. The effects will be immediately felt throughout the world. Briefly, these could be:-

* China would, overnight, become one of the largest and most powerful economies of the world.
* With such economic clout China would be able to single handedly displace the economic centres of gravity of the world from Washington, New York, Tokyo, London, Zurich and Frankfurt to Beijing and Shanghai. (The cliché "shanghai-ed" would then have assumed a literal meaning).
* The World Bank and IMF would stand diminished unless they accommodated China on its own terms. The same would apply to WTO.
* The European Union would loosen its bonds with USA and look more in the direction of China.
* Russia would become militarily more insecure having to contend with the Eastward expansion of NATO and the Northwards expansionist urge of China.

* Japan, at some stage, would have to loosen its military bonds with USA and reach accommodation with China. (Japan's position would become untenable with 80 percent of its energy supplies having to pass through the South China Seas).
* Most of South East Asia would follow suit.
* China would become the legatee of the concept mooted by the Japanese in a different era of the Asian Co-Prosperity Sphere.
* Australia would be economically crippled if it did not reach suitable accommodation with China: being obliged to sever its links with the USA.
* India?

What has been mentioned above is one possible outcome of a 'rapid' (peaceful) incorporation of Taiwan by China. In spite of a number of imponderables – and an even greater number of variables – the core hypothesis would, in all probability, remain the same. The question mark in front of India should be read the way it is meant to be read i.e. a question mark. It connotes a whole range of interesting possibilities whose consideration is outside the scope of this discussion.

GENERAL ASPECTS

The Perception of 'Threat Perception'

In the most simplistic derivation of the 'perception' of 'threat perception', any country which is larger and more powerful constitutes a potential threat to its neighbours. Whether that threat manifests itself in a military form or in any other form becomes a matter of detail. There have been neighbours who have co-existed peacefully for generations on end and there have been neighbours who have fought with each other a number of times in almost every century. Whatever be the case, history is replete with examples of countries losing their freedom *per se* or their freedom of action whenever they failed to take adequate measures to safeguard their security against more powerful neighbours. The present century and the post-colonial period have been no exceptions to this historical phenomenon, the frequency of whose occurrence makes it an historical verity.

In the light of what has been stated it becomes obvious that, in a manner of speaking, China constitutes a threat to India. Even if it had not been a permanent Security Council member with veto power – whose formidable nuclear and military might keeps increasing rapidly – China would still have constituted a threat to India in keeping with the historical truism just elaborated. Possibly, the reverse proposition would also hold true for a person examining the same hypothesis from the point of view of China. Therefore, going strictly by (elementary) logic, China would constitute a "potential" threat to India no matter how one looks at the matter. Hence, China's fierce reaction becomes incomprehensible when the obvious is stated. The US military establishment has been citing China as its principal threat since the end of the cold war. Nobody in China has taken exception to it. In fact, the relations between the two countries have actually been improving since both sides realised that they constitute the biggest threat to each other in the next century. What is the reason for this improvement in relations between these two mighty powers? The reason is that both of them shed hypocrisy in this regard from day one. In the case of India, hypocrisy linked to an inability to face reality, has (generally) been the hallmark of defence planners. Patently false pronouncements for decades on end engendered a feeling of overlordship in the minds of China's leaders to the extent that when the truth – a natural extension of the universal hypothesis just mentioned – was finally articulated for the first time at the highest levels of government it sounded like a provocative and bellicose statement.

It was nothing of the sort. Nor was it intended to give offence to a giant neighbour. It was a wake up call given to the country's defence establishment. What should have happened in the early 1970s finally took shape after another quarter century had gone by. It is an entirely different matter that the ham-handed manner in which the Government of India justified its momentous decision gave needless offense to the neighbour in question. It demonstrated lack of experience and diplomatic finesse. The Government of China should have realised then-and should certainly keep in mind for the future that in a democracy – and especially during the phase of coalition governments – individuals holding high office could make statements that show an independent drift. China should appreciate that in a democracy dissent cannot be muzzled. Loose canons cannot be always controlled.

The Nature of Colossi

After slumber and subjugation of several centuries China is again becoming the great country that it was throughout most of its history. It already looms large on the horizon of its Asian neighbours. At the dawn of the new century it will assume the shape of a colossus. When that happens it will begin to exhibit the 'nature' of a colossus. What exactly is the nature of a colossus? The nature of a colossus is that it begins to develop an appetite for aggrandisement. By making this statement it is not the intention here to attribute any malign intent to China's leadership. The discussion is on historical phenomenon. They closely resemble natural phenomenon. Throughout history its colossi have, almost without exception, manifested this urge. Kingdoms that became large grew into empires. Empires, after consolidation, started becoming larger and larger through a process of conquest till they assumed gigantic proportions i.e. they had become fit enough to burst. The nineteenth and twentieth centuries were no exception. The British Empire grew so large that ultimately it had to give way. The Soviet Empire is a more recent case from our century. The lone superpower, unless it shows self-restraint, will come to the bursting point any time in the first half of the next century. This time around, the difference would be that when the explosion occurs it could possibly destroy much of the world as well. It is the reality of nuclear weapons and weapons of mass destruction.

Reverting to China, whether its present leadership wishes it or not, the country will automatically start showing the symptoms of a colossus in the next century. The military build up in Tibet is sufficient, at the present, to enable the mounting of a full-scale offensive against India to threaten the 'entire' North East of the country. As if this were not enough there is no let up in the pace of augmentation of this capability, regardless of the so-called tranquility along the border. The countries adjoining China, especially the defence planners of this country, better take heed. Samuel Butler is reported to have said, "man is the only animal that can remain on friendly terms with the victims he intends to eat until he eats them". Once again it is reiterated that nobody is assigning evil intent to China's honorable leaders. The expansionist urge inheres in the nature of colossi. In the case of China the situation will be exacerbated by growing scarcities in the region in the next century. To cite an example, arable land in China is shrinking at an alarming pace.

The Effect of Globalisation

It is not the intention here to merely repeat what has been oft-repeated i.e. that globalisation is inevitable and those who do not adapt will go under. Here it is proposed to examine as to what happens to countries like China and India and many others like them when the inevitable does overtake them. Taking the case of China, the first realisation that must have come to the post-Deng Xiaoping leaders, when confronted with the partially-liberalised economic atmosphere, would have been that there is a stiff price tag attached to it. Economic liberalisation must lead, beyond a point, to dilution of the absolute single party monolithic structure that prevailed in China during the second half of the twentieth century. The architects of globalisation in the West – again USA being the chief architect – had planned the invasive globalisation model with a bigger aim. The aim plus had twin objectives. The first being to maintain a pace whose rapidity would keep the lesser developed countries off balance so that they could never pause to regain their balance and take stock to effect mid-term corrections. Put in another way, the globalisation model launched from the West was specifically designed to maintain a state of disequilibrium in the Third World. Unless the leaders of Third World countries appreciate this fact and get their act together – to plan counter strategies – the Third World will not ever be able to catch up.

In as far as it pertains to China, the second major objective, riding on the coat tails of globalisation was to force democracy on China; again at a "pace" at which the transformation from a stable system of government – whatever its ills – to the Western democratic model would create disequilibrium, if not outright anarchy. It should be noted the emphasis here is on the destabilising "rate" of change rather than the question of democracy *per se*.

India and China have a common interest in ensuring harmony in Asia so that the long suffering peoples of the de-colonialised nations of this continent are first able to stand firmly on their own feet before they find their place in the sun. For, should the two largest countries on the globe, start modernising rapidly as per the American gospel of modernisation the planet would become uninhabitable somewhere before the end of the next century – even without a nuclear holocaust. To elaborate, one need take only an example or two by way of illustration. Should China and India adopt only a few of the consumerist habits of the average US citizen it would mean the adding of such numbers of automobiles so as to create a global inferno. The accompanying increase in energy consumption and waste generation would reduce the two countries to becoming environmental graveyards, and junkyards. Culturally, they would have become clones of

USA, as many of the Japanese have been induced to become.

The gravity of what is being stated must be comprehended by the leaders and the peoples of these two countries, China and India. They must strain every sinew to maintain their ancient heritage and their cultural identities. They owe it to themselves and to the generations of the human race to follow. To give another example, the Chinese people right up to the eighties decades were mainly poultry consumers. Many of them have changed their habit to become beef eaters, in the Western mould. It requires one ton of grain to raise a ton of poultry, whereas a ton of beef requires eight tons of feed. Already grain shortages are anticipated in China in the coming decades. A Wall Street Journal article published in January 1999 had it that by the year 2030 China's grain shortage would assume such proportions that the country would require to mop up all the grain surpluses in the world to meet its grain requirements. Indian economic planners and the burgeoning Indian middle class must take heed before they too are irreversibly mesmerized by the great American dream. A dream whose end result would be the eco-destruction of the Planet. Recent studies carried out by the World Bank have made stunning revelations. When Thailand doubled its GDP its industrial pollution load went up ten times.

The point that is being highlighted is that while globalisation is upon the Third World these countries will have to take stock every now and then; so that they are able to sit back and calmly assess for themselves the beneficial and deleterious effects of the rapid change being inflicted upon them. Unless this exercise is expertly undertaken the underdeveloped and developing countries will start ruing their folly, when it would be too late – shutting the stable door after the horse has bolted. They will mature only after they have mortgaged the economic freedom of their successor generations in unequal and imperfectly understood global protocols devised by the West. None, if any, of these protocols originated in the

Third World. The underdeveloped countries, already reeling under an unsupportable debt burden, have no means to prevent the organised plunder of their remaining assets. This is where China and India can join hands to remove the shackles with which the underdeveloped countries have been subtly bound. China must play the role of a responsible global leader of the 21st Century. It must ensure that it does not desert the world to which it belongs and be enticed into the rich man's club in the manner of Japan.

China, the United Nations and the New World Order

China no doubt is a permanent member of the UN Security Council with veto rights. In the second half of this century when the country was in the process of growing to its natural size it needed the veto right to protect its vital interests against the two superpowers of that time as it could have been thwarted by either of them in its quest for occupying its rightful space in the world. This is no longer the case. One of the erstwhile superpowers is now itself in a vulnerable state. The remaining superpower is no longer in a position to dictate terms to China. China has come a long way, a very long way indeed. It is an unquestioned global power at the close of the twentieth century.

The world of the next century has to change. If global destruction is to be avoided then a more equitable world order will have to replace the expansionist and exploitative order of the centuries that followed the industrial revolution in the West. A strong China will no longer find it necessary to take shelter behind its Security Council veto. Hence, it must play a leadership role in seeking a restructuring of the Security Council so that it becomes more representative of the whole world. The next century will not countenance the victors of the Second Great War of the twentieth century lording it over the rest of the world, a good fifty years and more after their victory. China has prospered after a long hard struggle. Its people, like most of the people in the Third World, have had to endure great hardship over the centuries. It can only now begin to enjoy the fruits of its labour. Such enjoyment is only possible if the world order is generally in equilibrium. The peoples of China will find no rewards in a fragmented world order. The present lopsided world order handsomely benefited the West. It had hardly any attraction for the non-Western world. China, Russia and India have a very big stake in working collectively to bring in long overdue changes in the UN system.

Concluding Remarks

Were China and India to gaze through the same lens at the global horizon deep into the next century they would realise that they would have far more in common in the future than they had in the troubled twentieth century. This would become apparent from the ensuing chart.

Areas of convergence of interest between China and India and time frame in which they start influencing decision-makimg

Area of Convergence	When Become Apparent	Joint Approach
Himalayan Environment	First decade of the 21st century	Joint eco-restoration in border areas and Tibet
Further Eastward or Southward expansion of NATO	First decade of 21st Centruy	Commonality of interest with Russia
Any further weakening of Russia	immediate	Several Possibilities
Increasing US military presence in Central Asia	Immediate	Commonality of interest with Russia

Asian stability	immediate	Several Possibilities
Global stability	Any time in the future	In conncert with UN

China is a great country with great potential. At this juncture it still has a conscious choice, before it is irrevocably entrapped in the American model of growth, as have so many other countries. While certain changes are inevitable in countries that have to modernize to survive in the present day world, it is to be hoped that China will not completely shed its civilisational values in the process – as Japan seems to have done and India seems to be doing. Should China decide to take a wrong turn then there would hardly be any future worth contemplating for the human race on this planet in the millennia to follow.

Section II
Subcontinental Affairs

Introduction

7. A Farewell to Arms
8. Leadership in the Army
9. National Security: The Dangerous Drift must Stop
10. Force Multiplication at the Intermediate and Lower Ends of the Technology Spectrum
11. India's Security Imperative
12. Restructuring the Armed Forces
13. Subcontinental Realities at the Turn of the Century
14. Strategic Challenges for India in the 21st Century
15. Remoulding the Subcontinent

Subcontinental Affairs

Introduction

If there was a "Human Misery Index", the Indian subcontinent would rank with sub-Saharan Africa as a place where hope barely survives. Although it is home to one of the oldest existing civilisations, its late-history has been a history of foreign subjugation which has left its mark on its people and its culture. It has chained its future, till the subcontinent is able to transcend the many divides (not only of "lines drawn by its colonial masters") and comes together to address its myriad problems. If, however, it is able to emerge from the dark and shed light on the present and future of humanity on earth then its deep spiritual reserve will enrich the world immeasurably and may be even show it a path beyond its greed for more things, more consumption... and at the same time less happiness and less culture.

In this section, Vinod Saighal expounds on the destiny of the subcontinent which according to him cannot be reached till its people start thinking and acting in the "subcontinental mode". The implications of these are analysed clearly and a case is made for remoulding the subcontinent so that it can become more accountable to its people and its destiny, and not merely viewed as the "most likely place for possible nuclear armageddon". He also makes an intriguing proposal that "Tibet become the *bridge* between: India and China; China and the West; and China and the rest of the world. Such a reversal could become an historical turning point, not only for the future of Tibet, but for the future of India, of China, and for mankind as a whole."

7

A Farewell to Arms

Another war between India and Pakistan would be physical suicide for Pakistan, economic suicide for India, and a catastrophe for the subcontinent. War – conventional, nuclear or even proxy – has ceased to be an option for India and Pakistan. For Pakistan it is just not winnable in military terms and for India it is simply not affordable in economic terms. Besides, the region is being overtaken by events whose import is being discerned by the vast majority of people on both sides of the border even if it is not being comprehended by their ruling elite.

Pakistan has neither geographical nor historical depth – major reasons for the innate fear that governs its behaviour. Strange as it may sound, the country is running out of options as well. It does not have the strength to inflict a military defeat on India, now or in the foreseeable future; and one does not go to war unless one has a reasonable chance of winning. When Pakistan went to war in 1965 it suffered a reverse; in 1971 it suffered mortification; a lost third round would almost certainly write *finis* to its tale.

Pakistani generals of today are no longer of the Yahya mould. They are sound professionals and hardheaded realists. The military reality could not be lost on them, as it is not lost on the rest of the world. The US could conceivably tilt the balance somewhat in their favour, but unless India is caught totally unawares, it can never be sufficiently tilted to cause serious military reverse.

So far as the nuclear scenario is concerned; the amount of verbiage generated on the nuclear capabilities of both countries in Western reviews is disproportionate to the dimensions of the problem. Three aspects need reiteration: Indian and Pakistani leaders, their public posturing notwithstanding, would be as responsible or irresponsible as any Western leader was during the height of the cold war. Any miscalculation or irresponsibility on the part of the cold warriors would have resulted in the devastation of the globe; a similar miscalculation on the part of the subcontinental adversaries would mostly harm the poverty-stricken populations of both countries. And last, but not least. Pakistani leaders, if it came to the crunch, would be reluctant to unleash a nuclear attack on India because the retaliation would be swift and massive. The damage to India would be unacceptably heavy. Pakistan would cease to exist.

Having realised a long time ago that a conventional or nuclear war against India was unwinnable, the Pakistani strategists embarked upon the covert war. After nearly ten years, the so-called low-cost option too seems to be losing its relevance. A strategy remains viable if the damage to the opponent is substantially higher than the cost to oneself. The profitability of the covert option to Pakistan peaked with Charar-e-Sharief. The law of diminishing returns will soon set in.

The covert war does hurt India (more due to the ineptness of its leaders than anything that Pakistan can do); but due to its vastness and amorphousness it is well able to absorb the shocks. Not so Pakistan. The proxy war strategy is now not only proving counter-productive but may well have begun to boomerang. Unless Pakistan pulls in its horns and eschews war as an option, it might suffer losses as severe as the loss of Bangladesh even before the turn of the century.

For nearly five decades the people of Pakistan had no choice but to put their destinies in the hands of their military leaders. The blindfold and straitjacket cannot remain in place indefinitely. They see India, whatever its (trumpeted) failings, surging ahead. The colossal waste of 50 years of their national earnings and energies, channelised, solely towards India-baiting, is manifesting itself in more ways than one.

At the same time, the realisation is dawning that if a war against India is unwinnable, now or in the foreseeable future, then expending such a disproportionately large portion of their national income on an insatiable military machine is an insult to their intelligence and a mockery of their indigence. (In real life, the leaders themselves seldom have "to eat grass").

The average person in Pakistan may be ready for a change, having realised the futility of prolonged hostility which never seems to bring tangible results but adds only more misery. He may also have realised that his government is not in control of the situation. The Inter Services Intelligence agency (ISI) monster might have gotten out of hand and started feeding on the people of Pakistan themselves. Karachi is paying the price for the destruction of Kabul. The higher price for the destruction of the Sufi shrine of Chrar-e-Sharief might again have to be paid in Pakistan.

If Pakistan has artificially stunted its growth by remaining in India's shadow for nearly half a century, the Indian leadership too became ostrich-like by adopting a Pak-tinted world-view. Whatever the sins of omission or commission in the past, the Indian leaders must appreciate the altered ground realities. Today India and Pakistan are seen to be the most painful squabblers of the second half of the 20th century. The sorry spectacle that their representatives provide at every global forum has reached levels that self-respecting Indians and Pakistanis feel ashamed of. Mr. Klaus Naturp, a specialist on the Indian subcontinent, said in a despatch in the *Frankfurter Allegmeine Zeitung* about the dilemma of foreign dignitaries visiting Pakistan over the Kashmir issue. "No guest can escape it (Kashmir). Pakistani politicians and military are obsessed by the theme," he wrote.

At the very least it is hoped that India will be able to pull the subcontinent out of the cul-de-sac into which we stumbled several decades ago. A stage will soon come where the world will actually die of 'ennui' if they are exposed to more of the Indo-Pak slanging matches. Not only the rest of the world but even the people of the subcontinent are fed up with the tired old rhetoric. At the ordinary levels of existence, the vast majority of people of India and Pakistan would like nothing better than to consign the politicians, diplomats and defence planners of both countries to the nether regions, in perpetuity.

If the impasse has got prolonged beyond its natural life span, the Indian leadership is as much to blame. Just as war is not an option for Pakistan it is no longer an option for India. The threat from Pakistan will soon become non-existent if Indian leaders show cohesion and competence. Other threats, more insidious than that posed by Pakistan are looming on the horizon. India has the wherewithal to prepare for them. Are the leaders locked in their petty squabbling, able to perceive them? Do they have the will to create an array of options that will be required by the coming generation if they are to find a place in the sun.

Meanwhile, India has to take care of Pakistan itself. India should not depend on others to pull its chestnuts out of the fire. To begin with, it can tell the world that since a stable subcontinent would be a necessary precondition for the global equipoise of the next millennium, the world must leave India and Pakistan alone for a while. The leaders of the two countries must learn what the people of India and Pakistan may have instinctively begun to realise, albeit belatedly after decades of mistrust and violence: that they will have to speedily resolve their differences before they are overtaken by events that neither side would be able to control. If India and Pakistan do not pull themselves up by their bootstraps, the world will leave them behind to wallow in their self-inflicted miseries.

8

Leadership in the Army

Today I shall talk to you on a subject which is fundamental to every aspect of military activity. In war, it is critical to the successful outcome of battle and, in the interregnum between wars which we call peace, it goes a long way towards ensuring that the army remains in a trim state to meet any challenge.

In the next hour or so I shall speak on the subject of leadership in the army. A number of eminent military men throughout the ages have reminisced and written about the qualities and attributes that make men into successful leaders. The biographies of these men and their writings are an inspiration to us. These books are available in your library and I would recommend that you make it a point to read them. More recently we have had a spate of books on leadership by experts who have probed the human mind. These bring out the complexities of present day societies and how they affect the men in uniform. They too provide fascinating psychological insights into the make-up of a soldier and his reaction under stress in battle.

From what I have just said it may have become apparent to you that I am not going to follow the well-trodden path of a straightforward talk on leadership in the classical mould. Instead I am going to dwell at some length upon the crisis of leadership that has developed in most modern societies and which by extension has had a not inconsiderable impact on military leadership at all levels.

This is a crisis that you will confront and have to squarely face. I do not mind admitting to you, at the very outset, that the challenges (as commanders of men) that "you" are likely to face are greater than was faced by my generation when we joined the army of a newly independent India. Regardless of other aspects, we had inherited a system where the officer class was respected 'per se' and any one commissioned as an officer automatically enjoyed a status, obedience and respect which was quite different from what it is today. I do not intend to go into the reasons for this decline. They are manifold: ranging from a straightforward decline in values and standards to subtle forces which are imperfectly understood. What this means is that when you go to your units each one of you will have to "prove" to the men that you are fit to be their leader. The moral weight of tradition would be available to you only upto a point.

Inspite of what I have said so far, there are, nevertheless, certain attributes and qualities of a leader which are elemental. We can safely say that they have been uniformly applicable throughout history. The upright man, a fair-minded man, a man with initiative and courage will still be respected anywhere. These are basic qualities. Many others can be added to complete the picture of a well-rounded personality and a good leader of men. I shall touch upon some of them as we go along. Please remember one thing, however. Once you have built up a mental picture of a good leader you must then stand back and take an objective look at yourselves; because, the person who emerges from such a description would be a perfect man. Human beings are seldom perfect. So, in a detached manner, take stock of your strengths and weaknesses and "aspire" to develop as many of the qualities as you can. This development is an on-going process and each one of us changes, or should change, with age and experience.

I see a leader as a man of vision. Raising himself from the humdrum of daily chores, a man of vision can look beyond to the farther horizons. Not only can he perceive these himself but he is also able to provide a glimpse to the men he leads so that their faith in him, and their own ability to reach those goals, remains unimpaired. But this is seldom the case these days. It is with sadness that I behold the majority of youngsters today starting their army careers with a lack of idealism or belief in themselves. As a formation commander, when I had occasion to go around my formations and units, instead of seeing young officers bubbling with energy, ideas and a sense of adventure, I generally saw deflated "young old men" worried about their careers, their courses and their age of retirement. Gentlemen, if you are constantly worried about "yourself" what sort of leadership can you provide to your men. How will you lead them in battle? They see your concern for yourself writ large on your face and are disheartened. If at the tender age of 20 you have lost your ideals how can you hope to inspire others to have visions of a great army and a great country. Gentlemen, let me tell you that if you start life in this fashion there can be no "real" rewards for you at the end of your career, no matter how successful it may appear from the outside. With such an attitude you might attain senior ranks but you will get no joy from it. You will be an embittered man because you would have made all sorts of compromises during the best years of your life. You would have missed out on life and nobody would be able, at that belated stage, to restore to you the joyousness, spontaneity and camaraderie that should be yours in a healthy and happy environment. You will end up a supposedly successful man: looking back upon a sterile life. So, I would like to say to you that please do not limit your horizons. Please cherish and safeguard the quality and freshness of your dreams at the start of your life. Keep alive a spirit of adventure and take life as it comes.

The next aspect I wish to touch upon is professional pride. I use this word in its positive sense. As a soldier, and especially, as an officer, you must have pride in your unit, your profession and your country. Remember, the profession of arms has always been an honorable one. If you are not proud of your uniform, and all that it stands for, you have no business to be wearing it in the first place. Our country has a volunteer army. Each one of us who is here has come of his own volition. Hence, whatever your reasons for entering the service always emphasise the positive side to your men. In the army you may not find all the money or perquisites that glitter at a distance when you see some of your counterparts in the civil. There are other rewards, other forms of recompense: ones which we take for granted. We in the Army always possessed, what the Field Marshal (Sam Maneckshaw) referred to once, as a 'reverse snobbery'. We always put up a bold front. Whatever our travails and tribulations we never communicated our misgivings to outsiders.

The army is not only a fine profession, it is a way of life. Don't let cynical people destroy your values or your beliefs at the start of your careers. Don't let your head be turned by a vulgar display of wealth that you so often behold amongst a new breed that has come up in the metropolitan cities. They must be viewed against the backdrop of poverty and misery that still afflict the majority of our people. You must not underestimate your own worth. You must keep your hope and ideals alive in the turmoil all around you for, when all else fails, "you" will be the ultimate guarantors of India's integrity and sanctity.

9

National Security: The Dangerous Drift Must Stop

"*Hunooz Dilli Door Ast*". This line in Persian from India's tragic past, attributed to a King of Delhi, aptly sums up the security environment in the country; or, at least the mind-set of those responsible for India's security at the highest levels. The pointers towards this dangerous drift are frightening; and yet the powers that be show a complacency that is even more chilling. What are these pointers?

We begin with the decision-making hierarchy at the national level. It defies analysis. India is perhaps the only country in the world with modern armed forces that deals with its security planning in such a cavalier fashion. It is ad hoc; it lacks cohesion; and at the apex level it is handled mostly by people who cannot possibly have anything more than an armchair acquaintance with security in the field or its global dimensions.

Insignificant

India's largest neighbour is leaving no stone unturned to strangulate it should the need arise. China with a permanent seat and veto right in the Security Council is yet straining every nerve to augment its not inconsiderable nuclear and conventional military might. India's capacity to inflict any 'real' damage on China would perhaps be insignificant.

China's potential to inflict damage on India, in comparison, would perhaps be of an order of magnitude. Not remaining content with such lop-sided military superiority, it is continuously making inroads into every country neighbouring India. The writing on the wall is as clear as it is ever likely to be. While no effort should be spared in improving relations with China, it would be both imprudent and unpardonable to leave future generations wholly at the mercy of China's goodwill.

In an unequal military relationship a portion of the country's sovereignty remains permanently impaired if the very thought of a deepened frown impinges on foreign policy decision-making. Here, it would be pertinent to recall the statement made by Singapore's Lee Kuan Yew in a recent interview. To the question, 'Some Asian countries already feel threatened. Is that worry legitimate?' Lee replied 'I think so. Not that they're going to be captured, but it's about freedom of action. In decisions you make you have to factor in the reaction of a very big and important neighbour. By letting China develop such an overwhelming military disparity India will not only curtail its own freedom of action (for decades to come) but would, by extension. become instrumental in forcing smaller neighbours, historically and culturally inclined towards India, to curtail their freedom of action as well. Whether we like it or not, whether we wish to admit it or not, the policy followed by India's defence planners is pushing the country headlong into this corner.

Coming next to the USA, that country has declared its intent to try and foreclose several options for India. The intent has been spelled out so often and so unequivocally that it cannot be stated in plainer language. For nearly four decades the USA and many of its allies have been undermining the stability of India, either directly or through hostile neighbours. It requires a special type of abstruseness to misread the past. Such abstruseness is not lacking in this country. Nothing under these circumstances, could be more ridiculous than to lament before Pakistan's backers that by arming Pakistan the donors would be forcing India to spend more on armaments. But that is exactly what the whole exercise is about: to force India to spend more on relatively useless types of armaments; armaments that can only inflict damage on its partitioned limb; armaments that can only lead to fratricide and nothing more, nothing beyond. This policy ensures that not enough money is left for armaments that can make India a world player.

In as far as it relates to Pakistan, realization is fast dawning on both sides of the divide that protestations of its leaders notwithstanding, Pakistan is not the prime mover. Here a small illustration from the field of economics will suffice. When a banker bails out a client it makes sure that it gets leverage with that client. These days financial institutions put their own nominees on the board of firms to whom they make sizeable loans.

Unstable

In the case of our neighbour the bailing out has taken place so often that if any freedom of action still remains it would only be by sufferance of the donor. Should the threat of rapprochement between the subcontinental neighbours (as perceived by the global power brokers) become real a way out would be found to make available the next tranche of weapons to Pakistan. Hence, India's security environment will continue to be unstable until the day the peoples of Pakistan throw off the yoke of their 'programmed democracy'.

Coming back to India, the internal security dilemmas have been well brought out in a series of articles by several responsible persons. They hardly need elaboration. A plethora of security agencies continue to work in an uncoordinated manner, often at cross purposes. The recent exposures make even more dismal reading. What is beginning to stand out clearly is that the enemy within is potentially far move sinister than the enemy without. It is also becoming equally clear that the enemy within has nothing to do with communities *per se*. It has to do with failure of intelligence, lack of clear direction and misgovernance. Even more dangerous, it has a lot to do with the subversion of the governing hierarchy at various levels of governance. It should be apparent to most concerned citizens that the Government *of* India is no longer in control of the Government *in* India. What is true in the field of internal security could equally apply to the field of defence. Should that be the case, some urgent steps will have to be taken to check the dangerous drift.

Irreversible

The churning taking place at the hustings provides an historic opportunity to set things right before irreversible and unacceptable compromises are made to India's long-term security interests. A coalition government need not, in itself, indicate a state of affairs more degenerate (or ineffective) than the one preceding. Similarly, just because coalition governments failed in the past it does not automatically follow that people have not learned a lesson and that coalition governments must fail for all times to come. The mental association formed by the words "hung Parliament" in relation to the type of politicians that people have become used to, could have one meaning. It could have an entirely different connotation for a new set of representatives who just might have a changed concept of national security and parliamentary decorum. Not carrying any dead wood from the past, they might decide to first supply a vital dose of oxygen for reviving democracy before starting to bicker about the spoils of office.

Seeing that vital decisions would have to be made in the next few months, if not weeks, it should become the first order of business of the new Parliament and the new Government to give this issue the priority it deserves. An independent national security council is the ineluctable need of the hour. The time for debates is long past. The President of India would be well within the bounds of constitutional propriety to advise the new Government to set up the requisite machinery within a stipulated time frame in the overriding interest of national security. *'Dilli'* must forever actually remain *'door'* for those casting baleful glances at this ancient land. The ships that henceforth come to its shore must come to trade and not to invade. The destiny of India is once again in the hands of its citizens. The new parliamentarians, the repositories of the nation's hopes, can ensure that it remains so.

10

Force Multiplication at the Intermediate and Lower Ends of the Technology Spectrum

Like much else since the Second World War, military neologisms have preceded the sale of military equipment to the Third World. A whole generation of military leaders of nations emerging from their colonial past were conditioned into a mindset that prevented them from seeing that there was very little resemblance between the military needs of their countries and the military doctrines taught to them in the West, and later the USSR. It was a pathetic sight to see newly-established war colleges of emerging nations wasting time on doctrines of NATO and Warsaw Pact countries. Even more ridiculous examples can be cited. Fighting skills, pertaining to their own sectors, were allowed to atrophy. China and Vietnam were exceptions.

Over fifty years have elapsed since the end of the Second World War. Even the Cold War seems a long time ago. Other nations have since fought major wars. Their military leadership has become more professional and self-assured. And yet, the majority of the developing countries still keep falling into the trap set for them since the end of the Great War – the technology trap. Not only does this become a heavy drain on their exchequers but also results in their defeat in detail at the hands of forces possessing superior technology. What then are the answers? How do these countries get out of the technology trap without impairing their defence capability?

Global technology spectrum

At a seminar on "Global Competivity for Indian Industry" in November 1995 the global technology horizon was analysed by the writer under the following heads.

* Technology Thrusts
  ⇒ Long term
  ⇒ Short term
  ⇒ Prioritisation
  ⇒ Re-focalisation

* Technology Upgradation
* Technology Obsolescence
* Technology Degradation, Technology Extrapolation, Technology Interfaces
* Technology Trap
* Low Tech Back-Up
* Technology Marketing (Strategies)
* Technology Assessment
* Threats and Challenges

While most of the items covered in the global technology round-up relate to military technology as well, here it would be possible to dwell only on a few of the more important ones concerning military acquisitions.

Fighting through high-tech paralysis

Since the domination of the West in military high-tech can hardly be challenged in a hurry it would be suicidal for developing countries acquiring armaments to place over-reliance on high-tech warfare. It should not have come as a surprise that the Gulf War was over even before it was fully joined. This had hardly anything to do with the relative fighting skills of the adversaries. It had a lot to do with serious miscalculations and high-tech paralysis. The high-tech paralysis was brought about in several ways. Even before the actual fighting started, the so-called friends of Iraq, who had benefited handsomely from Iraqi largesse through arms purchases running into several billion dollars, abandoned their star client without batting an eyelid. Electronics and armaments firms of world repute took no time in handing over details of the Electronic Counter Measures (ECM) packages fitted on Iraqi weapons systems as well as the means to counter them. The Russians followed suit. So much for the worth of international contracts, for purchases made in free foreign exchange. Not related to the justness or otherwise of the war, several questions of military relevance have not only remained unanswered but were never even posed. The first question which should have been asked by all importers of armaments immediately after the war can be framed simply thus: If an Iraqi type of intransigence had been committed by an advanced country, would these firms have passed on the ECM packages and their neutralisation modes to those attempting to right the wrong? The next question which should automatically follow would relate to the sanctity of future purchases made by developing countries from armaments firms of advanced countries. (What is applicable to purchases applies equally to generously off-loaded surplus armaments, donated to fuel an arms race).

The less developed countries have a natural ability to fight and sustain low-tech wars in their own milieu. The moment they shed their native as distinct from primitive warfare skills and go overboard on high-tech they are asking for trouble. The lesson of the Vietnam War (overlaid by the more recent Gulf War) was again highlighted in

Somalia. The two examples which follow should help to illustrate the point.

One of the observers at a NATO exercise a few years ago disconnected the supply to the computer network at an artillery command post. In the consternation that ensued it was found that amongst all the artillery officers present at the Command Post not one had retained the elementary skill of taking an ordinary shoot without the help of computers. The second, more general, example relates to a phenomenon which is very rare in developed societies – power breakdown of a grid. Where the breakdown continued over a long period of time entire communities failed to cope, plunging urban conglomerates into nightmarish chaos; representing possibly a civilisation breakdown. In poorer societies similar occurrences seldom result in near total breakdown.

Prudence dictates that resource-poor countries do not allow themselves to be sucked into high-tech traps, based on doctrines which do not apply to them; which, in any case, they should not be adopting without an incisive analysis of the type of warfare specific to their region. For developing countries, whose economies might occasionally be coaxed to cater for certain high-tech acquisitions, it would still be prudent to retain well-honed abilities to fight on through high-tech paralysis. Their short term adversaries might be regional neighbours. Nevertheless, it would be military folly of an extreme order not to plan for the potential adversaries of the next century; adversaries whose potential to inflict real damage would be of an order of magnitude compared to the 'brother enemy'.

Fighting on ground of one's choosing

The literal meaning of the term "fighting on ground of one's choosing" would be known to any military commander. It is the extension of this term, in its figurative sense, to other aspects of warfare which requires to be gone into. An example could be the neutralisation or diminishment of the high-tech advantage of outside powers that come to project their forces, to safeguard 'their' national interests, in countries thousands of miles away (which presumably are not supposed to have national interests of their own). When such force projections are carried out by the great power(s) in the next century, in concert with their true and trusted regional allies, the operations will almost invariably commence with the suppression of electronics of all weapons systems that can be used by the defender to inflict damage on the aggressor. In the past such suppression was generally through electronics fitted on aerial platforms of various types or through jamming systems positioned in close proximity, where feasible. In future conflicts, the masters of high-tech warfare will, with impunity, use mini nuclear air bursts to create total Electro-Magnetic Interference (EMI) paralysis before moving in for the kill, again with impunity, if the CTBT is ratified (in the form presented at the end of June 1996). When that happens costlier high-tech will soon enough become available on the high-tech vendors lists in the form of nuclear-hardened equipment to withstand EMI effects.

One can go on in this vein to bring home the point that while tanks and aircraft will be around in the inventories of armed forces for some time to come countries of the developing world will have to re-evaluate their weapons mix for the emerging threats of the next century, and whether they wish to place total reliance on systems which can hypothetically be swamped before they have even begun to do their job. There are several ways of getting around such high-tech traps. Each developing country must carry out a reassessment of its armaments needs to ensure that it is not led meekly to slaughter by friends of yesteryear who one fine morning decide that 'their' supreme national interest mandates turning erstwhile friends into foes. As a corollary weapons purchases from the leading manufacturers might have to be shifted to other more reliable manufacturers.

The tank provides a good example of the difference between affordable and extreme high-tech. Most modern armoured fighting vehicles have a first-round hit probability of above 75 per cent up to intermediate ranges. For achieving first-round hit probabilities of above 90 per cent at higher (direct fire) ranges of the tank gun retrofitment updates of a million dollars plus would be available in the market. Many countries have gone in for such updates. Here it would be pertinent to note that most tank versus tank battles have been fought at ranges below 1000 metres. Additionally, in countries where soldiers spend many years in active service (as opposed to the short service period in conscript armies) it is possible to hone the skill of tank gunners to very high levels of accuracy, coupled with retrofitments which are far more affordable.

Recipient-related specificities

It would be difficult to lay down a general yardstick for what exactly constitutes a technology trap and how it should be avoided. There are several factors which go into (or should affect) such considerations by military hierarchies of countries making these purchases. In the earlier decades after the War there were attempts by donors to close the gap (in the minds of the recipients) between the perceived need of the acceptor and the induced need created by the donor. This is where military courses in advanced countries, military exhibitions and military attaches came into play. As the value of military sales improved so did the skills of the salesmen. By the late 1970s, after the sudden spurt in oil prices, the skills of the representatives of leading arms manufacturers worldwide surpassed the marketing skills perfected by the business enterprises in their countries over a hundred years. All this has been well-documented by researchers and experts writing on the subject. By the end of the Cold War it should have been past history.

Since history keeps repeating itself, the Gulf War gave fresh impetus to high-tech arms sales. The quantum of high-tech arms pushed into the Gulf region 'after' the Gulf

War, at exorbitant prices, has not enhanced the security of that region as would be obvious from recent developments. If force multiplication were simply to be a multiplication factor of pounds, shillings and pence then certain countries would not have to worry about their security for a long time to come. This is obviously not the case. In spite of high-tech acquisitions running into tens of billions of dollars the level of insecurity experienced by most of the Gulf countries is actually higher today. Even another ten or twenty billion dollars spent on 'more of the same' will not significantly diminish their insecurity.

Acquisition of military high-tech must relate to the threat perceptions, both short and long-term, as perceived by the recipient and not as 'perceived for them' by the think tanks of the countries pushing the sale of arms; and not even by the native think tanks sponsored at their behest. Not many in the developing countries seem to be able to avoid this pitfall.

Most people who go in for high-tech purchases do not seem to have consciously analysed the technology degradation factor. The more complex the technology the higher the technology degradation factor is likely to be for imported military technology when measured against all the variables. Some of the variables that need to be mentioned here relate to the cost of upkeep; enhanced security requirements for guarding the very costly equipment; continued availability of spares at affordable prices for the high-tech equipment, as well as spares for the maintenance equipment specially designed to maintain the complex high-tech equipment; and the degree of dependence on outside experts for special maintenance and repair needs, linked to their dependability when the need is greatest, i.e. during war. An important 'rapid' technology degradation factor that should also be included as a variable concerns the relationship between the client and the supplier and the maintainability of the status quo in case of change of regime in the recipient country. For example, what happens in the case where the new regime does not meet with the approval of the country (or countries) supplying the high-tech armaments – a very likely possibility in the Middle East and even Pakistan in the not too distant future.

It is amazing that given the variables sufficient debate on these inter-related issues has not taken place in the Gulf countries or other developing countries going in for miltech purchases at the higher ends of the technology spectrum. Would the equipment purchased or donated be regime-specific or country-specific or would it have other specificities for unforeseen eventualities? Should the present configurations change, will the essential component of the equipment self-destruct in battle under certain conditions? The recipient may never know (until it is too late) as to what self-destruct instructions the high-tech exporter (global player) has programmed into the export package for developing countries for certain specific contingencies.

Paradigm shift

What applies to weapons acquisition applies equally to research and development. For well-nigh fifty years many developing countries decided to spend the bulk of their R&D funds for fabricating tanks and aircraft. It is tempting to speculate where these countries would be today had they made a 'timely switch' to development of weapons systems which will dominate tomorrow's battlefields.

The history of warfare from times immemorial is replete with instances where a superior technology changed the face of war. It is nobody's case that higher and more lethal forms of technology will not continue to dominate the battlefields of the next century, supposing always that mankind is still around to fight those battles. These technologies might technically 'dominate' the battlefield but generalship on the part of possessors of lower orders of technology demands that they plan their wars in a manner that such higher technologies are not allowed to 'prevail' on the battlefield. That is what generalship is all about. What is being stated is that blindly following the high priests of high technology to fight the battles on the ground of 'their' choosing (high-tech warfare) will spell doom for less developed countries till the time they are able to match the high-tech leaders chip for chip and all the rest that goes with supertech. In the interim lesser mortals have to draw their inspiration from the biblical story of David and Goliath. What would have been David's plight had he chosen to fight Goliath with weapons wielded by the giant?

11

India's Security Imperative

By now it should have become eminently clear to almost everyone concerned with India's security planning that over the years the country's vision had become totally distorted by its Pakistan-centricity. But the blurring of vision continues due to a refusal to empty out the distillate that remains after half a century of diplomatic (and defence) swirling around the brew concocted at the time of partition. The principal architects of partition having disappeared from the world stage, the time may have come for India to chart an independent world vision more attuned to meet the opportunities and threats looming on the world horizon. For this to happen, it would be necessary to first carry out a realistic re-appraisal of the ground reality as it is today, delinked from the fixations that developed in the post-indepenence decades.

While India itself may not have realised it, the world became alive to India's potential quite some time ago. Even before the end of the cold war (before German reunification) one of the members of a Eurpoean group of financiers, trying to peer into the hazy future mused, almost presciently, that Berlin and Bombay could well be amongst the financial capitals of the world in the year 2025. India lagged behind not because it did not have the potential to be a world player but because the powers that continue to hold dominion in South Asia were able to induce a tunnel vision in the leaders of the nations of the subcontinent.

If India still continues to lag behind after the scales have been brutally removed from its eyes, then it must be prepared for the rawest of deals in the next century. This level of vulnerability could not have been reached if its leaders had not allowed themselves to become hostage to the machinations of forces inimical to the country's quest for a better deal for its people and a more equitable world order. Should that be the case, it would be prudent for the country to appreciate that in the world order as it is currently shaping up, it is swimming unprotected in a sea of sharks.

There is no hyperbole in what is being said. In every international treaty relating to economic and security spheres – both spheres being the cornerstones of a country's security edifice – the handwriting on the wall is as clear as daylight: those who are unable to guard their turf will be squeezed out (or eaten up by the sharks). If there is one country in the world which should never have forgotten this lesson, that country is India. In 1487 when Bartolomeu Dias came to the wealthy trading ports of the Malabar coast, he returned to Portugal with stories of great wealth. He also carried back tales of "vulnerability". It was a case of history repeating itself. For the same (historical) reasons the reappraisal of India's security imperatives must take on a realism that it has lacked so far.

By now, India's security planners should have grasped an essential fact: that Pakistan's governing hierarchy had long ago mortgaged its freedom of action. If this fact is grasped by India's defence and foreign policy establishments, everything will fall into place. More importantly, it will allow the country to plan more realistically for the perils that lie ahead: perils which are far more grave than any faced by it to date. The reasons for the loss of decision-making freedom of Pakistani governments – except to keep moving in the direction in which it is propelled by invisible hands – have been clearly spelled out by several writers on the subject.

Since, on its own, Pakistan never had the capacity to be anything more than a thorn in India's flesh it can be reasonably inferred that those who provide the poison for the tips of fresh thorns being prepared to be pushed into India's side are no friends of India. Conceivably, by their recent actions, they have rendered a great service to India. At long last, the country has been impelled to call a spade a spade and face up to the stark reality that it too was well on the way to mortgaging the options of future generations of Indians. India's real enemies can only be those countries that continue to arm and embolden Pakistan's ruling hierachies. The ordinary people of Pakistan are not, and cannot be, enemies of India.

Having identified the 'real' enemies, it behoves India's security planners to orient its defences to meet the 'real' threats darkening the country's security horizon. Here again we run into a nearly insurmountable difficulty. As in the case of Pakistan, albeit to a lesser degree, the governments of India, in recent years, too lost their freedom of manoeuvre. The reasons are well-known. This was best summarised in one of the talks delivered by the author last year at a renowned forum in the capital. "Many of the leaders are no longer independent actors. The government of India may drag its feet over prosecution of people who acted against the interests of the country while holding positions of power. The intelligence agencies of several foreign governments would not have left any stone unturned to gather such evidence. It is anybody's guess as to how this evidence is being used."

Not many people doubt that, whatever the reason, India's long term security interests were being compromised at the political apex. But for a timely electoral change, irretrievable damage could have been caused. Damage limitation, however, has not proceeded apace because of a "residual security dilemma". The electoral change, while it led to re-shuffling (for better or for worse) in ministerial berths, did not lead to meaningful change in the hierachies that underpinned the political decisions. It is not inconceivable that over the years many in these organisations were subverted along with their political masters. It will not be an easy task to remove all such people from positions of responsibility. As in the case of a neighbour, these entrenched officials continue to support the grand (global) designs of the international power brokers. Even sworn enemies of India could not have retarded India's march towards security self-sufficiency to the extent that it was retarded by the packing of security decision-making organs with officials who did not, and perhaps still will not, allow India's real security needs to be met. In the long run this trend is far more dangerous than the suppresion of promising scientific programmes.

12

Restructuring of the Armed Forces

Another war between India and Pakistan will be physical suicide for Pakistan, economic suicide for India, and a catastrophe for the subcontinent.

A stable subcontinent of India at peace with itself is an essential prerequisite for the global equipoise of the next millennium.

Introduction

There appears to be a vague uneasiness at the heightened insecurity in and around the region. The Government strives valiantly to make the best of a far from satisfactory situation. There is a suspicion that the country may have led itself into a morass from which it finds difficult to extricate itself. Without speculating as to where our predecessors went wrong in this regard we should make a determined effort to look ahead for making the leap into the next century.

The time may have come for India to chart out an independent world vision more attuned to meet the opportunities and threats looming on the world horizon. For this to happen, it would be necessary to carry out a realistic reappraisal of the ground reality, de-linked from the fixations that developed in the post-independence decades.

The first major change that has taken place is that the geostrategic emphasis has shifted from the plains of Punjab and Rajasthan to the mountains and the seas, not only for the subcontinent but for the continent as a whole. We have been slow to appreciate the change. Our adversary of yesteryear, having realised the futility of waging a conventional war against India left the middle ground and moved to the nuclear and the Low Intensity Conflict (LIC) ends of warfare. For ten years or so, the country kept on pumping resources into areas where the enemy was not and thereby missed a golden opportunity to become a global frontrunner in several fields. Having said that, it needs to be added, that the situation that has developed is not entirely an uncomfortable one for India and the strengths created will stand us in good stead during the time required to make certain strategic shifts.

India is a potential world player. Even for basic survival in the next century it must learn to be a global player. The whole of South East Asia and several other regional countries will lose their independence, in one way or the other, if India continues to whimper.

In the Twenty First century, India has to match the larger security threats looming on the region's horizon. It is axiomatic that if one is able to take care of the bigger menace the lesser threats automatically get taken care of. Pakistan must be allowed to go its way. It must be allowed to nuclearise, acquire whatever armaments it wishes to acquire, either for its own safety or as the superpower's (or the emergent super power's) "Trojan Horse" on the subcontinent. Even Pakistan's nuclear deterrent is not an independent deterrent. The project was financed by Libya and Saudi Arabia. USA and the Western world cannot wish this mortgage away. The word 'Islamic bomb' has to be taken in its literal sense, in more ways than one. If it is ever used it will be responsible for the destruction of more adherents of Islam than any other faith. China too has an indirect lien on the bomb. The possibility of a lien on it by the great superpower's clandestine agency cannot be excluded.

Therefore, India must free itself from the nuclear, missile and every other non-pacific linkage with Pakistan. Should that country wish to come into the subcontinental fold it should feel free to do so. Should it wish to remain outside the pale, either of its own volition or for circumstances beyond its control, it must again be free to do so. It is well within India's capability to cater for threats to the nation and the region in which it must co-exist with neighbours.

Threat Perceptions

There is a tendency at the national level to downplay the threats to national security. While India may not be in a position to match the outlays of its potential adversaries, there is a threshold below which India cannot "ever" afford to go unless it wishes to jeopardise its security. The present outlays are already below that threshold. It may not be out of place to cite the case of a country, which has not fought a war for centuries. The country faces no threat in the foreseeable future. Yet it will not compromise on its security. Reproduced below is an extract from an interview given on 11 Feb 97 at Jerusalem by Lars Reke, Sweden's State Secretary for Defence.

> 'We regard the risk of an hostile attack on Sweden as being NIL currently. But you do not know what will happen in Russia. This is the reason we need strong armed forces in the future".

India is intrinsically a strong country. If a feeling of helplessness has been engendered in a nation of 980 million people, it cannot be attributed solely to the machinations of outside powers. The real demoralisation has been brought about by the incapacity of the leadership to take the right and 'timely' decisions. Even if the leadership continues to be weak, the country can progress if the vital aspects of security are not neglected. No country can force India to give up on its minimum security needs. China is not only seeking parity with the leading military power of the world but has also added to its military posture against India in several ways. Not so India. Instead of creating options for the coming generations, India excels in foreclosing them. Not paying heed to one's security needs is a cardinal sin which no nation can afford to commit.

Geo-Political Time Horizon Power Asymmetries

Certain asymmetries can develop with some of the key players whose activities in the region may impinge on India's security. The projections upto 2010 are given in the chart.

Military
1. India – China   Factor of 8 to 1 0 (-ve)
2. India – USA   Factor of 15 to 20 (-ve)
3. India – Pak   Factor of 3 to 5 (+ve)

Economic
1. India- China   Factor of 2 to 3 (-ve')
4. India – USA   Factor of 8 to 1 0 (-ve)
5. India – Pak   Factor of 3 to 5 (+ve)

The asymmetries with USA and China keep increasing; almost exponentially with the USA and significantly with China. With Pakistan the asymmetries improve in India's favour with each passing year.

India does not have to wage war against anyone. The only credible way to ensure that war does not take place is to make it clear to potential adversaries that the country has the wherewithal and the "will' to inflict irreparable retaliatory damage. The perceived threats to India's security in the short, intermediate and longer time horizons are as under.

Time Horizon 2000	Time Horizon 2010-25	Beyond 2025
1. Externally Induced LIC	1. China	1. China
2. Demography linked to bad governance.	2. Demography	2. Goblal Environmental Threats
3. US-induced distortions to security preparedness.	3. Western World.	
4. China-induced threats.	3. THI	3. THI
5. Pak-related threats.		
6. Time Horizon Imponderables (THI).		

Threat from Pakistan.

A gradual diminution of the threat from Pakistan is likely. Two distinct streams are manifesting themselves in the Pakistan social milieu – one deeply rooted in the traditions of the subcontinent and the other coalescing around the traditional governing elites. The leadership is being taken over by pragmatic entrepreneurs, who are inclined towards a rapprochement with India. The latter, centred around the military establishment, are feeling increasingly beleaguered. They have been in the ascendant for fifty years. At the end they do not have much to show for it. The fissures in Pakistan society are deepening. They must find their own adjustments, both within and with India. A military hierarchy now under siege, must "never" be allowed to harbour any illusions that it would be allowed to get away with adventurism.

Pakistan might "itself" fall into the trap that it has set for others, at the behest of others, by agencies not fully under the control of the national governments. Hence, whether the Taliban succeed in unifying Afghanistan, or fail to do so, the problems for Pakistan will get exacerbated, either way. The agenda being set for Afghanistan did not originate in Pakistan. The Agency in Pakistan, sponsoring the agenda on the ground, is answerable to its foreign handlers and not the Government of Pakistan.

Time Horizon Imponderables (THI)

Time Horizon Imponderables relate to events over which human agencies might not have control. As an example, much-vaunted American way of life may devastate the globe in about fifty to hundred years if the pattern of unrestrained over-consumption is not modified. The American model is being rapidly extended to other regions of the world, notably the ASEAN and Pacific rim countries. Like the Japanese, the Chinese too are fast becoming Western-oriented in their consumption patterns.

These consumption patterns put Japan, an otherwise affluent society, in a precarious position. From domestic security perspective, that dependence on imports makes it hostage to many calamities like changes in the weather patterns, world famines and so on. Japan is perhaps the largest importer of grains. China too imports huge amounts of grain. Both nations thus contribute in a big way to the hike in world grain prices. In China the consumption of meat is increasing rapidly. In particular, the demand for beef has risen much faster than that for the more traditional pork and chicken. It takes eight tons of feed grains to produce a ton of beef whereas a ton of pork and a ton of chicken need only four and two tons respectively.

China's Expansionism

The factors which will dictate the behaviour of China towards its neighbours, is the large size of the unemployed population which, in the next century, could reach the figure of a few hundred million. The arable land in China is being lost to industrialisation and urbanisation at a rapid pace. In spite of its huge size, China has only limited space for cultivation; it has less arable land per capita than India.

China has already shown its hand. It would be extreme folly on the part of India and South East Asia to continue to harbour illusions. The ground reality is that the final solution in Tibet has been put into effect. The Han-isation of Tibet and the decimation of the native population will be completed within the first three decades of the next century. After Tibet is fully digested, the dragon's appetite will only have been whetted. The ecology of China has already been severely degraded. The ecologies of Tibet, Western Bhutan and portions of Nepal and Myanmar under Chinese sway are being systematically destroyed. The southward march of China began in real earnest a long time ago. It has taken India nearly thirty years to wake up to the magnitude of the threat.

Demographic Threat

The demographic threat may be linked to the social unrest. It includes political uncertainties. For India, this threat has internal and external dimensions. It would suffice to say that unrestrained demographic proliferation could destroy the quality of life and the social cohesion of the subcontinental societies more comprehensively than any military threat. India being the more vibrant democracy and economy will continue to attract the deprived segments of the populations of Nepal, Bangladesh and Pakistan. The migrations are unidirectional. Reverse migration almost "never" takes place. This problem has to be addressed urgently and concertedly by all the governments of the subcontinent and at fora like SAARC.

Necessity For Restructuring

Some of the reasons for the restructuring of the armed forces are:

* *No structure can be permanent.* Restructuring is long overdue.

* *Certain options that were available to India ten years ago perhaps are no longer available:* In like fashion options not exercised today may not be available tomorrow.
* *Converging geo-centricities.* With ASEAN and IOR.
* *Breaking the bureaucratic mindset to ensure India's continued viability.* Twenty five years moratorium is recommended on the use of certain phrases like "time honoured", "withstood the test of time" etc. as an excuse for not moving ahead. Since Independence India has been boxed in "mentally", not physically.
* *Geo-strategic shift to the mountains.*
* *Non defence mutualities.* All understandings with like-minded regional neighbours to improve the region and to cater for mutual security, short of mutual defence pacts should be explored and reached.
* *Time Horizon Imponderables.* There is need to cater for cataclysmic events that could effect South East Asian security much before these countries prepare themselves for such eventualities i.e. the sudden capitulation, almost overnight, of Taiwan, contrary to all present indications. There could be several reasons for this, not excluding a secret trade-off between China and the USA, or the latter not thinking it worth its while to get involved in a full-fledged fight with an emerging super power on an issue over which an impartial international body could well concede China's claim upon the territory, if not the manner of settling the claim.
* *Post Cold War geopolitical restructuring.* Super power matrix of the next century is likely to be quite different.
* *Shedding historical amnesia.* China will soon be a super-power. Throughout history the strong powers have invariably attempted to exercise some form of

suzerainty, over their neighbours. China is no exception. As a corollary, weak and whimpering neighbours, displaying a singular lack of courage, are invariably the first to be gobbled. India, tragically, is again developing the symptoms that kept it under the heel of foreign invaders for a thousand years. Whether this state results from an ingrained pacifism, irresoluteness, or an inability to appreciate the gravity of the situation, the result is the same. What is even more stupefying is that an entire political and military hierarchy has, over the decades, refused to face up to the reality. A millennium of suppression, colonisation and deprivation has taught the rulers of post-independence India no lesson. While the soldiers on the frontline have been willing to make every sacrifice, there has been a frozen immobility in the mindset of the governing hierarchies. Unless an immediate change in direction takes place future generations of Indians might be condemned to second or third class status in world affairs.

* *Sleaze as a form of Warfare.* Enough examples have emerged from Washington and some of the Middle Eastern and European countries – and more recently in Afghanistan. This form of warfare is likely to play an increasingly important role in the next century as the spread of multinationals dilute nationalism. As it is, India is plagued with a number of scams involving large sums of money.

* *Giving Clausewitz, Mahan and other Western military thinkers a well-deserved rest and concentrating instead on India's specific and palpable needs.*

* *Safeguarding India's intrinsic strengths.* The Indian Army, in spite of working under the most trying conditions, remains the most important bastion of the country's sanctity. *Where it is a question of sheer guts and grit and fighting at impossible*

heights, under impossible climatic conditions, the Indian Army remains one of the finest battle forces in the world. High technology domination of the battlefield by the armed forces of the more advanced countries falls into an entirely different category. That category, referred to as force multiplication in military parlance, is actually multiplication factor based on pounds, shillings and pence. India can afford to shed a few tanks, guns and aircraft including carriers. It should never dilute its strengths in warfare spectra where it is second to none in the world, especially when there has been a geo-strategic shift to the mountains which will continue to affect world affairs for a long time to come. If anything, there is need to accentuate and safeguard these strengths — which require almost a lifetime to develop and are not amenable to degradation by the electromagnetic spectrum.

* *Full spectrum domination elsewhere — not on India's turf.* Refers to the stated US policy. The same applies to its efforts to "deepen and widen" its military to military cooperation with friendly countries. It could be the beginning of full scale undermining of the armed forces of the countries targeted for the purpose.

* *Comprehensive security approach.* There is hardly any informed person in the country who questions the need for the setting up of a National Security Council. If, in spite of the well-articulated and universally-conceded need, some elements have been able to consistently thwart the setting up of this body for several decades on end, the country must assume that moles of powers inimical to India's security interests have established themselves in the corridors of power.

Restructuring parameters

The proposed restructuring model is based on the parameters given below :

- * Optimised utilisation of "existing" budgetary resources.
- * While seeking global parity in certain areas in the longer term security horizon, obtaining force multiplication at the intermediate and lower ends of the technology spectrum in the interim.
- * Not falling into the high-tech technology trap set for Third World countries.
- * The ineluctable need for meeting India's vital needs in the region-specific priority areas.
- * Denial of Tibet and other regional neighbourhoods as launchpads against India.
- * Containing and "adequately" dealing with emerging threats.
- * Meeting, and safeguarding, regional aspirations.
- * India is not a party to any containment of China at the behest of any other power. It will take its own minimum defensive measures within the region as deemed fit from time to time.
- * Catering for Time Horizon Imponderables.

Fighting through High-Tech Paralysis

Since the domination of the West in military high-tech can hardly be challenged it would be suicidal for developing countries to place over-reliance on high-tech warfare. The Gulf War was over even before it was fully joined. This had hardly anything to do with the relative fighting skills of the adversaries. It had a lot to do with serious miscalculations and high-tech paralysis. Prudence dictates that resource-poor countries do not allow themselves to be sucked into high-tech traps, based on doctrines which do not apply to them. For developing countries, whose economies might occasionally be coaxed to cater for certain high-tech acquisitions, it would be prudent to retain well-honed abilities to fight on through high-tech paralysis. Their short-term adversaries might be regional neighbours. Nevertheless, it would be military folly of an extreme order not to plan for the potential adversaries of the next century. While tanks and aircraft will be around in the inventories of armed forces for some time to come, countries of the developing world will have to re-evaluate their weapons mix for the emerging threats of the next century. Each developing country must carry out a reassessment of its armament needs, to ensure that it is not led meekly to slaughter by friends of yesteryear who one fine morning decide that supreme national interest mandates turning erstwhile friends into foes. Acquisition of military high-tech must relate to the threat perceptions, as perceived by the recipient and not as 'perceived for them' by the think tanks of the countries pushing the sale of arms; and not even by the native think tanks sponsored at their behest. Not many in the developing countries seem to be able to avoid this pitfall.

The Tibet Question and India's Security

India's largest neighbour is leaving no stone unturned to strangulate it, should the need arise. China with a permanent seat and veto right in the Security Council is straining every nerve to augment its not inconsiderable nuclear and conventional military might. India's capacity to inflict any "real' damage on China would perhaps be insignificant. Not remaining content with such a lopsided military superiority, it is continuously making inroads into every country neighbouring India. While no effort should be spared in improving relations with China, it would be both imprudent and unpardonable to leave future generations wholly at the mercy of China's goodwill.

In an unequal military relationship a portion of the country's sovereignty remains permanently impaired, if the very thought of a deepened frown impinges on foreign policy decision-making. Here, it would be pertinent to recall the statement made by Singapore's Lee Kuan Yew in a recent interview. To the question, "Some Asian countries already feel threatened. Is that worry legitimate?' Lee replied "I think so. Not that they are going to be captured, but it is about freedom of action. In every decision you make you have to factor in the reaction of a very big and important neighbour". By letting China develop such an overwhelming military disparity India will not only curtail its own freedom of action but would, by extension, become instrumental in forcing smaller neighbours, historically and culturally inclined towards India, to curtail their freedom of action as well. Whether we admit it or not, the policy followed by India's defence planners was pushing the country headlong into this corner.

Whatever future historians of the Nehru era might say; there is a suspicion that the handing over of Tibet to China on a platter without obtaining any safeguards for this country was a pure and simple act of appeasement. For the hapless Tibetan people it is settled question. That, however, should not prevent people in India from taking stock of the enormity of the changes wrought in Tibet by the Chinese over nearly fifty years of unfettered exercising of their sovereign rights over a subjugated people – genocide coupled with large scale demographic changes. If the Chinese are not checked, the Tibetans will be reduced to the status of the aborigines in Australia before the next fifty years are out. The Tibetan landscape will soon become spiritually, culturally and ecologically sterile. Besides Lhasa and the other big cities Han populations will soon overflow from the Chumbi Valley and other areas on the borders with India. If there is any country in the world which has the deepest historical, emotional, cultural and spiritual links with India, it is Tibet. The country can do nothing retrospectively about the historic blunder committed half a century ago. It can, however, look after its own interests and those of the region prospectively by not mortgaging its freedom of action in the future.

Restructuring

Regional
1. Bay of Bengal Maritime Pact.
2. IOR. Region – specific strengthening. No potential Trojan Horse(s).
3. Quadrilateral of stability. (Longitudes 80º East to 105º East; Latitudes 0º to approximately 22º North).

Missile Coverage
4. Accelerated development to be maintained.
5. Short range (upto 350 kms) saturation coverage by 2000.
6. Medium range (upto extremities of Indian Ocean). Moderate to dense coverage by 2010. Separate radii of action charts.
7. If no verifiable cutbacks announced by China, provision of short range missiles to friendly countries bordering China.
8. Integrated Tri-Service Missile Command to be established by 2000. Personnel to be re-assigned from within the Services and DRDO.

Nuclear
9. Declaration of Intent.
10. Rationale for support by ASEAN and IOR.
11. Establishment of Integrated Nuclear Command.

Armed Forces
12. Gradually relegating high-tech, high cost weapons systems, whose utility generally is confined to Plains warfare, to lower priority with immediate effect and re-allocating resources elsewhere. Discarding dubious utility high tech ventures, or

relegating them to low priority; and re-assigning resources elsewhere.

13. Establishment of high-tech, high reliability sensor belts and surveillance systems.
14. Eastern Naval Command to be re-designated as Bay of Bengal Maritime Command with re-defined roles and with dedicated tri-Service resources placed under command. To be activated by 2000.
15. Coordination of tri-Service air defence resources in Peninsular India under an Unified Command.
16. 100 per cent increase in Intelligence resources. Positioning of Defence Attaches in all Asian and African countries. Essential restructuring of the Intelligence services.
17. Streamlining of MOD decision-making and establishment of structures considered essential for the prosecution of war in modern times.
18. Downsizing of MOD, MES, DGOF establishments and other such establishments on priority. Restructuring to be completed in phases by 2000.
19. Restructuring in the DRDO and re-prioritisation of research.
20. Augmenting, in a phased manner, the strength of specialist and sector-specific forces in the North and North East.
21. Quantitative increase of forces for operations in the North and North East. Offsets to be made from within the resources of the Army.
22. Priority restructuring of Air Defence.
23. The imperative of reducing casualties in LIC type operations.
24. Force multiplication by reinforcing the morale factor of the field forces, the ordinary soldier at the business end.

25. Ecology protection as a military necessity.
26. Rejuvenation and revitalisation of the Armed Forces.
27. NO "full spectrum' domination by 'any' power of the subcontinent of India.. Military priorities and foreign policy to be adjusted accordingly from time to time.

Bay of Bengal Maritime Pact

1. *First Contracting Parties:* INDIA, BANGLADESH, MYANMAR, MALAYSIA, THAILAND.

2. *Second Stage Adherents:* INDONESIA, SINGAPORE, SRI LANKA.

3. *Salient Features*
   (a) Overriding priority to environmental Protection and Conservation of fisheries.
   (b) Safeguarding bio-diversity and marine ecotone at the terrestrial and marine interface.
   (c) Preferential trade.
   (d) Maintenance of ethnic diversity.
   (e) Customs Union.
   (f) Safeguarding peace and tranquility in the region.
   (g) Geographical contiguity and littoral presence essential for membership of the Pact.
   (h) NOT a military Pact.

Nuclear issues

India took a principled stand at the CTBT negotiations at Geneva in 1996 and again at the UN General Assembly thereafter. In its own way it might have changed the course of world history. Many great things have small beginnings. At the level of international diplomacy, especially in the case of Western governments and their allies, India's stand might have been roundly and soundly condemned. But there were others who took note of the arguments put forward by India's representative at Geneva. At the UN General Assembly, however, for reasons that have not been made clear India narrowed the scope of its objection; to the extent that the main plank of its argument that had given heart to proponents of universal nuclear disarmament worldwide was suddenly removed. The universality of the theme was abandoned for a very restricted India-specific perception. The country has to now look ahead and subtly restore the grandeur and universality of the original vision put forward by India.

Surprisingly, ASEAN countries have, in a way, already stolen a March. In a series of decisions, flying in the face of deeply ingrained Western views on the subject, these countries decided to give primacy to regional interests by admitting Myanmar into their fold. From there it is just a short step to backing India's CTBT position, again in the regional interest. For, should India decide to sign the CTBT the non-aligned world will lose its leverage with the nuclear weapons states for restricting further refinements and augmentations of their nuclear weapons stocks as well as for a time bound nuclear disarmament regime. By the same token ASEAN countries would always be looking over their shoulders, sick with worry about Chinese sensibilities, before making any move in case an independent deterrent, no matter how small, did not obtain with India. The same logic applies to countries of the Indian Ocean Rim who are not irrevocably allied to the West or China.

13

Subcontinental Realities at the Turn of the Century

For several decades India has been tackling its security problems in an ad hoc manner. The country must now look ahead. The first line of India's defence is not at its borders but in the USA, Russia and Europe. The second line is in Central Asia, Iran, Indian Ocean Rim, Middle East and South East Asia. The implications of what is being said must be clearly understood. Most independent countries have long term aims; and strategies to match those aims. China is prepared to wait another fifty years (or so they say), if need be, to incorporate Taiwan.

India's natural frontier is at the Hindu Kush. The subcontinent of India begins at the Hindu Kush historically, culturally and tectonically. Irrespective of what happened in the past, irrespective of the partition of India in 1947, and irrespective of the world-view of the global powers of today the global equipoise of the next millennium can only be attained through a stabilisation of the subcontinent preferably along the northern perimeter, as defined earlier.

After fifty years as an independent country India should give up the "tentativeness" in its external dealings. Of late, the tentativeness could have crept in for any of the following reasons:

* Fear of annoying the USA.
* Fear of annoying China.

* Fear of annoying the Arab world, OIC and a host of others.
* Fear of blackmail of decision-makers by foreign powers and their agencies especially those persons who have been compromised or those who have been the recipients of ill-gotten monies (stashed in foreign banks).
* Fear that exists amongst non-professionals or incompetent people holding sensitive jobs when confronted with professionals who have a lifetime of expertise in their respective fields behind them. Many similar fears that should remain unstated.

The fearful tabulation made above reflects the downside. It betokens the indecision that overtook the governing hierarchy, especially in the 1980s and the 1990s. There is, of course, a brighter side as well. Whatever the criticism levelled against India's foreign policy it has to be conceded that as things stand the country can still emerge as a strong nation in the coming years if good governance is restored and if the country's leadership can get its act together. This writer is of the view that the decision-making process will mature, sooner rather than later, and that a national consensus as to where India's real interests lie will emerge in the near future.

One of the difficulties faced by both insiders and outsiders who are frequently accused of treading on India's toes is in failing to discern as to what really constitutes the country's turf. The aim of this presentation is to outline a set of parameters that might help in sending a clear message to the world at large as to where India wishes to draw the line beyond which it would not tolerate trespass or interference. One hesitates to use the term "*Lakshman Rekha*" as that might connote a stance far more rigid than that intended. A clear definition along the lines being indicated would allow India's neighbours and well-wishers to take note and mesh in. Should the others, who have been in the forefront of actions to artificially limit India's natural growth, see things India's way, well and good. India does not wish to have an adversarial relationship with anybody. It wishes all countries well. However, it will not allow outside interference in its legitimate spheres of growth and development. It will have been noted that once again the phrase chosen has been "spheres of growth and development". The phrase "sphere of interest" has been deliberately avoided on account of the threatening military connotation; largely conferred upon it due to its usage by (dominant) groups in pursuit of unrestrained global power.

Cardinal Principles of India's (Suggested) Foreign Policy for the 21st Century

(Tenet of Faith as well as a Declaration of Intent)
1. Dynamic pursuit of general disarmament and complete abolition of nuclear weapons.
2. Concomitantly, India will remain in the forefront for eco-revival of the subcontinent and the planet.
3. NO foreclosing of ANY option for future generations of Indians unless the option being curtailed, or closed, is part of globally enforceable, non-discriminatory global protocols.
4. Abiding faith in the need for strengthening the United Nations system along with democratisation of the UN.
5. India should give up "canvassing" for a permanent UN Security Council seat. This body is in need of major systemic reforms. Thereafter, India will "automatically" get its due in a more rational global governance order.
6. India is against nobody, be they global powers, emergent super powers or anybody else. However, it will, hereafter, exercise all rights and options in conformity with globally acceptable limits on such rights to pursue its national interests as deemed fit.

The national interest is defined as the interest of the country as perceived by the people of India.
7. India will view any destabilisation attempts on the subcontinent of India by outside powers as hostile acts and react accordingly – commensurate with its capabilities and in the manner best suited to counter such threats. For the purpose of this enunciation the subcontinent of India – both tectonically (geographically) and historically comprises all lands South of the Hindu Kush. The same configuration obtained up to (perhaps) the sixth century AD; and then again at the peak of Aurangzeb's empire except in the South of India. The claim of the British that they were the first to unite India is untenable.
8. Any attempt by foreign powers to establish military bases in the subcontinent as well as the Bay of Bengal will be viewed as an act of (potential) aggression calling for a full-scale review of India's options to deal with the threat.
9. After fifty years of intermittent wars and foreign-inspired terrorist activities India considers the Kashmir question as finally closed. Hereafter, the only basis for talks will be the "peaceful" merger of POK and the so-called Northern Areas into the State of Jammu & Kashmir.
10. From 1 January 2000 India will consider the threat of use of nuclear weapons by any state against another state as a form of nuclear terrorism – at par with nuclear terrorism by non-state actors. Following the declaration India will persuade the UN General Assembly and other groupings to make similar declarations.

Subcontinental Perspectives

No political leader, defence planner or diplomat can afford to ignore the statements made by persons who are generally able to influence the US establishment. These are being reproduced in the chilling terms used by some of them while defining the US objectives in the developing world.

"To prevent the development by non-Western societies of military capabilities that could threaten Western interests". (A respected US intellectual). "In every situation that I have seen so far, nuclear weapons would not be required for response. That is, we could have a devastating response without the use of nuclear weapons, but we would not foreswear that possibility." (Statement made in April 1997 by former Defence Secretary Perry).

Similar statements have been made from time to time by military and intelligence heads before Congressional and other committees. All developing countries need to take note of these pronouncements. The threat is not being taken seriously enough. Instead one is confronted with the phenomenon of defence hierarchies rushing into military to military cooperation on their own soil and on their own continental shelves. It is worth reading the text of the talk delivered by the US Secretary of Defence William S. Cohen, "Continuity, Change and Commitment: America's Asia-Pacific Security Strategy" at the Institute of Defence and Strategic Studies, Singapore on 15 January 1998. That the US is committed to a `forward' presence in the region and military to military cooperation provides 'access' becomes apparent from the talk.

The next set of extracts reproduced below have been selected as a backdrop for many of the formulations that are made subsequently in this paper.

"The discrediting of socialism, epitomised in the collapse of the Soviet Union, is something the world will regret in time, now that market forces are unfettered and dominant and greed has been sanctioned". (One of the Members of the Canberra Commission in a private communication to this writer). "There will be no big wars in the future; but a thousand deadly (small) tribal conflicts shaping up all over the world". (Jacques-Yves Cousteau in a fax sent shortly before his demise).

One has to be conscious of the fact that whether one is for it or against, the agenda for global debates, whatever their nature, is set in the West. Therefore, unless the focus and locus of these debates can be changed, so-called independent decision-making will remain a chimera. In the short review that follows an attempt has been made to look at the geopolitical spectrum of the region around India with such a perspective.

Pakistan

Throughout the second half of the twentieth century Indian leaders, irrespective of their hue or persuasion, kept saying that the breakup of West Pakistan was not in India's interest. Most genuinely believed in what they said. Still others expressed this view in public because it was fashionable to do so. It made the speaker appear statesmanlike. Governments of India, well-wishers of Pakistan in India and the majority of the intellectuals working for a genuine rapprochement with Pakistan have failed in their endeavour. The military defeats have not worked either. Primarily because they were called off inopportunely when Indian forces were poised to gain major advantages. After the conflicts too many unilateral concessions were made in the hope that these might make the other side more amenable to reason.

The past must now remain a closed chapter. India has to bring into play an entire range of options "excluding war" to effectively demolish Pakistan's ability to create further mischief in India or, for that matter, 'anywhere' in the subcontinent. Several pathways suggest themselves. These can be summarised as follows:

* Detaching the Pakistani hawks (generally known as the Punjabi elite comprising the military, civil services and the upper classes) from the ordinary people and the other provinces.

* Fully exploiting the vulnerability of the Province of West Punjab.
* Direct economic links (pipelines, railroads etc.) between Iran and India via the provinces of Baluchistan and Sind.
* Inviting Baluchistan and Sind to forge direct economic links with India and the rest of SAARC, through India.
* Offering a loose confederation (largely for economic benefits) with India to the provinces listed above.
* Several other interesting options not exercised before.

It needs to be reiterated that India does not consider (counter) terrorism or war with Pakistan as an option to be exercised as the other options just spelled out could demolish the war-mongers in that country far more effectively. However, Pakistan should never be allowed to harbour any doubts that India would deal very decisively with any misadventure by that country.

In pursuance of the interest of the dominant group (the Punjabi elite) the backwardness of the other (larger) provinces was perpetuated. Consequently, from the very beginning i.e. in the nineteen fifties and the sixties, well before the advent of missiles, heavy industries including the military industrial infrastructure was concentrated in Punjab, in a handful of core areas. Therefore, in an all out conflict, it would be very easy for India to demolish the Punjabi heartland with a few hundred short range Prithvi missiles without resorting to the use of tanks or aircraft.

It was stated, however, at the very outset (in this and many earlier articles by the writer) that war is NOT an option that India should ever exercise unless the adversary forces one upon this country. In that eventuality, India could even assure the other provinces of Pakistan that it would not like to inflict damage upon them. The people of India and Pakistan are ready for a rapprochement. At the very least they would like the SAARC common market to develop fast so that economic prosperity comes to the subcontinent. This development is retarded solely by a few thousand wielders of power in the Punjabi heartland as well as their foreign backers.

The accolades that the Pakistan Army Chief has been receiving in the USA during his recent visit should be viewed more gravely by the Prime Minister of Pakistan than India. In this country it has been known for several years or should have been known that the Pakistan Army represents the American bridgehead on the subcontinent. It is the instrument with which the USA hopes to keep the SAARC region divided in the next century. The pattern should now be familiar to most people. In the early 1980s, after the loss of Iran to the Khomeini revolution, Saddam Hussein was "encouraged" by the Americans to attack Iran. The weapons of mass destruction were supplied to Iraq mainly by USA and UK. The suppliers would have known that they would be used on the Iranians. They 'were' used on the Iranians; and the Kurds. Although both Iran and Iraq were ready to call off the war much earlier, the Western military-industrial complex saw to it that it continued for nearly a decade. The governments and peoples of both countries must take heed.

Going just one step further it should by now have become clear to Indian defence planners that the US does not really want China to cut off the supply of nuclear material and missiles to Pakistan. Their protestations, notwithstanding, the US military establishment could tacitly encourage Pakistan to use them against India. Pakistan's principal backers are hell-bent upon fuelling a mutually debilitating arms race on the subcontinent for the reasons stated earlier and for the more important reason that India be made to concentrate on the lower levels of defence technologies.

US interest in curbing technology transfers of this nature is limited to Iran. Should China curtail supplies to Iran the US will have no further interest in the matter.

China

China has persistently, and deliberately, been increasing Pakistan's capability to inflict damage on India. The policy which has been vigorously pursued for well over two decades does not spring from any love for that country or its people. It is motivated solely by a desire to encourage a mutually destructive conflict between Pakistan and India which, in turn, could weaken both countries sufficiently for China to be the dominant player in Asia in the next century. Should the military in Pakistan remain in the ascendant, it will also prevent or retard the growth of the SAARC common market, a development viewed with dismay by Beijing.

What is far more worrisome is that defence planners in India have invariably under-played the Chinese threat and over-played the Pakistan conventional military threat. Even if a grand reversal takes place now — after a full-scale strategic review — it will take the armed forces, at least one or two decades to simply undo the effect of wrong priorities of the previous decades.

What is true of the thinking of defence planners applies equally to the external affairs community. China has, no doubt, taken a neutral stand on Kashmir in recent years. This shift was necessitated by China's internal re-appraisals, based on its own security dilemmas and the post-cold war global power plays. It had little to do with Indian sensibilities. A beleaguered foreign ministry of India indulged in patchwork remedies in the face of rapidly changing governments and the incertitude at the political apex. It was felt that appeasement of China was the best policy. Gratitude for China's shift on Kashmir made the Government of India blind to the extremely dangerous moves made covertly by China to comprehensively undermine India in the next century.

Therefore, India's China policy while stressing the need for normalisation of relations with that country should comprise the following elements:

* Firmly announcing to China and the world that transfer, sale or technological assistance to Pakistan to create an offensive capability against India, especially in the nuclear weapons and the missiles fields is viewed by India as an unfriendly act.
* India should not remain a passive spectator in the face of attempts by China to establish any form of military presence in the Bay of Bengal or elsewhere on the subcontinent.
* Speeding up a retaliatory capability. (Without using the nuclear option there are several equally efficacious ways to retaliate, if forced to do so).
* The world has started realising that water shortages might become one of the great concerns of the next century. In this regard what if China were to decide to modify the course of the mighty Brahmaputra with nuclear demolitions. It is not known as to what extent it would be geologically feasible. But should it be effected, even partially, it would sound the death knell for a few hundred million people in the North East and Bangladesh. These and a few more issues of an allied nature, especially those relating to demographic transitions in South Asian societies, will concern the region far more closely than the security concerns highlighted by some of the most eminent persons connected with national security.

Before closing the short resume on China and regardless of the measures that India must take, in the face of the military growth of its giant neighbour, to ensure that the security of the coming generations on the subcontinent is not compromised it should nevertheless be the constant endeavour of Indian statesmen to bring home to their Chinese counterparts that India regards China as an essential pivot for the global equipoise of the next century. Hence the quest for a harmonious relationship with China should continue to be an essential element of India's foreign policy.

Russia

No matter how one looks at the international power equations of the next century one thing that stands out clearly is that under almost every conceivable scenario there does not appear to be a likelihood of a clash of interest between Russia and India. In fact, what does stand out from any review of this nature is the growing commonality of interest between the two countries. Therefore, in as far as it relates to Russia, India should continue to strengthen the good relations established over the years with that country. In concrete terms it calls for a fifty or hundred years accord with Russia in the fields of science and technology, space ventures, and many other related fields.

The attempts by the US to establish a military presence in Central Asia would result in greater instability in that region in the next century. While economic penetration by US and Western multinationals can be viewed as an extension of globalisation military intrusions in any form would have to be viewed with dismay by Russia, China, Iran and the subcontinent of India (excluding for the time being Pakistan). These nations would be well advised to act in concert 'now', before the presence is enhanced, to exclude the possibility of greater militarisation of Central Asia before the situation gets out of hand.

Iran

There should be no "tentativeness" in extending full-scale economic cooperation with Iran. India has long-standing historical and cultural ties with Iran. This country must not allow others to lecture India as to who it should be friendly with and the extent of that friendliness; especially in its own backyard. Should the Governments of India and Iran decide to set up a joint commission for full exploitation of the hydro-carbon reserves in Central Asia they would be able to arrive at mutually beneficial solutions which could turn out to be far more attractive than those being planned by the Western cartels. All of them ultimately need to sell their products in the enormous market of India. At a later stage even Iraq could be brought into the fold.

Afghanistan

Without breaking off relations with the Northern Alliance India must open a dialogue with the Taliban in Afghanistan. Even if the Northern Alliance maintains its tenuous unity it is unlikely that they would be in a position to retake Kabul or the greater part of Afghanistan under Taliban control; as long as the Taliban have the backing of USA, Pakistan and Saudi Arabia. Should at any stage, in the near future, good relations get established between the Taliban in Afghanistan and the Government of India, Pakistan might start feeling decidedly uncomfortable; for more reasons than one. It needs to be reiterated that establishing good relations with the Taliban does not mean that India would abandon its support to the Northern Alliance; provided, of course, that the Alliance continues to hold. It also needs to be added that it is in the greater interest of the Taliban to maintain good relations with India. When they come around to this point of view India should be prepared to listen; and to act.

Japan

When one looks at the geo-political horizon of the coming decades it becomes increasingly clear that India and Japan have far more in common than is currently perceived to be the case, either in Japan or in India. The Japanese dependence on the USA might have served the country's interest admirably in the twentieth century. It is hardly likely to be the case in the twenty first century when Japan starts looking afresh at its global options without the dead-weight of the US Japan Defence Treaty. After the end of the cold war the Soviet threat, which included the threat from communism, ceased abruptly. Instead of comprehensively reviewing its geo-strategic options the Japanese establishment was railroaded into another cul de sac. The emerging threat from China was played up to a degree far greater than the ground reality necessitated. The Japanese public was not given a chance to debate the issue. Had an expert reappraisal been carried out it would have brought out quite clearly that the Chinese military, even perhaps after another fifty years, would be incapable of mounting a threat to mainland Japan of the same magnitude as the Soviets in an earlier era. The dispute over the Spratly group of islands is a separate issue.

It is beyond the scope of today's presentation to dwell at length on this vital issue. It would take up too much time. Today it would be sufficient to state that, delinked from the American strategic intent in the Asia Pacific region, there could be complete harmonisation of Japanese and Indian perceptions for ensuring stability in South East Asia.

India and Japan, possibly linked to Taiwan and South East Asia, have a big stake in developing greater economic cooperation. The cooperation should extend to jointly developing space and ocean technologies of the next century. The Japanese, because of their economic prosperity, have been coopted into the Western alliance, in more ways than one. They will realise in the twenty first century that they have more in common with South East Asia and the Indian peninsula than with the West.

Taiwan

Coming straight to the point it is felt that India should:
* Consider enhancing economic and cultural relations with Taiwan to a level which obtains with some of its closest trading partners.

* Establish technological cooperation with that country in the aerospace sector. At a later stage, technology transfer for manufacture of missiles of less than 1500 km range, under license, should be considered. (Setting up joint defence production ventures with Vietnam falls in the same category).
* Greater cooperation between the navies of the two countries.
* Any other cooperation that could strengthen relations between the two countries.

The world at large accepts that at some future date Taiwan could become a part of the PRC. However, there is a near global consensus that the merger, when it takes place, would have to be through peaceful means. Since the people of Taiwan do not appear to wish to become a part of China in the foreseeable future treating Taiwan as an outcast for decades on end simply because China can rattle its military sabre cannot be a proposition for stability in the next century.

South East Asian Meltdown

The devastating effect of the crash of many South East Asian economies, including that of South Korea, has not yet been fully appreciated by most of the developing countries – as a collective body. The reason being that the global media is in the hands of the developed world. First rate analyses made in India by economic experts will get infinitely less coverage worldwide than third rate analyses by their counterparts in the developed world; and the IMF and World Bank. There are lessons to be drawn from the traumatisation of the ordinary people in Indonesia, Thailand, Malaysia and elsewhere. Lessons which will be lost on India and the developing world unless they get their act together. Before going further in this regard it may be worth pausing to look at some of the comments that have been made recently:

* There's a feeling that basically the rich caused this problem and they're getting bailed out while the poor are being shafted (Walden Bello. A social analyst at Bangkok's Chulalongkorn University as reported in Asia Week, 6 March 1998).
* "A visceral engulfing fear" Alan Greenspan, Chairman of the Federal Reserve.
* Messrs. Edward Mason & Robert Asher, the historians of the World Bank cautioned the Bank against pursuing "ideology based conditionalities".

The penetrating remarks are not far off the mark. IMF and other aid packages will merely bail out the rich. The rich bankers, that is, in the developing world who not only made imprudent loans for unviable schemes contrary to good banking norms but actually induced the privileged elites to mortgage the future of their countries. The western banks have perfected the system. IMF packages are primarily intended to ensure that western banks do not collapse under the weight of unsecured loans that turn sour. The economy of the South East Asian countries 'will' be revived in due course. The ownership pattern, however, of several national assets would have changed. It was the case in Argentina and Mexico. It will be the case in South East Asia.

Shortage of time does not allow for analyses in other areas which, in their own way, are as important as the economic analysis. At this juncture the following measures could help in limiting future damage:

* Full-scale, independent reviews by expert panels nominated by the G-15 to study the global pattern of destruction of Third World economic independence engineered in the West. Russia having been a victim of similar activities would also benefit from the exercise. The G-15 panel to finalise their report within 12 months and

thereafter present it at a G-15 heads of state meeting. The Panel should repeat the presentation before public bodies in each of the G-15 nations and other nations who might show interest.

* Similar exercise to be undertaken by SAARC; over and above the exercise undertaken by the G-15 countries.
* The South East Asian countries (South Korea is excluded) should declare a moratorium on the purchase of prohibitively expensive offensive weapons systems like aircraft and tanks for twenty years till their economies stabilise fully. Meanwhile, China, Japan and India to collectively guarantee the maintenance of territorial status quo of the countries of the region. (As far as possible Asian security should be secured in Asia).

India need not take fright at what has happened in South East Asia to backtrack on its globalisation. The major lesson that has emerged is that India should not allow itself to be 'pushed' in any direction by the western powers and their vast army of supporters in this country. Economic liberalisation will become necessary after careful evaluation of what is in the best interest of the country. The other important lesson which the new government of the country must learn is that "crony capitalism" needs to be completely wiped out. This can be implemented through guaranteeing the independence and competence of regulatory mechanisms as well as through decentralisation and transparency. Heads of financial institutions, public sector banks and enterprises should be nominated by independently constituted panels. The procedure should be transparent.

India's development has been artificially retarded; not by lack of resources but by the siphoning off of resources. The fodder, telecom and fertilizer scams and the Bofors and HDW rake offs were not the only cases. There would have been several hundred such cases that were not investigated or exposed. Collectively they represent astronomical sums of money which could have more than doubled the "real" outlays for the Five Year Plans of the country. India is not a poor country. It still has enormous resources which can be effectively mobilised. Should the bureaucracy be re-vitalised and good governance restored India can make spectacular progress in the years ahead. The world needs India's markets as much as India needs foreign investment. It is a sobering thought to remember that the current telephone density of India is 2 compared to 80 in the USA. Even if telephone density rises to just 10 the number of telephones required would exceed all telephones currently operating in the western world.

India's Defensive Posture for the Opening Decades of the 21st Century

The utilisation of the defence budget by the Ministry of Defence (MOD) and the three services has hardly been geared for optimum utilisation of resources in the national interest; as opposed to the narrow service interests. The problem has been compounded by unwarranted interference by bureaucrats and politicians, often swaying to the tune of outsiders. There were several reasons for this state of affairs. These have been cogently articulated often enough by any number of respected professionals across the national mainstream for almost fifty years. They have had no effect on the bureaucracy of the country which can be squarely blamed for India's lack of preparedness in several areas. There have been some outstanding bureaucrats. However, in as far as it relates to defence they were exceptions rather than the rule.

While the new government ponders over the composition of the National Security Council (NSC) – and before the NSC is able to start making independent formulations for decision-makers at the political apex – it would be prudent to immediately set up a National Defence Review Panel. This Panel must not comprise solely of Chiefs, Cabinet Secretaries, Defence Secretaries and the like. They all had their chance and their say. It is time to induct new blood and experts from areas not normally associated with such reviews in India. The Panel should make its recommendations within 12 months to the Government as well as to the Parliamentary Committees associated with defence. After that the Panel should be wound up. Its recommendations should be implemented within a time bound period, regardless of bureaucratic opposition. Meanwhile, an interim National Security Council could be set up. This body would also be wound up once the recommendations of the National Defence Review Panel are implemented. These recommendations would include the organisation and structure of the National Security Council. Should the NSC turn out to be a repeat of past exercises, i.e. the same set of people sitting in a different room, donning fresh hats and calling themselves the NSC, it would turn out to be an exercise in futility.

Finally, it needs to be reiterated that at the very minimum the following capability should inhere for the defence of the Indian subcontinent:

* The Indian Navy to have a meaningful capability and presence in the Indian Ocean region. (India does not have the desire to extend this capability beyond the Indian Ocean Rim. The building of this capability is primarily a "defensive" measure to counter threats to the subcontinent of India in the next century. India does not wish to get into any confrontation with any power)
* The Indian Navy to develop full-scale capability to deal with outside interference – to regional stability as well as marine eco-systems in the Bay of Bengal.
* The Indian Coast Guards to be strengthened in a similar manner

* Projection radii (especially seaward) for the Integrated Missile Defence Forces (IMDF) by the year 2010 to be spelled out by the National Defence Review Panel
* Projection radii for IMDF beyond 2015 depending on global environment
* Maintaining the highest regard for fighting potential and readiness of the Indian Army in the changed geo-strategic environment in the North and North-East of India
* Developing and maintaining a capability for fighting through "high-tech paralysis" in any future conflict. No developing country should allow a repeat of what happened in the Gulf War.
* Developing a first rate space surveillance capability

14

Strategic Challenges for India in the Third Millennium

Introduction

When I first looked at the subject for this morning's talk I was straightaway struck by the amplitude of the time horizon involved. Instead of mentioning the millennium the proponents could very easily have limited its scope by asking me to speak on the strategic challenges faced by the country in the twenty first century, or its opening decades. Not knowing whether the choice of those who selected the subject was deliberate or otherwise I have decided to take a mental leap into the wide blue yonder; making sure at the same time that our feet remain on 'terra firma'.

And this brings me to a major dilemma. Where should we situate ourselves while looking at the future? Where we happen to be now, i.e. at the close of the twentieth century? Around the year 2025? In the middle of the twenty first century? Or even beyond? Putting it in another way, should we make the projections while our thoughts are shackled by the immediate problems in which India and South Asia are mired, or should we have faith in our ability to overcome these problems and look beyond?

I have chosen to overcome the dilemma by flitting between the different points of the time horizons just elaborated.

What Is India?

Before we make global projections for India in the third millennium (after Christ) we must be clear in our minds as to what is India. As a professional military man who has spent his life in this environment I have no hesitation in stating that when we talk of India in the coming millennium, and the millennia to follow, India means the "subcontinent" of India. I see no future for this country, or the other countries of the subcontinent, in any futuristic projections as non-harmonious, dissonant and fratricidal entities. This aspect has been clearly perceived by the majority of the people in these countries. It has yet to be comprehended by their governing elites. Hence, as the largest entity in the region, India's single biggest endeavour in the opening decades of the next century – which translates into its foremost strategic goal – will have to be the harmonisation of the countries of the subcontinent, regardless of the difficulties involved, and in spite of outside interference.

Strategic Challenges (or the Existential Imperatives)

I had presented the Cardinal Principles of India's (Suggested) Foreign Policy for the 21st Century in a talk that I delivered at the USI on 25 March 1998 (page 126), a few days before the swearing in of the new government:

What I am going to now put before you is a natural extension of the earlier presentation. The strategic challenges for India in the next millennium are based on three existential imperatives. In order of priority these can be listed as:

* Demographic-Ecological Imperative.
* Globalisation and the Economic Imperative.
* Technological and Military Security Imperative.

We will discuss each one of these in turn.

The Demographic-Ecological Imperative

The greatest threat to future stability in the subcontinent remains its burgeoning population. Unless all segments of society are mobilised to reverse the horrendous population growth the future will not only remain stark but become bleaker with each passing year for the majority of the inhabitants of these countries. It must be appreciated that in South Asia we have gone beyond Malthusian self-corrections. Taking the example of AIDS, were this scourge to spread faster in South Asia than is the case in many parts of Africa, it would make no difference to the population growth on the subcontinent. Were it to become technologically feasible to project ten thousand people every single day (including holidays) to a colony on the Moon the population would still not decrease.

Here I would like to quote two short statements from a talk delivered at this very podium in January 1985 on the "Population Problem of India". I quote: "The family planning programme in India at the end of 1984 suffers not so much from a resistance on the part of the population to adopt the small family norm but from an organisational infirmity". Since then the organisational infirmity referred to a good fourteen years ago has permeated all aspects of governance. Here is another extract from the January 1985 talk, "Sex is no joy to most women in the slums. In fact, many of them weary of the daily grind and barely recovering from the last pregnancy dread the inevitable onslaught of the drunken male. In a male dominated society that semi-starved woman, battered both by fortune and her spouse, would welcome a deliverance from constant child-bearing. We have failed to reach her".

While the political class dithers the horrors of sub optimal growth for hundreds of millions below the poverty line stare us in the face. I believe that over thirty percent of the pregnancies today are unwanted pregnancies. At the very least, it should be possible to achieve almost zero population growth in as little as ten to fifteen years in the urban agglomerates where large populations are concentrated in slum clusters.

And this brings me to my next point. There has been considerable talk in environmental circles and among political reformists calling for minimising government role in various areas. While such thinking can be seen to be a very healthy development in the Indian polity a word of caution needs to be sounded in this regard. The problems of India and the Indian subcontinent are so monumental and, on the face of it, so intractable that any talk of demolishing the government's role beyond a given point would be premature. The need of the hour is good government. Not no government. There is scope for bringing about transparency in government and for de-centralising in a manner whereby local communities are able to utilise the resources allocated to them optimally. However, while de-constructing government machinery in sectors where it has consistently failed to perform it has to be concomitantly ensured that the transition that takes place is not towards the "Bihar model of governance" which, if one is not careful, could become the norm over larger swathes of the sub-continent.

The government may have displayed its inability to manage resources optimally. Complete privatisation and absence of controls, however, could give free rein to private sector greed. The common man, caught in between, would invariably continue to suffer and the environment to diminish. Therefore, the answer lies in finding a via media that incorporates the strengths of both parties and rejects the worst ills of either side. There would be many who would look askance at such compromises. While one can understand their misgivings one must realise that in present day societies the governments are generally here to stay. With the awesome power available to the state it would perhaps be well nigh impossible to displace it. Hence the need for sensible accommodations that reduce government role in designated areas and allow for bringing in outside talent to wrestle with the enormous problems confronting developing societies.

I believe there is an immediate requirement for the setting up of an independent national – possibly international – commission to go into the entire gamut of rapid industrialisation and its ecological consequences. I would not be too surprised if such a commission decided to recommend limits to the number and types of industries that could be set up in ecologically fragile zones. We need to reverse the pace at which the automobile revolution has overtaken the world, and now India. Sooner or later, we will have to put quotas on the number of automobiles and chemicals that can be produced in different regions of the world. Similar limits will also have to be placed on aircrafts and ships. THE AGE OF OPEN-ENDED GROWTH IS OVER.

Globalisation and the Economic Imperative

No matter in which direction one looks these days one runs into some aspect or the other of globalisation. It is upon us. One can neither shut it out nor wish it away. If those at the helm of affairs understand the intricacies and nature of globalisation they would be in a better position to regulate and monitor the pace of globalisation, thus avoiding many pitfalls.

The subject of globalisation is much too complex. It is being brought up, in passing, to stress the point that developing societies are unable to grasp the real nature of globalisation. It has become a 'they versus us' debate; perhaps rightly so, in the short term. To begin with all, or most, of the advantages are stacked with the developed economies. The reason is that the process of globalisation having begun in the advanced societies they were better positioned to take advantage of it. The same applies to the pace of globalisation. It is the developed economies who are forcing the pace in order to keep the vast majority of developing economies off balance; and hence the

treadmill effect as would be apparent from the data given below:
* Of the 100 largest economies in the world, 51 are now global corporations; only 49 are countries.
* The combined sales of the world's Top 200 corporations are far greater than a quarter of the world's economic activity.
* The Top 200 corporations' combined sales are bigger than the combined economies of all countries minus the biggest 9; that is they surpass the combined economies of 182 countries.
* The Top 200 have almost twice the economic clout of the poorest four-fifths of humanity.
* The Top 200 have been net job destroyers in recent years. Their combined global employment is only 18.8 million, which is less than a third of one one-hundredth of one percent of the world's people.
* Not only are the world's largest corporations cutting workers, their CEOs often benefit financially from the job cuts.
* Japanese corporations have surpassed US corporations in the ranking of the Top 200.
* Over half of the sales of the Top 200 are in just 5 economic sectors; and corporate concentration in these sectors in high.

The figures just read out have been appearing in the media with regularity. I have taken them from an economic affairs daily. They are garnered from a study by the Washington based Institute for Policy Studies. Another set of figures released by United Nations Conference on Trade and Development (UNCTAD) indicates that Foreign Direct Investment (FDI) might reach 440 billion dollars in 1998. The Secretary General of UNCTAD has pointed out that, "while traditional factors, such as the existence of a pro-FDI regime, natural resources, market growth prospects and market size, as well as labour conditions, continue to remain important, increasingly firms are also seeking investment locations that offer people-made advantages, so-called 'created assets' from technological advantages to particular labour skills".

Having heard the statement of the Secretary General, UNCTAD I would like you to take your mind back to the 'time horizon imponderables' with which I commenced my talk. You would recall that I had mentioned several time scales in which we could position ourselves while evaluating our future strategies. This situational placement becomes very important. Viewed in the time frame of the next twenty-five years the societies that have held sway over the globe for the best part of this century will enjoy the advantages of unidirectional globalisation flows. The moment, however, one crosses this time horizon segment (of say twenty five years) one will find that the prime movers of today are not likely to retain their ascendancy in the manner in which they are constituted today and in the geographical entities in which they are nested. An elaboration is necessary.

Trans National Corporations (TNCs) that have effectively broken country-specific global barriers on very large economic scales will not continue to support national policies of their country of origin if these interfere in their global activities and diminish return for their invested capital. They have already started influencing the policies of USA and several other countries, both developed and developing. Electronic commerce and information flows will transcend the sanctity of national borders. A few years down the road global companies will shift their headquarters, R&D and capital to those parts of the globe where there is the least interference with their operations. By the middle of next century, if not earlier, the concept of nationhood in as far as it relates to military strategy and commerce will have lost its relevance.

Technological and Military Security Imperative

When we now talk of the technological and military security imperative, in the light of what has gone before, it becomes abundantly clear that it is "this" generation, and possibly the next, which has to worry about military security in its limited sense, as currently understood. Mind boggling technological breakthroughs visible on the horizon will rebound soon on their handlers unless these are globally harnessed to provide security – both military and economic – to the whole world. I would like to strongly advise this prestigious institution and many other like it around the world to pay greater heed to the post nationalistic phase of globalisation when they plan their geo-political, geo-economic, geo-environmental and demographical studies in the years ahead. We must learn to differentiate between the problems that beset developing societies due to lack of good government and proper management of resources and those which result from military and clandestine activities of external agencies. The latter activities invariably result in greater mischief in societies that lack internal cohesion.

The military dimension has been submerging other existential dimensions throughout mankind's history. Talk is proliferating the world over, at a frenetic pace, that the Revolution in Military Affairs (RMA) is going to overwhelm those who got left behind. I look at RMA differently. It is a menace to global harmony in the short term, i.e. till the time that sober people around the world realise that RMA is being pushed by the people who do not wish the world to derive the peace dividend after the end of the Cold War. Therefore, in the short term most developing countries threatened by the lack of keeping up with the RMA will have to perhaps devote more time, money and energy towards it. In actual fact, it is a red herring that is keeping the world from strengthening the UN system. The moment that the UN system is perceived by most countries in the world to be a just system it will automatically result in substantial decrease in military spending, leading to release of much-needed funds to restore the health of an environmentally decaying planet. The moment the transition takes place the very concept of RMA becomes redundant.

The brief reference to RMA brings me to the centrality of India's strategy for the coming millennium. The country must spare no effort to ensure that a more rational global order is ushered in as quickly as possible. Under the rubric of this overarching strategy it must guide the developing world towards the strengthening of the United Nations by breaking the stranglehold of the five nuclear powers. Military power, by itself, cannot save developing societies from the fate that has befallen Indonesia; where inspite of a strong military the country faces disintegration due to nearly one hundred million people suddenly coming below the poverty line in the short span of a year. Hypothetically, doubling or trebling Indonesia's military strength would not be able to solve its existential problems.

Inevitably, when talking about technology, especially military technologies, countries like India with a strong technological base but with economic constraints that do not allow the full exploitation of that technological base, will have to ponder over the question as to where to put their scarce resources. I believe that the highest priority has to be given in the short and medium term to securing future energy needs.

Externalities Impinging on Independent Decision-Making

Independent decision-making, across the entire national decision-making spectrum, may not be possible for national entities in the next century. Not even a superpower, or superpowers, will enjoy the same freedom of manoeuvre that they did in the past.

I would like to highlight a few global trends that could influence the geo-political strategies of India and the world. They can be tabulated under the following heads:

* Global environmental concerns that transcend national boundaries·
* Rise in planetary consciousness
* The inevitability of UN reforms and the consequent strengthening of the UN system
* Increasing influence exerted by China on global affairs
* The moderating influence of a stronger European Union on global events
* Trends in Africa
* Direction taken by USA in world affairs
* Technological breakthroughs – especially in the energy field

Regardless of external factors that could influence its strategies we can, nevertheless, discern core strategies where India is unlikely to compromise. These can be stated as:

* Engendering subcontinental cohesion
* Strengthening the UN system
* Retaining an independent deterrent up to the time that global, co-equally enforceable protocols are adopted
* Harmonisation of space and outer space activities
* Maintaining peace and tranquility of the Indian ocean region
* Subcontinental and intra-regional aspects of demographic-ecological interface

Conclusion

As I come to the concluding remarks I cannot help re-iterating that unless sane people around the globe put the military dimension on the back-burner the world may be overtaken by existential stresses over which mankind may lose control. This is not a pessimistic note that is being sounded at the end of my talk but a realistic appraisal derived from a host of factors – both military and non-military – that are likely to exert much greater influence on human societies than has been the case in the past. I have deliberately not touched upon global scarcities which could aggravate global tensions or of the social stresses multiplying exponentially across the world due to increasing income disparities.

I heard someone mention the other day that the power to predict the future goes with the power to shape the future. To date, it has been mostly individuals and hierarchies wishing to hold on to power who have tried their hands at shaping events: sometimes with success but more often with disaster. Global society could be hurtling in the latter direction. India's strategic options are no longer merely this country's strategic options. They are global concerns which uniformed fraternities around the world can join hands to address together or simply watch while the world sinks into an existential slime the likes of which have not been witnessed before by man – or nature.

15

Remoulding the Subcontinent

Introduction

It is not perhaps known how the last millennium (going by the Gregorian calendar) ended. It is known that the current millennium seems to be ending on a dismal note. On the human plane, the forces in the ascendant are propelling the world towards:

* Eco-Destruction of the Planet.
* Remilitarisation of the Planet; and
* Dehumanisation of the Planet (due to the breakdown of the social cohesion of societies).

As the close of the century approaches, two events have intruded rudely on to the global consciousness. Reference is made to the "K words:"

KOSOVO AND KARGIL

In the first case, that of Kosovo, the Western powers, in their collective might, fired a warning shot of 'unilateralism' across the bows of the established international order – which was based on the primacy of the United Nations to sanction military interventions.

In the second case, the Kargil intrusion was a 'wake up' call to the Indian nation; to shake it out of its self-induced somnolence. Monumental inadequacies in the ascending hierarchical spiral – an invitation for Kargil to happen – were magnificently retrieved at the business end, at the lowest end of the military ladder, albeit at great cost in life and limb. The saga of gallantry and sacrifice galvanised the nation as never before. It demonstrated that the nation is as united as any nation can hope to be in this day and age. It clearly brought out that the divisions had been artificially induced, over the years, by the self-serving policies of the governing hierarchy – a class apart.

Where do we go from Here?

If India has to come to the forefront in the 21st century – which it must if it wishes to survive in the emerging world order – then it must respond firmly to the threats that loom large on the time horizon of the next century. The foremost threat still remains the internal threat, brought about through venality and misgovernment. Taking a leaf out of the book of the valiant youth of India who fought at the front, the public must proceed to deal in like manner with the elements 'within' the land who have sapped its strength for full fifty years. Acting in unison the nation can now give short shrift to all such elements.

To deal effectively with external, or externally inspired threats, it behoves a nation the size of India to clearly define its security parameters; and even make transparent its pattern of future response to the type of mischief that nearly tripped up the nation in a very big way.

India's external security parameters in the next century would have to have two distinct components: the core component and a complementary component. The policy statement relating to the core component would explicitly lay down:

* The centrality of India's commitment to universal nuclear disarmament.
* Strengthening of the UN system to introduce a more equitable and universally respected dispensation.

* Creation of sufficient military and economic strength to: (i) exclude outside interference on the subcontinent; (ii) maintain the security and peaceful coexistence of India and its trading partners in the Indian Ocean region; (iii) harmonisation of the subcontinent for the peaceful development of its member states.
* Strengthening efforts for the demilitarisation of the Himalayas as an ecological imperative.
* Unequivocal support for the ecological revival of the planet.
* Demilitarisation of space.

The complementary, or supplementary, component relating to India's security policy would centre around:

* Maintaining the economic viability and physical integrity of South East Asia, in concert with all the regional powers, notably China and Japan.
* Maintaining the inter-relatedness and harmony of the Central Asian Republics in concert with the regional powers, namely Russia, China, Turkey and Iran.
* Diminishing, or demolishing, the ability of Pakistan to create further mischief in the region.
* Maintaining the regional sanctity of the Bay of Bengal in concert with the littoral states.
* Eliciting global support for the doctrine of primary responsibility which states that " a state transferring or selling nuclear weapons or nuclear material to any group would be held responsible for all damage resulting to another state from such transaction i.e. the action of the group or groups to whom the nuclear weapons or material had been transferred. The transferring state would thus become liable to be dealt with as if it had itself used those weapons in an act of aggression against another state." (The doctrine can be endorsed after due deliberation by

the International Court of Justice and the concerned UN agencies).

As it transpires none of the above statements, taken singly, or collectively, fly in the face of the emerging global consensus on these issues. In order to meet its primary and secondary objectives India should progressively endeavour to:
* Maintain its defence expenditure at between 3 to 3.5 percent of the GDP, at constant prices. (Even with slight improvement in governance, transparency and accountability it would be possible to bring down the budget deficit considerably).
* Maintain a 'robust' nuclear deterrent sufficient to deter any threat to its interests in and around the subcontinent as well as in the Indian Ocean.
* Maintain a viable (independent) defensive posture with separate 'credible' offensive components in the North and North East.
* Maintain sufficient naval strength in the Indian Ocean to ensure the primacy of its interests in the region.
* Progressively create a Rapid Action Force of sufficient strength for deployment anywhere in the region, for dealing with adverse situations.
* In case of sustained terrorist activities, sponsored from outside, India will reserve the right, with effect from 1 January 2000, to take all necessary measures to neutralise such activities at source. (Sufficient warning is thereby given to 'all' regional states harbouring individuals who have been persistently indulging in extortion, terrorism or mayhem in India). By the same token India reserves the right to strike at any camp, in any state, where mercenaries are being trained for terrorism on Indian territory. India's actions will be limited to

elimination of such camps. Should the sponsoring state escalate tensions, thereafter, it would bear full responsibility for further retaliation by India.

* India has abjured the use of nuclear weapons to settle international disputes. It has no desire to invade the territory of any other state. It hopes that such self-restraint will not result in adventurism on the part of other states.

The interesting definition of 'aggressive patrolling' provided by the Army Chief of a neighbouring state in a recent interview to the international media would no doubt have been taken note of by his Indian counterpart. It would doubtless be put to effective use for dealing with cross border terrorism in future. Local commanders could well be given the initiative to destroy build up of infiltrators at assembly points across the border before they are able to infiltrate across to kill women and children. In order that there is no misunderstanding as to the intent and 'limited' scope of the exercise, Army Headquarters would lay down the radii up to which such actions could take place with the permission of the sector commanders, not below the level of divisional commanders; from resources "integral" to the formation taking the action. The Government of India should also make an official announcement to this effect – limiting the action to sectors where infiltration routinely takes place.

Global Ramifications of the Restoration of the status quo in Kargil: Actions of the Indian Army

While the nation takes legitimate pride in its armed forces, analysts around the world are only now beginning to take stock of the global ramifications of the demonstrated prowess of the Indian Army at the lowest end of the technology spectrum. Before coming on to these global ramifications which will, hereafter, have to be factored into the defense planning of nations in the next century it is relevant to reproduce an excerpt from an article written in a national newspaper in 1995:

> " Where it is a question of sheer guts and grit and fighting at impossible heights under impossible climatic conditions, the Indian Army remains one of the finest battle forces in the world. High technology domination of the battlefield by the armed forces of the more advanced countries falls into an entirely different category. That category, referred to as force multiplication in military parlance, is actually a multiplication factor based on pounds, shillings and pence. In time the Indian Army will deal with the foreign mercenaries and elements working against the interests of the state. It is not inconceivable that in the process the unfinished agenda on the other side of the Line of Control too might get resolved to India's satisfaction thanks to the opening provided by the induction of mercenaries."(Time India Changed its Defence Perspective, by Vinod Saighal, appearing in The Hindu, 17 October 1995).

This passage was repeated in the talk, "Restructuring of the Armed Forces." (Reproduced in USI Journal, July-Sept 1997). It is being again alluded to because it is pivotal to several options that emerge for India in the national and regional security fields in the next century. It should be appreciated that regardless of the lack of international support for Pakistan's attack on Indian territory in the Kargil sector, and the support provided with high precison weapons by the IAF, the situation could not have turned to India's advantage unless the Indian Army had demonstrated its ability to physically recapture those heights, in spite of the very high casualties being sustained. The real pressure on the Pakistan Prime Minister was the realisation that the gambit had failed. He allowed himself to be persuaded only after it had become clear to him that reverses on the ground had indeed started taking place. Whereas, other skills and capabilities can be augmented rapidly through high tech purchases, the special skills inhering in the Indian Army take years, if not a lifetime, to develop. The military hierarchy must never lose sight of this aspect. The national security policy of the country should take into account this demonstrated prowess. It follows, therefore, that if pushed beyond its threshold of tolerance, the country has the ability to fight its way to the Hindu Kush to neutralise any and every threat to the sanctity and security of the subcontinent of India.

Dealing with Pakistan

It should have become eminently clear by now that pacific accommodation with Pakistan would be unlikely till the time that the establishment that has pushed that country into its fourth misadventure with India is demolished. Unless saner elements come to the fore, here onwards, the Indian policy towards Pakistan, stripped to its essentials, could well become:

* "the marginalisation of the elements that repress the natural growth of Pakistan and the subcontinent."

India has no choice but to lock in its Kargil victory in a manner such that the question of another action against India – covert or overt – does not arise. Translated into a policy directive it means that:

* The additional deployment forced upon India in Kargil should no longer be construed as a purely defensive deployment. If India's hand is again forced, it could just as easily become the launch pad, at the time of India's choosing, to rest the flanks of the Indian Army on the Hindu Kush.
* India might be obliged to create additional strike elements for the mountains in J&K. After due parleys with all concerned, India should establish a Counter Insurgency & Mountain Warfare School (CI&MWS) at a selected location in one of the Central Asian States.
* India will keep all options open for its rapid deployment force. Hereafter, the elimination of mercenaries that have infiltrated into J&K (and

elsewhere) will be carried out with the same despatch and vigour as the Kargil operation.

It is reiterated that Pakistan military establishment's ability to create mischief through religion-inspired terrorism should be made to end with the 20th century – for the sake of the region, for the sake of the world, as well as for the sake of the moderate elements in Pakistan itself. India will now take all necessary steps to ensure that the scope for such mischief is considerably curtailed in the next century.

This country continues to believe that, regardless of the emotiveness of the Kashmir issue, the silent majority in Pakistan, and especially its non-Punjab provinces would be ready to explore saner alternatives for a harmonised subcontinent; at peace with its neighbours and at peace with itself. To these elements, desiring peaceful co-existence, proposals should be offered for economic betterment of both countries. In the first instance, it is proposed to construct an oil and gas pipeline running from: Central Asian Republics – Iran – Baluchistan – Sind – to Rajasthan.

A task force to prepare the blueprint should be set up for the purpose. Generous partnership incentives should be offered to the leaders of Baluchistan and Sind at a special conference in Tehran, New Delhi or London. The consortium and its lead bankers should be identified. The Government of Pakistan can consider coming aboard in due course, failing which conditions should be created for the said provinces in Pakistan to break away, retain their autonomy in a subcontinental confederation and join the consortium as independent entities. Since it will take a few years to finalise the blueprint, the other stakeholders should proceed on the basis that in due course saner counsels "will" prevail in Pakistan. Should Western oil majors decide to back the proposal they will find that geologically, technically, environmentally and from the point of view of the economics of the proposal it provides perhaps the best alternative for marketing the hydrocarbon wealth of the Central Asian region.

The damage caused to the Himalayan ecology as a result of the military build up and confrontation cannot be fully appreciated by this generation. Its horrendous consequences will be felt by the coming generations in the subcontinent and China. It would be worth reproducing an excerpt from a UN report prepared consequent to the military intervention during the Kosovo crisis:

> "through explosive reactions, fires and the burning of great amounts of different materials and chemicals and through intensive actions of military airplanes, the millions of tons of oxygen that the living world needs, have been irretrievably spent." (Report of the Inter-Agency Needs Assessment Mission dispatched by the Secretary General of the United Nations to the Federal Republic of Yugoslavia).

Here is another excerpt from a paper circulated at the behest of the UN Secretary General to the task force set up for the purpose in the Balkans:

> "it would not be easy to make the world at large see the enormity of the harm being done to myriad life forms on the ecological plane – life forms that depend upon their inbuilt sensors to communicate, navigate, attract mates, find food or to ward off danger. There have been protests about the ecological damage to the Danube river basin but nowhere commensurate to the magnitude of the ecological impoverishment of the region taking place day by day with increasing intensity." ("The Ecological Consequences of the Kosovo Crisis," note prepared by Eco Monitors Society in April 1999).

As an alternative to the enhanced military build up being effected by both sides as a result of the Kargil conflagration, complete demilitarisation of the region is proposed along the following lines:

* Complete demilitarisation of all areas East and North of Zojila, to include Ladakh, Aksai Chin region under Chinese occupation, Baltistan –

Skardu and Gilgit. In the first instance, the demilitarisation to be effective for fifty years.

* The demilitarisation will respect the *de facto status quo* (present position of the three countries) without prejudicing their right to negotiate a more lasting settlement. Adequate safeguards would be incorporated for denial of infiltration to hostile elements — hostile to the concerned states as well as elements hostile to the spirit of the accord.
* The demilitarisation instrument to be deposited with the International Court of Justice as a binding protocol.
* The entire region will, thereafter, be turned into a giant Himalayan ecological park.
* A tripartite commission comprising non-governmental organisations and other nonmilitary elements to work out an hundred years ecological revival package for the region; All the concerned countries will act as co-guarantors for its ecological revival. UNDP and other interested organisations could be co-opted to assist in the ecological restoration package.
* Light border posts could continue to be manned by paramilitary forces till the time mutual confidence is restored.
* Local communities will be given employment as ecological wardens. A special fund — possibly one twentieth the cost of full military deployment — should be created for ecological restoration work. A corpus could also be created with the help of the World Bank and other national and international agencies. Personnel of these agencies would be debarred from entering should they be found to be acting against the interests of the region, or any of the members.
* Concomitantly, it is proposed that a joint Indo-Pak commission, possibly under the aegis of the Indian and Pakistan chapters of the World Wildlife Fund

for Nature be set up, to carry out a study of the ecological consequences of the Himalayan military deployments and conflicts.

It would have been noticed that while on the question of dealing with Pakistan several options, at both the sterner and softer ends of the spectrum, have been spelled out. The elements currently in the ascendant, successors to those others who can be credited with having engineered the break up of Pakistan, are likely to oppose the saner options. Indian media, the business fraternity, diplomats, Non Resident Indians (NRIs), and Non Resident Pakistanis (NRPs) must try and see to it that the debate is enlarged within Pakistan before that country hurtles further towards self-destruction. The moderate elements in Pakistan would be well advised to erect their own protective barriers in anticipation of the enactment of the Pakistan Shariat Bill and the resultant Talibanisation of Pak society. People who enforce their writ through the gun do not understand any other language than that of equal or superior force. The moderate elements should give a thought to raising their own militia to ensure they do not go the way of the hapless women of Afghanistan.

The Government of India and responsible media elements of both countries must make it their business to educate the public on the subcontinent as to the consequences of a nuclear exchange so that persons making such irresponsible statements are obliged to shut up and keep shut. This exercise needs to be undertaken on priority.

Dealing with China

For centuries on end Tibet has been considered as a buffer between the two giant Asian neighbours. It is proposed that this millennial mindset be shed and in the next millennium Tibet become the *bridge* between:

* India and China;

* China and the West; and
* China and the rest of the world.

Such a reversal could become an historical turning point, not only for the future of Tibet, but for the future of India, of China, and for mankind as a whole. If nearly forty percent of the total population of the globe decides to live in peace and harmony the prospect of world peace is immeasurably enhanced.

It is felt that it would be in China's long term interest to accept the autonomy proposal of the Dalai Lama; while it can do so from a position of strength, as an act of far-sighted statesmanship. In the process it could turn to advantage the formidable goodwill created by the Dalai Lama and the Tibetan diaspora in the last forty years. The moment that China's great leaders look at the proposal dispassionately, in the context of the conditions obtaining in China at the close of the century, they would not fail to realise the enormous advantage accruing to China from turning the Dalai Lama into one of their closest allies. The Chinese people should start regarding Tibetan culture as a unique world heritage. By preserving it China enriches itself.

Meanwhile, the inexorable consequences of the ecological ravaging of Tibet and the Himalayas will condemn the coming generations on the subcontinent, China and South East Asia to an existence far worse than is possible to imagine at this juncture, although the alarm signals are all there. The tragedy is that the two civilisations that pride themselves as being the repositories of the wisdom of the ages are ignoring it in a manner whose blindness is difficult to comprehend.

It is worth dwelling on this aspect for a while and to examine the evidence:

* Many great river systems trace their source from the Tibetan plateau, flowing into India, Pakistan, Bangladesh, Nepal, Bhutan, Myanmar, Thailand, Vietnam, Cambodia, Laos and China. They water some of the most productive croplands in the world.

* The population of the area between the Yellow River in the East to the Indus in the West comprises nearly forty-seven per cent of the world's population.
* Over-exploitation of the fragile environment of Tibet and the Himalayas is leading to grave ecological devastation. Pollution at the headwaters of rivers in Tibet, including from nuclear wastes, is leading to serious ecological and bio-genetic consequences.
* Massive deforestation, resulting from equally massive military deployments, has contributed significantly to siltation and destructive flooding in the Brahmaputra, Yangtse, Mekong, Indus, Sutlej, Salween and the Yellow rivers. These rivers flow into the South China Sea, Bay of Bengal and the Arabian Sea. The global scale of these ecological disasters has yet to be fully assimilated.
* The Tibetan Plateau plays a critical role in the stability of the global climate and the monsoons.
* Himalayan glaciers are receding at a worrisome rate.

One can go on endlessly in this vein. Each frightening statistic numbing the mind further. The Eco Monitors Society had presented last year a "Blueprint for the Demilitarization of the Himalayas as an Ecological Imperative". It is under consideration by several international agencies as well as the concerned ministries of the government. In keeping with the spirit of that proposal a blueprint for the demilitarisation of Tibet is presented. The salient features of the plan include:

* In principle agreement by China to commence demilitarisation of Tibet, as part of an overall understanding with India on the boundary question, with effect from 1 January 2000. China could continue to retain a reasonable military cordon around its existing nuclear and missile

facilities till 2025 unless genuine progress were to be made in the interim towards universal nuclear disarmament. It would undertake not to augment the existing facilities. Plans would concomitantly be prepared for safe dismantling, which could commence as soon, thereafter, as the global environment becomes conducive for such action.

* Five giant Ecological Reserves to be created in Tibet for the 'ecorevival' of Tibet over the next hundred years. Billion dollar ecorevival trusts to be created with monies contributed by international donors. The 'ecoreserves' would be jointly managed by the Tibetans and Chinese representatives. They would include the Tibetans in exile. The donor agencies would nominate their own representatives.
* Where the Eco Reserves straddle the Himalayas in India, Nepal and other such regions, joint management by all the concerned governments; with preference given to globally respected non governmental organisations from the participating countries.
* Establishment of an Eco Management Institute in Lhasa for training of Tibetans in scientific methods of revival of degraded areas.

China is in a state of flux. The surface stability is deceptive. The Chinese leadership faces very real dilemmas. Apparently, there is a common saying doing the rounds in China which goes something like: "if the communist party does not reform it will die, and if it reforms, it is seeking death".

The banning of the Falun Gong sect may turn out to be a controversial decision. It is not the aim here to criticize the Chinese government action, but to communicate an apprehension. It would be worth taking note of a remark attributed to Thomas L. Friedman: "I believe that the key problem the world will face with China in the next decade will be managing its weakness. China may grow richer, and it may grow more authoritarian, but it is not going to do both at the same time." (Thomas L. Friedman, "How to worry sensibly about China in transition", appearing in the New York Times).

Dealing with the Central Asian Republics

India must continue to strengthen its relations with the CAR states, not so much in the competitive mode with other global players vying for influence in the region, but in a manner that would strengthen the ability of these states to withstand outside pressures; pressures that could create tensions in the region. Towards this end it is recommended that:

* India should encourage CAR states to form a common policy for tapping the oil wealth of the region for the joint development of the region as a whole.
* Setting up, with Indian help, a regional Water Management Institute. At some stage the sharing of water resources would be crucial for the harmonious development of the region.
* Working with all like-minded people to formulate a policy that would exclude the development of fissiparous tendencies in the region. It is in the long-term interest of India, China, Russia, Iran and Turkey to ensure that they do not destabilise, or allow the destabilisation of the region. Such a policy may ultimately coincide with the interest of the United States of America as well as the European Union, should these latter countries take a long- term view.
* The setting up of a joint oil consortium between Gazprom, ONGC and the companies dealing in oil in Iran and China should be considered.

Dealing with South East Asia

Having dealt at some length on ASEAN in two earlier talks at this forum, notably "From Economic Intelligence to Strategic Intelligence" and "Subcontinental Realities at the turn of the Century", it only needs to be reiterated that:

* A tripartite guarantee by China, India and Japan to maintain the territorial integrity of ASEAN, both individually and collectively. No country should exploit, or be allowed to exploit weaknesses developing in these countries as a fall out from the economic meltdown in the region.
* China, Japan and the concerned ASEAN states to demilitarise the Spratly group of Islands and set up a joint holding company for the management of fisheries and the equitable sharing of revenues accruing from the oil or mineral wealth that might be found in the region in the next century.

It is believed that the non-regional powers that have interests in the region would not be averse to such agreements and could be expected to welcome them in the interest of ASEAN.

Military Aspects (General)

At this stage, it is important to bring in reforms that will strengthen India's fighting machine internally. Enough has been written on the aspects of joint defence planning and joint chiefs of staff system in the last fifty years to realise that without such a system the country will continue to suffer. If every modern fighting machine in the world has switched over to this system it requires a special type of obduracy to continue to oppose it. It is presumed that this time around the political hierarchy will itself introduce the long overdue reform regardless of the specious reasoning provided by the bureaucracy, or the individual service headquarters to counter it. The Kargil victory was a near run thing. It would be foolish beyond belief to be carried away by the military success achieved locally – literally at platoon, company and the battalion levels. It is more than made up by the professional inadequacies and intellectual dishonesty existing higher up the ladder. The National Security Council too needs to be revamped.

Meanwhile, it is recommended that a statutory five-member Military Commission be immediately set up. The Military Commission would comprise highly respected retired military officers (ex Chiefs do not automatically fall in this category) and a retired chief justice of the Supreme Court. The tenure of the members of the Commission would be limited to a single five years term. The Commission would not have any role in the formulation of defence policy, or its execution. It would be a watchdog body that would ensure that:

* Politicisation of the armed forces is totally excluded.
* That defence ministers, bureaucrats, or politicians do not exercise undue influence, to the detriment of the service, in promotions, postings or transfers.
* It would also serve as a review body for all statutory complaints relating to officers of the rank of Colonel and above (and equivalent ranks in the other two services). Its decisions would be final.
* It would *suo motu* examine, at random, defence deals, *post facto*, to reassure itself that extraneous factors had not come into play in the purchase of defence equipment. The Commission would be a body with extensive powers to order independent inquiries into matters where it felt that the national interest had indeed been compromised. It would under no circumstances get involved in the routine functioning of the Ministry of Defence or Service Headquarters.

Unless professionalism is improved in the top governance hierarchies, including the defence services, no amount of defence spending will ensure real security for the country. The Government of India must itself become more professional in the conduct of military affairs. As an example, it must lay down in the form of a directive, the minimum quantum of regular army formations and units that must be retained at all times in the Eastern theatre, regardless of the adversity of the situation that may develop in the Western theatre. The thinning out pattern that would have been established over the years would not have gone unnoticed. Exploitation of the vacuum created in the East, due to a misreading of the situation by Indian military commanders, could result in a disaster several orders of magnitude higher than what has been taking place in the West, from time to time. Attention has been rightly focused by a highly informed media on the need for acclimatisation of troops before committing them to battle at high altitudes. As any commander worth his salt would know, equal attention needs to be paid to terrain familiarisation.

As a general perception India's intelligence agencies are simply not geared to provide world class inputs that would be required by the country in the global environment of the next century. Without setting out an intelligence revamp blueprint in this presentation, some aspects that need to be kept in mind while undertaking such an exercise are mentioned below:

* Massive one time weeding out of deadwood.
* Bringing in outside talent from IIMs, IITs, colleges, industry, technocrats, military personnel (serving or retired) at the appropriate levels, commensurate with the quality that the inducted talent manifests. It could be permanent absorption, contract based employment for a given period or mission—specific appointment.
* National interest must take precedence over narrow cadre interests. The best minds in the

country must be allowed to contribute to the national interest. Those who are unable to see beyond their narrow service (or cadre) interests — which essentially means their own self interest — must be weeded out/phased out/ transferred to less sensitive departments.

* Massive retraining and specialisation of the personnel that are retained after special screening exercises should be carried out.

* If necessary, a *tabula rasa* approach must be taken while carrying out the intelligence revamp. The country is faced with a structurally deficient intelligence system. It is no longer a question of posting in professionally competent heads, whatever their provenance. What needs to be realised is that, as presently constituted, the system simply does not have the capability or capacity to perform at world class levels.

There has been a lot of talk, informed and not so well informed, on the reasons for the ingress that took place in the Kargil sector. Whether it was a command failure, intelligence failure or systemic failure in the way the defence of India is handled, the most obvious question that should have been posed has remained unasked. Simply stated the question is:

"If such was the state of affairs in the show window of national defence, what then is the real state of affairs in the other areas, far removed from the public gaze". (The Kargil sector would be reckoned to be one of the most (obviously) vulnerable sectors, where round the clock vigilance and instant reaction should have been the order of the day).

It is a most troubling question. One shudders to hazard a guess.

Concluding Remarks

In a way, strong global currents, far stronger than the forces that unleashed war and planet-destroying consumerism on the world, are coming into the ascendant to re-shape the destiny of the planet. These stronger, humanity-embracing currents represent the aspirations of ordinary people around the world.

The peoples of China, India and Tibet are civilisationally the best placed to use these currents, to harness them to their purpose, not only for the resurgence of China, Tibet, India and the region, but for the resurgence of the planet.

China is already a major force in world affairs. It might one day narrow the gap with the United States in nuclear and missile weaponry. It faces no military threat in the coming century. China could, instead, go under from the contradictions and pressures building up internally. Should its leadership, at the dawn of the new millennium, look at the world through different lens, they would be the first to realise that an historic compromise with the Dalai Lama automatically relieves pressure on practically all other fronts — the Western world, Falun Gong, internal unrest, and even Taiwan. The time has come for a great civilisation to turn a supposed adversary into an ally and thereby usher in a new destiny for the region and for the world of the 21st Century.

By the same token India and Pakistan would also need to come to terms with their shared history, geography and the abject misery in which the majority of their respective populations still live.

For India, the action in Kargil at the turn of the millennium could be the turning point in the country's march to greatness. A handful of young people with faith in their hearts and pride in their country have rekindled (modern) India's romance with the motherland. At the end of the day, and whatever the earlier failings, the armed forces hierarchy needs to be complimented for having restored an adverse situation with panache and skill. And finally: "if India's national security aim for the second half of the 20th century could have been succinctly defined as the preservation of India's unity, the country's aim for the first half of the 21st century could equally succinctly be defined as the preservation of the integrity of the subcontinent, as an essential prerequisite for the global equipoise of the third millennium."

Section-III
Ecology

Introduction

16. Ending the Menace of Poaching
17. Ecotone Restoration
18. Ecological Revival of the Planet
19. Revitalised Ganga Action Plan
20. Demilitarisation of the Himalayas

Ecology

Introduction

Without a doubt, the most pressing problem that is facing mankind at this juncture is the threatened ecological devastation of the earth. Despite the countless conferences and conventions, there has been little real action to address the fundamental issues at hand. While we need development to uplift those who live in poverty, what seems to be happening is that development is furthering the interest of the global elite. The credo seems to be "from each according to their ambitions, to each well beyond their needs" irrespective of the impact of this lifestyle on the environment. This is obviously not sustainable. What we therefore need is a new model of development that must necessarily emerge from the developing nations rather than the First World.

In this section, Vinod Saighal addresses a wide spectrum of issues pertaining to the ecological restoration of the world, with the emphasis on the Indian subcontinent. Of particular interest and importance is the farsighted proposal for the demilitarisation of the Himalayas – a region whose fragile ecosystem is currently being devastated by not only the military presence of China, Pakistan and India and frequent skirmishes but also by ill-conceived development of the nations that encircle it.

16

Ending the Menace of Poaching

Sansar Chand, the notorious poacher, has been making headlines. It is said that he has contributed more to the destruction of India's wildlife than anybody else. The tally: September 1974 – 581 skins seized; November 1974 – 539 skins; November 1975 –123 skins; January 1976 – 43 skins; May 1978 – 335 skins; January 1979 – 64 skins; March 1988 – 29,486 skins; February 1990 – 92 skins and 30 kg of tiger bones; 1992 – 82 skins; and so on up to the present day. An impressive record of nearly a quarter century.

Sansar Chand is actually a manifestation of a deeper national malaise. It is pointless asking how many Sansar Chands there are. The more important question is how this particular individual managed to get away after having been booked as early as 1974.

A stark fact that emerges from the widespread poaching coming to the public's notice is that vigilance on the part of NGOs, environmentalists and citizen's action groups cannot, in itself, be a substitute for effective governance. The state's failure to apprehend the culprits and bring them to book is the real cause of the rapid decline in India's wildlife, and of much else. Whether the blame lies with poorly equipped, ill-motivated, demoralised foresters, or the timber mafia, or the police-politician-criminal nexus, the result is the same. Hence, indifferent discharge of duty must be deemed to be as serious an offence as the actual destruction of wildlife and its habitat.

Whatever the reasons for this indifference-poor pay, lack of motivation, lack of training, lack of the wherewithal for effective monitoring, or undue interference by politicians – the functionaries of the state who are unable to discharge their duties effectively must be made to yield their place to those who are in a position to deliver. The taxpayers are paying them to perform a function. If they cannot carry out that function they must not continue to be a burden on the state. In addition to the permanent incumbents the greater culpability being that of the minister he too must be brought to book. Designated courts with judges like the incorruptible Italian magistrates must be empowered to investigate a minister's culpability. Being defeated at the hustings is not enough; the real plunderers of the country's wealth have also to be made to face criminal prosecution.

What is it that is preventing us from putting our house in order: lack of resources or lack of will? Certainly not the former. If an audit were to be conducted by an independent body of the allocations made in the last two decades to various government departments entrusted with forest regeneration and protection of endangered species and of grants received from the World Bank, UN agencies, foreign governments, private donors and all other allocations falling in these categories the final figure arrived at would be astronomical, even by standards prevailing in the developed countries. The problem has been one of squandering of resources. Immediate remedial measures that could be considered include:

* As a first step, the institution of regular independent scrutiny of accounts of departments suspected of mismanagement of funds. The existing institutional checks have obviously failed.

* Professional management of national parks, forests and wildlife habitats by properly trained and equipped wardens. The emphasis has to be on quality rather than quantity. One dedicated warden is worth more than ten indifferent performers.
* Speedy completion of satellite imagery of habitats and use of sophisticated photogrammetry techniques.
* Introduction of ecology monitoring in each of the remote districts. There must not be any more 'fait accompli'.
* Political interference with state functionaries, while in the legitimate discharge of their functions, to be made a cognisable, non-bailable offence.
* Much stiffer penalties for wanton or wilful destruction of protected forests, wildlife habitats and endangered species. (A new category of federal offences could be considered).
* Special benefits for dependents of forest guards killed in the line of duty.
* Ecotone restoration along natural water bodies.

A debate has been raging in many parts of the world on human needs versus animal needs. The human species is proliferating exponentially. A few more or less of this particular species will not impoverish the planet. The disappearance of a unique habitat or an endangered species will.

17

Ecotone Restoration

Why the Songbirds Have Fallen Silent?

Several months ago an article, *Songbirds Fall Silent Under Onslaught* had appeared in "The Times", London. In a report compiled by the Royal Society for the Protection of Birds an alarming decline was noticed in the numbers of several species for which surveys had been carried out, over several decades. The decline varied between 52 percent to 89 percent.

In India too several budding ornithologists in olive green who had good opportunity for extended studies while camping in the field for months and years on end were reporting similar declines. Then in 1979 and 1980 a specific survey was undertaken in a 600 square kilometre area in the Batala-Gurdaspur districts. As part of the survey the team set itself the task of attempting to find the reasons for this decline.

The chilling fact that came to light was that in the entire 600 sq. km. area surveyed there was no "eco-patch" (a term used in the report to describe any patch with continuous tree cover and undergrowth) except for portions around the Aliwal Escape. Finally the team watered down the definition of an eco-patch as any area of even 100 metres by 20 metres having continuous shrubbery with moderate tree cover". Again, except for Aliwal, no eco-patch was to be found. This meant that the ground and bush nesters had simply run out of undisturbed nesting habitats. Added to this was the fact that the "ecotone" along river banks and canals had already been virtually destroyed.

Synecological Studies of River Systems

Under these conditions the findings of the decline in avifauna came as no surprise. The ecotone destruction along rivers, canals, lakes and ponds due to over-grazing, and extension of cultivation upto the edges, was also an entomological disaster of a different order of magnitude.

The lack of an in-depth knowledge of limnology, with special reference to the pelagic/terrestrial interface in the coastal regions, has resulted in grave damage to the ecotone along rivers and the sea coast. This ecotone is the repository of the marine, entomological, avifaunal, faunal and vegetational diversity of riverine and coastal regions. Sufficient knowledge does not obtain in India of the spawning habits (and habitats) of anadromous species in the upper reaches. Perhaps no sustained research has been initiated for synecological studies of river systems in the subcontinent. There is an urgent requirement for the establishment of a national grid of synecological studies.

The immediate objectives of such studies would be: (i) To determine the pelagic/terrestrial interface in coastal/estuarine regions; (ii) to identify nesting/spawning habitats of anadromous species in their upstream migration; (iii) to recommend/initiate steps for preservation of the ecotone critical to spawning and nesting habitats for marine organisms, avifauna and fauna endemic to the region; (iv) to study pollution effects and recommend short and long term remedial measures; and (v) to prepare technical river profiles having an ecologico-geomorphological bias.

Making it Possible for the Songbirds to Sing Again

Since there is no scope whatsoever for losing any more ground (or being presented by *faits accomplis* in relation to the remaining virgin tracts (just about ten percent of the total area) the remedial steps now taken must be proof against further despoliation by vested interests and the indifference of local agencies. Ecotone restoration measures recommended below could go a long way in reversing the ecological decline. These measures would also reduce pollution and naturally strengthen river banks against erosion.

* Restoration of the tall grasses and forest belts along riverine tracts, canals, highways and railway tracks. In many places these are being restored for social forestry. In all such cases the concerned forest departments should ensure that whenever any felling is resorted to small sized *"eco-patches"* should be left intact. These could be patches of 100 metres in every kilometre. The undergrowth in eco-patches should also not be disturbed by burning or clearance of tall grasses. This measure will ensure that relatively safe nesting habitats are available to life forms that may have returned to the area over a period of time.

* Declaring certain patches along every waterway as protected wetland habitats. The minimum protected distance from the main water channel(s) in dry season should be laid down. Concomitantly measures should be adopted for enclosing these belts.

* Similar action to be taken for lakes where the minimum distance for exclusion of agriculture should be laid down from the periphery of the low water mark in the dry season.

* Where encroachment has already taken place upto the water channel, designated stretches should be resumed. Belts of 200 metres x 50 metres (ideally on both banks) for every ten kilometres would be sufficient to prevent an irreversible ecological change. When ordering resumption priority should be given for taking over patches where encroachment has been recent: the reason being

that a latent potential inheres in the soil for natural regeneration. Rather than going in for new planting of non-endemic species preference should be given for "natural regeneration" by effective closure of the patch. Other species can be introduced selectively at a later stage.
* Mid-channel islands, which can become natural habitats for a wide variety of bird species, should be immediately resumed and enclosed.

It has to be ensured that the problems that plague the ecosystem on land do not spill over to the marine environment; due to lack of foresight and the sustained pressure being put by developers to waive sensible restrictions which might yet preserve a modicum of the natural environment of the country for successor generations. Marine ecology is not confined to the narrow stretch of beach or shoreline but includes area upto the continental slope stretching sea-wards and ecotone (i.e. natural vegetation) adjacent to the shore which, in many cases, stretches along creeks and rivers many miles upstream. Instead of petitioning the central authorities to lift environmental restrictions the States should themselves enact supplementary safeguards to ensure that no further construction takes place on riversides, lake-sides and remote tourist spots. Almost every sublimely beautiful hill station of yesteryear has been ecologically ravaged beyond redemption. The pristine grandeur and solitude have yielded place to blaring transistors, loudspeakers, cheap eateries, garbage dumps and architectural monstrosities. As if this damage was insufficient hoteliers and travel agencies are vying with each other to penetrate the last bastions of remoteness for development – road access, heli-access and more of the same. Should present trends continue it is only a matter of time before this ancient land – of dense forests, magnificent flora and fauna, vast solitudes and mysticism – becomes an ecological and spiritual desert; all the way from Kashmir to Kanyakumari.

18

Eco Revival of the Planet

"The mode of living which is founded upon a total harmlessness toward all creatures or (in case of actual necessity) upon a minimum of such harm, is the highest morality." (*Mahabharata*).

The Eco Revival Summit comes at a time when realisation is growing all over that should the affairs of the planet continue to be managed as in the past the coming generations will have to live in a world which although technologically advanced would be spiritually and environmentally impoverished beyond recognition. The next generation would perhaps experience the change at the margins of the transition. The generation after that would not know the difference.

Not knowing the difference they would not care. A robotically-hedonised society taking its extravagant pleasures around the clock on press-button demand is not a projection from the third millennium. It is already upon us. The phenomenon can be perceived from coast to coast in the most advanced nation of the world. It can be demonstrated in pockets of affluence in many other parts of the world.

Not a good note on which to begin a keynote address. The fact is that herein lies the crux of the problem. Unless we confront this paradox squarely, while it is still possible to do so, the battle to ecologically revive the planet would be lost before it is joined. The statement has nothing to do with pessimism or optimism. It is our collective failure to grasp this nettle that is at the root of the global decline.

Just thirty years ago when I first became aware of the harm that we were doing to our surroundings the number of NGOs working in the field could be counted on the fingers of one hand. Nationally they did not exceed a few dozen. At the global level their number could have been a few hundred or, at best, a few thousand. Today as one looks around one would not be surprised if the number of NGOs in only one of the metropolitan cities were to exceed the national total of that time. Worldwide the number of NGOs, big and small, could well run into millions. Multiply this figure with the number of people in an average-sized NGO and one arrives at an impressive figure indeed. Thus, in spite of an exponential increase in the number of people doing good work, the rate of global environmental decline is steeper than at the time of which I speak.

I believe I have made the point. Unless this anomaly is addressed, and the strategies to meet the global challenges of today radically altered, there is little likelihood of achieving results commensurate to the effort put in. There is no dearth of shining examples of the remarkable work being done by dedicated bands all over the world. They remain beacons of hope. They cannot, however, by themselves, turn the tide.

Our aim in this conference will be to re-focus that strength; to give it the type of cutting edge that will bring decisive results in a battle that has already been lost in various parts of the world. Rhetorical though it may sound we must, nevertheless, ask ourselves the question, "When will we act decisively? When the meat from the last mink whale is offered at fifty thousand dollars a plate at one of the glittering restaurants in Tokyo or Taipei!" India though ecologically ravaged has not yet been psycho-spiritually devastated to the same extent as many of the more materially advanced countries. It is not yet subjected to worrisome amounts of acid rain. We have not yet accumulated "lethal" toxic wastes of the levels that threaten the ground water aquifers in the USA and which at conservative estimates would require clean up costs reckoned in hundreds of billions of dollars. Nor of the levels in some of the African countries used as dumping grounds for waste generated in the West – or of levels in the erstwhile Republics of the USSR.

I believe there is an immediate requirement for the setting up of an independent national – possibly international – commission to go into the entire gamut of rapid industrialisation and its ecological consequences. I would not be too surprised if such a commission decided to recommend limits to the number and types of industries that could be set up in ecologically fragile zones. We need to reverse the pace at which the automobile revolution has overtaken the world, and now India. Sooner or later we will have to put quotas on the number of automobiles and chemicals that can be produced in different regions of the world. Similar limits will also have to be placed on aircrafts and ships. THE AGE OF OPEN-ENDED GROWTH IS OVER.

A start can be made in India. We have to immediately put *cordons sanitaires* around the remaining virgin tracts before these too are stormed by frenzied developers. To prevent groundwater contamination the concerned ministries should begin by remotely sensing the underground water resources to study the permeability of the geological strata around the aquifers. This will give an indication as to the types of hazardous industries that should be prohibited within designated radii from the edges of the aquifers. I have touched upon just two or three critical environmental concerns that do not brook delay. There are others.

Remedial Measures

And this brings me to my next point. There has been considerable talk in environmental circles and among political reformists calling for minimising government role in various areas. While such thinking can be seen to be a very healthy development in the Indian polity a word of caution needs to be sounded in this regard. The problems of India and the Indian subcontinent are so monumental and, on the face of it, so intractable that any talk of demolishing the government's role beyond a given point would be premature. The need of the hour is good government. There is scope for bringing about transparency in government and for de-centralising in a manner whereby local communities are able to utilise the resources allocated to them optimally.

However, while de-constructing government machinery in sectors where it has consistently failed to perform it has to be concomitantly ensured that the transition that takes place is not towards the "Bihar model of governance" which, if one is not careful, could become the norm over larger swathes of the subcontinent. The government may have displayed its inability to manage resources optimally. Complete privatisation and absence of controls, however, could give free rein to private sector greed. The common man, caught in between, would invariably continue to suffer and the environment to diminish. Therefore, the answer lies in finding a via media that incorporates the strengths of both parties and rejects the worst ills of either side. There would be many who would look askance at such compromises. While one can understand their misgivings one must realise that in present day societies the governments are generally here to stay. With the awesome power available to the state it would perhaps be well nigh impossible to displace it. Hence the need for sensible accommodations that reduce government role in designated areas and allow for bringing in outside talent to wrestle with the enormous problems confronting developing societies.

Next Generation

This morning's Chief Guests are members of the young generation growing up under the shadow of the perception that the time for reckoning might soon be at hand. That someone will have to pay for the excesses of the generation that preceded them. Our young friends will soon enough have to assume the mantle of responsibility for the well-being of the planet. Looking at them I am reminded of my own youth. I was about their age, undergoing training at that magnificent institution, the National Defence Academy when the first Prime Minister of free India visited us. Even after forty years I can still feel the awe with which we beheld the great leader.

The great leaders of India have left the stage of history. The dreams which they nurtured have departed with them. I recall the incident from yesteryear because we had faith in our leaders at that time. This is no longer the case. And that is why we are appealing to the youth of India to be conscious of this betrayal. That such betrayal is global can be scarce consolation in a land where the levels of poverty and misery are perhaps the highest in the world.

We wish to tell our young friends in the audience that the lighting of the lamp by members of their generation goes beyond mere symbolism. We are making a direct appeal to the youth. Bestir yourselves. Your future is being mortgaged at an alarming rate.

In this gathering we have invited a cross-section of students and teachers so that when they go back they can, in their own inimitable style, initiate actions which will spread to many teaching institutions in India; and perhaps beyond India's frontiers. Towards this end we would like to suggest steps which, in our opinion, could lead to tangible results. We recommend, inter alia:

* The setting up of a Youth Ecological Revival Fund. This fund would not be dependent upon the benevolence of outside donors or government subsidies. Very simply, students in all recognised schools in Class, A, B & C, cities (of India) should take a pledge to donate one rupee a month from their pocket money towards the Youth Ecological Revival Fund. Other ways to augment this fund

could be thought of. For example, all middle class families and business establishments could be requested to donate just ten rupees from the monies that they spend every Diwali on celebrations, gambling and the bursting of firecrackers; the same pattern could be followed for Christmas and other festivals; NGOs across the country receiving grants and donations from the government or institutional donors in India and abroad would be asked to pledge one percent of their annual incomes towards this fund. Allied methodologies for building up an impressive corpus could be considered.

* The Youth Eco Revival Fund would be used in its entirety for implementation of Eco Revival schemes on the ground. No monies would be spent on conferences and the like. Vested interests would not be allowed to develop. The corpus would be invested in gilt-edged securities by a team of highly respected advisers. The manner in which the annual expenditure would be undertaken would be open for scrutiny to any member of the public. The managers of the fund would be changed periodically. In addition to knowledgeable, globally respected figures who would be guiding the affairs of the Fund, written suggestions would be invited from educational institutions from time to time. At the time of taking decisions youth representatives would be present, by rotation.

The youth in India have to be mobilised to reverse the horrendous population growth. We must appreciate that in South Asia we have gone way beyond Malthusian self-corrections. Taking the example of AIDS, even if this scourge were to spread faster in South Asia than is the case in many parts of Africa it would make no difference to the population growth on the subcontinent. Were it to become technologically feasible to project ten thousand people per day to a colony on the Moon the population would still not decrease. While the political class dithers, the horrors of sub optimal growth for hundreds of millions below the poverty line stare us in the face. I believe that over thirty percent of the pregnancies today are unwanted pregnancies. At the very least, it should be possible to achieve almost zero population growth in as little as ten to fifteen years in the urban conglomerates where large populations are concentrated in slum clusters.

An entire session will be devoted exclusively to analysing strategies whereby educated young India can rise to secure its future and that of its less fortunate brothers and sisters in the deprived strata of society. We would like to take this opportunity to suggest additional areas for consideration by the participants.

* India represents a sixth of humanity. We do not have to be herded into the globalisation pen like sheep. We "should" embrace aspects of globalisation that suit us and at the pace which suits us. It is not necessary to replace every camel with a truck in every part of the desert in a tearing hurry; or to tear apart the tranquility of every remote corner for the tourist dollar. We have to take a considered, long-term view.

* Natural intelligence is in danger of becoming submerged by artificial intelligence. Can we synthesise the two before it swamps the natural wisdom of so-called backward societies in many parts of the world. Preventing the campuses from becoming the battleground of political parties and divisive politics. Instead the younger generation could start the Youth Eco Revival Party of India – a "green" political party for saving the planet from the generation that was instrumental in destroying it. After consolidating in India the younger greens will embrace their counterparts in the whole subcontinent.

* Reviving the Romance with the Motherland & Mother Earth.

* *Planning of youth camps in eco-fragile areas during term breaks with the sole purpose of living with and interacting with the locals and assessing the actions to be taken for restoring the eco-balance. Each school to adopt areas over five year periods. We are all familiar with the idea of twinning of cities. Elite schools should now go in for eco-twinning with eco-fragile habitats. Well-endowed private institutions have tremendous potential to adopt, adapt and follow up. During such interaction they will monitor the effect of info-tech penetration in remote areas. There is an urgent need to study the effects and turn the phenomenon to advantage before the areas are ripped open for "development" and, inevitably "exploitation".

In this talk I have touched upon some areas where the educated younger generation, as part of the school system, can effectively step in to check the depredatory onslaught on the natural environment, or whatever remains of it. They have to go beyond being merely "aware". We expect the young representatives and their teachers to dwell upon these ideas and refine them. Having refined them they should go ahead and implement them without waiting for anybody to give them the green light. Today we have amongst us, the representatives of well-known educational institutions. We also have the Director General, National Cadet Corps and NCC cadets. The NCC in India is perhaps one of the largest youth organisations dedicated to nation building anywhere in the world. NCC cadets can be mobilised to act as vectors for social change.

There are several ways of reversing the near-universal trend towards gratuitous violence, at progressively younger ages. These too will be elaborated upon during the conference. We will attempt to analyse in some depth activities that are degenerative and those which can be described as regenerative. Meanwhile, we recommend that all schools and NGOs worldwide endorse resolutions to the effect that:

(a) Parades on National Days and Republic Days must become peace parades. No military weapons should be paraded. The demonstration of military might should be limited to marches by foot columns only.

(b) All concerned should work towards removal of toys for children that psychologically engender violence.

Macro-Dimensions of the Problem

If the pitiful remaining virgin tracts of the world are to be saved, a fundamental decision has to be taken to put humankind on the backburner for one or two decades; because every time some eco-restoration action is planned there is an hue and cry about job losses, income losses, profit decline and so on. It is a cruel dilemma. Whichever way one looks at it the have-nots will have to be compensated in some form or the other.

The foremost task facing the generation growing up to be the leaders of tomorrow in the subcontinent remains the eco-restoration of the Himalayas and the regeneration of the River Ganges. If the Himalayan forests are destroyed and the Ganga remains polluted to its present levels then India will lose its soul. The Himalayan forests and the Ganga are the very embodiment of India's cultural and spiritual heritage. Throughout the millennia sages, *sadhus*, and ordinary householders went there to find salvation or simply to live out the rest of their lives in the tranquility of the forest or on the banks of the sacred river. What holds good for the Himalayas and the Ganga applies equally to the forest belts and rivers in other parts of India.

When we talk of the Eco-restoration of the Himalayas it must be appreciated that to date the military dimension has been submerging all other dimensions – be they ecological or existential. The macro-dimension of the problem is intra-regional.

The Year of the Oceans

1998 has been declared as the Year of the Oceans. While it is heartening to see regional efforts taking shape for trying to undo the damage caused due to past heedlessness a new and potentially more lethal danger appears to be in the offing. Disturbing reports have come in of the death of whales in large numbers in some parts of the world on account of disorientation resulting from submarine communications in the very low frequency band, the spectrum thought to be used by the whales in communicating with each other. We recommend an immediate and concerted global action to investigate this phenomenon before one of the most wondrous species of mammals, already endangered, becomes extinct. This Conference appeals to the United Nations Secretary General to propose a five year ban on the movement of submarines under the polar ice caps and other designated zones while an international scientific study is carried out for ascertaining the damage caused to marine life by the proliferation of submarines for military use.

The close of the millennium offers an ideal opportunity to the great powers of the world to pause in the mad race for military exploitation of the oceans. It is the first time in this century – perhaps in many centuries – that no great power is militarily threatening the other powers. It is an opportunity the likes of which could not have been even dreamed of a few years ago. It would be extreme callousness on the part of the governments of the world to let it slip by.

Concluding Remarks

In a century which saw violence on a scale unprecedented in history Gandhiji was an outstanding proponent of *ahimsa*. Many followers of the older orders that took birth in this land still abide by the tenets of non-violence, in spirit and in deed. Violence invariably begets violence. In today's world, sadly, love hardly ever begets love. The gratuitous increase in societal violence is in turn leading to unprecedented eco-savagery. One can perhaps trace its roots back to the advent of Darwinism. The term "law of the jungle" took on a warped connotation. A brilliant scientific hypothesis was twisted out of shape to justify global plunder on a scale not witnessed before by mankind – or nature. Predation, no doubt, takes place at different levels of the food chain. But nowhere in the natural jungle is to be found the mindless savagery obtaining in the man-made jungles of today. In India the understanding of the law of the jungle was one whereby the great sages of this land were able to retire to the forests and live in harmony with the other dwellers of the forest. The picture that came to us through the ages was one of serenity and peace. It was the anti-thesis of the image created by the culture that arose after the industrial revolution in Europe and America to dominate the world. They first sought to destroy the cultures of the lands they conquered. The result is there for everyone to see.

Unfortunately, the dominant culture of those who guided the destiny of the world in the present century has permeated into the better off classes of India as well. Eco-ravagement is, in fact, eco-violence. The source from which it springs is the same: "the unalloyed domination of pure capitalism and its anti-thesis pure communism". Both systems at their extremes have savaged the planet. Hence, unless a way is found to live in the middle ground between these two systems the absolute ecological destruction of the planet will be completed in less than fifty years from now. Man will not perish. The monumentally-egotistical being will perhaps continue to survive – and thrive – on the rotting corpse of global diversity. By then, without knowing the difference, he would have descended into a different type of existential slime, far grimier than the primordial slime from which he arose. Therefore, if we wish to save our natural environment and preserve its bio diversity we will again have to call upon the youth of today to lead the way. Even a small beginning would suffice.

Civilisation tearing eco-catastrophes are already upon us. We fail to appreciate them fully because of the gradualness (in relative terms) with which the majority of the human beings on the planet, especially in the developing countries, are descending into the next sub human levels of existence. The eco-revival battle cannot be won unless the older traditions of this land, so ably re-enunciated by Vivekananda, Aurobindo, Gandhi and Tagore, are first revived.

Several thousand millennia ago nature lifted from the ground one among the myriad species inhabiting the Earth to an upright position. In elevating man to an erect posture it wanted this being to be able to look farther than the others, physically and metaphorically. For the latter faculty to emerge, it bestowed upon him a superior intelligence. Then just a few millennia ago the newly raised being whom nature had so favoured began to use his intelligence to gain dominance over his fellow species on the planet. In the millennium of our race just coming to an end the most intelligent creature on Earth began to devastate his surroundings. It is our hope that as humankind enters the next millennium this "intelligence" will graduate into "wisdom". When that happens the coming generations of humans, having forsaken their inhumanity, will again "walk" the Earth. They would have ceased to "trample" it.

19

Revitalised Ganga Action Plan

Well over a decade ago a youthful Prime Minister fired the imagination of the nation by outlining his vision for the purification of the Ganga. Unfortunately, despite huge outlays, there is very little to show for it on the ground. The dream of the former Prime Minister lies as shattered as lay his body after the assassination, before his cremation. Should we then give a decent burial to the Ganga Action Plan as well. We don't think so. As much as the Himalayas, the River Ganges embodies the very core of India's civilisational continuity and its quintessential spiritual flow - past, present and future. From the mists of antiquity, when the first great *Rishis* meditated on its banks, to the eternity of mankind's quest in the millennia to follow the Ganga has to retain its purity for the millions who come to worship on its sacred banks - at a myriad sanctified places along the course of "*Ganga Mayya*".

To revitalise the turgid Ganga Action Plan we recommend the setting up of a national task force, freed from all political and bureaucratic control, along the following lines:

* The national task force (NTF) to be constituted by an enactment of Parliament or under a directive by the Supreme Court of India or by any other means which would guarantee the independent functioning and efficacy of the programme.

* The NTF to be headed by any person of outstanding ability. Suitable guidelines to be incorporated in the initial enactment for ensuring the impartiality of the selection as well as the competence of the person selected to carry out the mandate.
* The allocation for the Action Plan to be made directly by the Planning Commission to the NTF.
* The NTF to have an accompanying special court or an empowered tribunal to ruthlessly eliminate all obstructions to the speedy implementation of the Action Plan. No subordinate authority in any of the States would have the power to interfere with, question, or stay the progress of the Action Plan.
* The NTF would be empowered to requisition the services of any qualified personnel of the Central or State governments for periods of time determined by the apex body of the NTF. In like manner, the NTF would have lien on any law and order forces of the Central or State governments for ensuring compliance with the decisions of the NTF and/or the empowered tribunal headed by a serving or retired Justice of the Supreme Court.
* Guidelines for the standards of purity, beautification and ecotone restoration to be attained, as well as the time frames in which these are to be realised would be laid down at the time of establishing the NTF.

The key ingredients of the revitalised Ganga Action Plan have been highlighted. Sensible modifications and mid-term corrections for the scheme could be carried out from time to time as the scheme progresses. It is possible to concomitantly set up national task forces along similar lines for some of the other major river systems on the subcontinent. The methodology recommends itself for application for long term flood control measures on a subcontinental or interstate basis.

It must be kept in mind, however, that the setting up of the NTF for the Ganga Action Plan and other task forces of a similar nature must, from their very inception, have a proviso for winding up of the task forces within stipulated time frames. Failing which, the country will be saddled with one more massive bureaucracy which would add further deadweight to the leviathan already crippling the country's growth. A contract-based, performance-oriented Action Plan, which would automatically get wound up on completion, would be the answer. After setting up the NTF mechanism the government and bureaucracy would remain totally out of the loop. Benign over-watch could be maintained by a non -governmental oversight committee.

20

Blueprint for the Demilitarisation of the Himalayas as an Environmental Imperative

The military dimension has generally prevailed over most other dimensions of human existence since the dawn of history; but never to the extent that it has in the 20th century. Coming closer to our day and age it now tends to preponderate over the other dimensions to the detriment of the planet as a whole.

As a landmass the Himalayas, and the regions adjacent to the great mountain chain, have the dubious distinction of playing host to perhaps the largest concentration of military forces and destructive weapons systems anywhere in the world. The collective concentration of forces of China, India, Pakistan and a few other states could destroy one of the most magnificent natural habitats in the world.

Individually, countries like India, Nepal, Bhutan and China "have" started perceiving at the periphery of their military vision that all is not well with the ecology of the region. In non-military segments there is greater awareness that an irreversible decline may already have set in its extremely fragile ecosystem as the armies of China, India and Pakistan have been waging war to gain control over the awe inspiring peaks and passes for decades.

In fact the day of reckoning for all the countries that derive sustenance from the mighty Himalayan sources is not far off as each year the evidence that all is not well with the ecology of the Himalayas is piling up. For instance, no one in these countries needs to be reminded of the suffering caused to hundreds of millions of people by unprecedented and ever-worsening floods every year. The ever-worsening character of these floods is primarily due to the indiscriminate and widespread deforestation in the foothills of the Himalayas.

In this article we will dwell upon the inter-regional dimension of the problem in order to highlight the fact that unless the countries of the region come to their senses and join hands to reverse the eco-destruction of the Himalayas, the future generations of Chinese, Indians, Tibetans, Nepalese and Pakistanis will not have much left to fight over. The eco-restoration of the Himalayas is now an ineluctable "survival imperative" for over a billion people living in an and around the Himalayan region.

This eco-revival plan put forward for consideration divides the portion of the Himalayan region into four segments, i.e. areas West of the 75º E Meridian, that is the Pakistan-Afghanistan sector; the India-Pakistan sector; the India-China sector; and other relatively dormant sectors. The first sector, the Pak-Afghan sector, West of the 75º E Meridian is outside the purview of the presentation, being the battleground for power play of very many outside powers. In the following pages we will take the remaining sectors turn by turn.

Indo-Pak Sector (J&K Sector)

This sector can be further subdivided into two sub-sectors: The Ladakh sector and the areas north of it; and the rest of the areas of the state of Jammu and Kashmir. In the Ladakh sector the main dispute centres around Siachen (and now also around Kargil) which is also the highest battleground in the world. In addition to the human suffering undergone by troops of both sides in surviving in the hostile climatic conditions, the actual environmental devastation will only be known once the troops pull out.

However, it is not widely known that tens of thousands of tonnes of human waste, oil and lubricants and other contaminants have penetrated the snowy vastness, not to mention the millions of rounds of small arms ammunition and mortar and artillery shells. Undoubtedly the phrase "pure as the driven snow" has acquired new meaning in much of this Himalayan landscape. We recommend an immediate demilitarisation of the Siachen region along the following lines.

* Non-military joint commissions to verify the exact position of the belligerents on the ground. After verification, the documents to be deposited by the respective governments at the International Court of Justice (ICJ) at The Hague. Both countries would give written undertakings not to remilitarise or change the *status quo* in Siachen after troop pull back, for a minimum period of 25 years. In case of infringements, the ICJ to be empowered to impose heavy fines on the defaulting party. Concomitantly, China would give a written guarantee not to, in any way, take advantage of the demilitarisation to the detriment of the countries pulling back their troops.
* After submission of the documents to the ICJ, complete demilitarisation upto designated lines would be effected within 180 days.
* The Prime Ministers of India and Pakistan to jointly dedicate a memorial to the fighting spirit of some of the best soldiers in the world. They have been fighting under conditions which test the limits of human endurance.

* Thereafter, joint Indo-Pak teams to study the environmental impact of militarisation of the Siachen region and remedial measures that are required to be undertaken for limiting damage to future generations.

India-China Sectors

The India-China sectors can again be further subdivided into three zones from the point of view of past hostility as follows:

<u>Zones of Absolute Tranquility</u>: These are the areas where no skirmishes or fighting has taken place since after the occupation of Tibet by Chinese troops, i.e. continued tranquility for nearly fifty years.

<u>Zones of Continuous Tranquility</u>: These represent those areas where for over thirty-five years there has been no fighting or skirmishing, i.e. since the Sino-Indian conflict of 1962.

<u>Zones of Hostility</u>: or skirmish zones.

Having delineated the sub-sectors we recommend the following pattern for gradual demilitarisation of the Sino-Indian border as well as the ecologically fragile zones of Tibet.

* In the first instance, the Siachen demilitarisation model to be applied to the first two zones of the Sino-Indian border, i.e. the absolute tranquility zones and the continuous tranquility zones. Similar deposition of documents before the ICJ along with identical pledges and penalties for infringement. China being a permanent member of the Security Council with veto powers, that body has been given a wide berth and the ICJ route taken instead.
* Establishment of joint eco-restoration commissions to undertake joint work without prejudice to either country's stand on the boundary dispute.

* Pledge before the ICJ that neither country would ever use the eco-restoration zones for military activities in the future or to launch any military operations through those areas.
* The Chinese government to set up an independent commission for the phased de-nuclearisation and demilitarisation of Tibet in anticipation of international movement in that direction. Regardless of the rate of international progress the Chinese government to unilaterally chalk out a massive twenty-five year programme for the eco-restoration of Tibet. The World Bank and the Tibetan diaspora to assist without prejudice to the position of the Chinese government on the Tibetan issue.
* The government of India, in concert with the government of Nepal, to chalk out a similar twenty-five year programme for the full-scale eco-restoration of the Himalayas in the entire sub-Himalayan and trans-Himalayan regions. Gorkha pensioners in Nepal and Indian ex-servicemen, hailing from the region, to be incorporated in this mammoth task.

Section IV
Demography

Introduction

21. Population Problem in India
22. Doomsday Clock Ticks Away
23. Defusing the Population Bomb
24. For Operation Population

Demography

Introduction

India's population has already crossed a billion and under current projections is poised to overtake China before the middle of the next century. This frightening projection and its dire consequences seem to have been completely overlooked by the decision-makers in India. The author contends that if immediate steps are not taken to arrest this growth path in the next decade and begin to reverse the current trends, then all efforts aimed at development will be rendered fruitless. With only 2 per cent of the world's land area supporting more than one-sixth of the world's population, all progress that has been made has already been diluted.

In this section, Vinod Saighal argues that despite having an infrastructure that can reach the vast majority of the population, we still have not been able to achieve any real success in the most populated northern states. Of these the worst are Bihar, Madhya Pradesh, Rajasthan and Uttar Pradesh where despite surveys which indicate that a large number of pregnancies are unwanted, the family planning programme has not succeeded in meeting this demand for birth control.

With considerable foresight and well before the Cairo conference, the author had in 1985 already presented his views on stabilising population growth. These views were well ahead of their time and had there been political will, the issue of population growth would not be so critical to the future of India.

Population Problem in India

The subject of my talk today is the "Population Problem in India." Now, before I go any further, I would like to place before you excerpts from a 1980 paper titled the "The Approach to Family Planning."

> "We have perhaps entered the last decade where we still have the semblance of an option for a reasoned approach to the interrelated problems of over-population and environmental conservation. And should we not succeed there can be no doubt that by the year 1990 any government, irrespective of its hue, will have to legislate draconian measures to ensure even a mean level of subsistence".

> "The problem looks insurmountable only because we cannot muster our will to overcome it. We are wrong to believe that (all) people want large families. In many cases it is the male child syndrome and in most others the children merely keep coming along. Sex is no joy to most women in the slums. In fact, many of them, weary of the daily grind and barely recovering from the last pregnancy, dread the inevitable onslaught of the drunken male. In a male dominated society that semi-starved woman, battered both by fortune and her spouse, would welcome a deliverance from constant child-bearing. We have failed to reach her."

It may be noticed that these excerpts contain an element of both hope and despair; and today, at the beginning of 1985, when we are half-way through the fateful eighties decade the situation remains the same: there is cause for optimism as well as for alarm. But essentially we still have a choice; and we have to exercise it now because it will not be there a few years hence.

I am going to divide my talk into three parts:
 I. Historical perspective of the population problem in India;
 I. An assessment of the national policy to date; and
 II. The choice before us – future perspectives

Historical perspective

The question of population growth affects the future of India as perhaps nothing else. If we are ever to improve the quality of life in this country then each one of us who perceives the challenge will have to get involved in the national effort to overcome it. I feel that this process is well under way and today I will concentrate on highlighting trends that hold a distinct ray of hope.

In order to proceed further, I am giving a canonical definition of some of the standard demographic terms that will be used in the course of my talk:

* <u>Crude birth rate</u>: number of births in a year per thousand mid-year population
* <u>Crude death rate</u>: number of deaths in a year per thousand mid-year population
* <u>Age-specific fertility rate</u>: number of live births in a year to a thousand women in any specified age group
* <u>Total marital fertility rate</u>: average number of children that would be born to a married woman if she experiences the current fertility pattern throughout her reproductive span (15-49 years)

* **Infant mortality rate**: number of infants dying under age one in a year per thousand live births of the same year
* **Natural growth rate**: the difference between crude birth rate and crude death rate
* **Gross reproductive rate**: includes only the number of girls born in a specific year. A simple way of calculating GRR is to multiply the total fertility rate by the population of female births among live born children
* **Net reproductive rate**: represents the number of girls who would be born per woman and survive to the age of their mother at the time of their own birth. In other words, NRR gives the rate at which the current generation of mothers is being replaced by a future generation of potential mothers
* **Expectation of life at birth (life expectancy)**: average number of years a new born child is expected to live under current mortality rates
* **Sex ratio**: the number of females per thousand males

Not long ago somebody calculated that if the current rate of world population growth were to continue for another 6500 years people would be accumulating so rapidly on earth that human bodies not only would cover the sphere but would be piling up away from the earth at a speed exceeding the velocity of light. I remember reading elsewhere that the same growth pattern could, in very finite time scales, fill the entire solar system and the milky way galaxy with human beings packed end to end.

India with nearly seven hundred million people has the second largest population in the world, i.e. nearly 15 per cent of the world's population lives in an area which accounts for only 2.4 per cent of the total area of the landmass of the earth. The population of India doubled itself in thirty years from 1951 to 1981. At the beginning of the current decade the annual growth rate was estimated to be 2.25 per cent. At this rate the population will again double in about thirty two years and by about the year 2012 AD reach the staggering figure of fourteen hundred million.

While the magnitude of the problem may not have been appreciated at that time, our planners after independence, nevertheless, appear to have been worried on this count as India became perhaps the first country in the world to accept population control as a major plank of national planning. Our growth patterns since the turn of the century reveal that though our birth rate has slowly declined (except for the small rise between 1951 –1971) since then, our death rates have, in fact, gone down much more precipitously since the second decade. Thus, at the beginning of the eighties, ironically through our achievement in decreasing the death rate (without commensurate success in decreasing the birth rate), our natural growth rate accelerated further and was estimated to be around 2.1 per cent.

An assessment of national policy to date

In order to go straight to the heart of the matter we have to address the following question: *Is India going to implode under the weight of a runaway population growth?*

In reply to this question I am going to give an unequivocal answer: *India is not going to implode. The infrastructure that independent India's planners established could enable us today to meet the targets set for the year 2000 AD by 1995 and even as early as 1990.*

So, what is the reason for my optimism? I will try and share with you the thought process that has led me to this conclusion. Later we will see how we could conceivably go about achieving the desired results.

First, let us see what we have been able to achieve since independence:

In the short period since independence – and it is short if we measure it against the millennia of subjugation – we have progressed to a stage where millions in this country no longer die on account of famine. Over 50 per cent of the population may still be below the poverty line but deaths due to actual starvation, wherever they do occur, are now reckoned in dozens, or at worst in hundreds, but never in the lakhs and millions that used to be the case before. In addition, we have engineered: (i) a fall in mortality rates, which in the first decade of the twentieth century were averaged around 352 for males and 332 for females; (ii) a substantial increase in the life expectancy figures from around 22.6 for males and 23.3 for females in the first decade of the twentieth century to around 50.8 for males and 50 for females in 1971-77 and (iii) a dramatic decline in the crude death rate for the same period (42.6 in 1901-1910 to 13.9 in 1977-1979)

Many other such achievements that have a definite positive impact on controlling the population can be projected. However, their message is the same:

> "A reduction of this magnitude in such a large population could not have been brought about without the establishment of a massive infrastructure across the length and breadth of the country. This self-same infrastructure, *if properly harnessed*, could now enable us to meet our population goals well before the turn of the century."

The operative phrase is "if properly harnessed". Before I elaborate upon this let me give you an idea of the magnitude of the work done towards the creation of this infrastructure.

> "The government proposes to establish one primary health centre for every 30,000 population in the plains and 20,000 population in the hilly and tribal areas. To provide at least minimum services nearer to the people, a village health guide, preferably a female, is being provided in every village. Upto April 1982, two hundred thousand village health guides had been trained. In order to improve delivery services to pregnant women in rural areas, about 350,000 traditional birth attendants (dais) have been trained upto April 1982 to undertake better

delivery under hygienic conditions. These measures are expected to strengthen availability of basic health and medical facilities in the rural areas which, in turn, would have a salutary effect on mortality rates with particular reference to infant mortality. They also provide a channel for supply of material and services to rural areas besides providing inter-personal communication, education and motivation for acceptance of the small family norm."

(Country Statement, September 1982)

By the end of 1982 over 6,000 primary health centres and more than 60,000 sub-centres had already come up. When we refer in such glowing terms to the country's achievements since independence then one is tempted to ask: *Why then the alarm? Why do we keep on talking of the intractable population problem in India?"*

The reason is two-fold: *"The demographic profile and the inability to capitalise on our initial successes."*

With respect to the demographic profile we find that we are confronted with a paradox: the population growth is directly attributable to successes of the earlier decades in the field of health and family welfare. This has led to what is called the demographic gap. As shown before, both death and infant mortality rates have registered a steep fall since the beginning of the century and should fall much further in the next fifteen years, to bring down the death rate to about 9 per thousand and the infant mortality rate to less than 60. Hence, even if the present trend of decline in birth rates continues, we are still going to be confronted by another spurt in the population.

Another factor that has led to this inexorable rise is the distribution of population by broad age groups which is heavily skewed towards youth. Given below is the distribution of population (in percentage) by age group for 1971 and 1978. The thing to note is that population under 15, about 40 per cent will start to move in the reproductive age group.

Age Group	1971	1978
0-14	42.02	38.69
15-59	51.82	55.71
60+	5.99	5.60

What all this boils down to is that unless we do something "rightaway" we are going to be driven into the dreadful morass of a burgeoning population with the attendant decline in the quality of life – if it is not abysmal enough already – and an ecological disaster of an order of magnitude.

From the above analysis, it is clear that short of a catalysmic event the demographic cycle was something we could not escape from and would have to go through in our process of development. However, with respect to the second reason outlined above for the alarm (*the inability to capitalise on our initial successes offered by the extensive infrastructure laid out in the earlier development plans*), we could have and can still do, a lot to reverse the ominous trend.

We may have failed to perceive a fundamental change that has come in our people. They may be subsisting below the poverty line but are no longer as ill-informed as they were a few years ago. They are aware today, as never before, of problems confronting the country. The message of the small family norm has permeated far and wide. Those who manage the family planning programme have not fully appreciated the revolution that has taken place. If there has not been a dramatic decline in the birth rate it is not because of reluctance on the part of the majority of the people to limit births.

> "The family planning programme in India at the end of 1984 suffers not so much from a resistance on the part of the populace to adopt the small family norm but from organisational infirmity."

On the face of it this seems a harsh indictment. However, as the following example about the primary health centres, main and sub centres network in Uttar Pradesh, the most populated state of India, shows that despite the fact that there would be over 14,000 of such centres established, much remains to be done to operationalise them. At a conservative estimate at any one time over 50 per cent would be without permanent incumbents: either not posted; posted only on paper; posted but not reported for work; not attending regularly; or they would be away at the headquarters seeking transfers. The rapaciousness of some of the motivators also leaves much to be desired. This state of affairs is exacerbated by an unhealthy rivalry between the paid social workers of the Department of Health and voluntary workers. As if that was not enough to cripple any programme we have the instances of refrigerators working on electricity being supplied to sub-centres where, at the best of times, power is available for only a few minutes, or a few hours, each day. The wastage of perisahble drugs is colossal.

I am not exaggerating one bit. The actual state of affairs in the most populous states of Uttar Pradesh and Bihar is much worse. The point that I am repeatedly trying to make is that some of us may still be thinking that the family planning programme is not making sufficient headway due to a resistance to the programme. The resistance is there in some quarters, but not to the extent that existed before. I would not be far wrong in saying that with the same outlays we could improve the results by 200 or even 500 per cent by putting dedicated professionals and social workers to oversee the programme at all levels; in the centre and the states, i.e. by organisational overhaul and better management; not by coercion.

Future perspectives

There has been endless debate on the impact of economic betterment on population stabilisation. I do not think that many people seriously refute this. In any case the debate is academic. Every country – developed or developing – is attempting, by whatever path, to better the lot of its people. This is an on-going process. Meanwhile, India is faced with the dilemma of a runaway population growth outstripping and even negating most of its development effort. More and more people are falling behind the poverty line. So, by the time that we actually see the rosy dawn of plentitude leading to population stabilisation, the country would be writhing in the agony of a billion and half people.

It has been the underlying theme of my talk that at this juncture in the country's development we have the wherewithal to limit our population without resorting to draconian measures. If I were to be asked to re-order the priorities for the family welfare programme I would list these as:

* Reduction in infant mortality
* Women's emancipation
* Reorientation of the approach to family planning

Reduction in infant mortality

Before starting with the analysis, I would like to quote an eminent civil servant and demographer, Asok Mitra:

"The tragic emotional exhaustion – augmenting a sense of insecurity, defeat and apathy, generating in its turn a desire on the part of the mother to forget and 'prove herself' by having yet another conception – that stillbirths, neonatal and post-neonatal mortality inflict on the mother and the household generally cannot be comprehended at all by anybody who has not had direct experience of such tragedies"

According to a survey report published in 1971 the high infant mortality rates in India are mainly due to the persistence of exogenic causes arising from environmental and nutritional conditions. The post-neonatal infant deaths, i.e. deaths occurring after 28 days of birth, are mostly due to these causes and these account for nearly 50 per cent of the total infant mortality in India.

Currently, the infant mortality rate is over 100 for the country as a whole and its decline to levels achieved in developed countries could still lead to a new spurt in population. However, social scientists and demographers all over the world agree that a decline in infant mortality rates gradually yields to a reckonable decline in the birth rate. As a result of this an impetus is being imparted to the immunization programme for children.

Infant mortality remains a field in which a dramatic decline is possible in the near future as these excerpts from a UNICEF handout of 1983 make clear:

* On a rough estimate anywhere upto two million young children die in India as a consequence of diarrhoeal infection. Many more suffer but survive, the more malnourished for each episode. Each increase in malnutrition increases the risk of another infection. The real threat to the life and well-being of children is not diarrhoea but the attendant dehydration. The answer to this is with the mother at home – a mixture of sugar and salt in water in a reasonably right proportion. If the mother in the village or slum is made aware of this answer, then child deaths will be far fewer and child health will be far better.

* Hundreds of thousands of young children die in India from common childhood diseases like measles, diphtheria, tetanus, whooping cough, poliomyelitis and tuberculosis. By and large vaccines are available but vaccination does not take place. Here again, the answer is social awareness and social demand for preventive health services.

* Infant mortality is in a state of crisis – for no reason at all. For there is no shortage of infant food, at any rate for the first few months of the child's life. Yet more and more mothers, well-to-do and poor, in towns and even villages, give up breast feeding their babies relatively soon. They opt for the expensive and inferior alternative of artificial

feeding – opening the way to malnutrition as well as infection. Regulating the irresponsible sale of milk powder is one aspect of this problem. Even more important is the education of the mother for restoring the baby to the breast.

Women's emancipation

Concomitant with the reduction in infant mortality we need to hasten the process of women's emancipation. If we can somehow liberate our women from the shackles that bind them we will not only turn the corner as far as family planning is concerned but will see a marked improvement in the quality of life in this country.

Women's emancipation does not necessarily lead to women's lib — the type of movement much heralded in the West. In our limited sense it relates to:

* An increase in the age of marriage; and
* Greater female literacy.

It has been the constant endeavor of social reformers and the government to raise the age of marriage of girls which remained at about 13 years till 1931. Thereafter it has risen to the current level of 17 years (presently the minimum legal age of marriage for girls is 18 years)

Literacy among women increased from one half of one per cent in 1901 to nearly twenty five per cent in 1981 but still lagged behind the literacy rate for males.

> "In 1981 for every 201 literate males only 100 females were literate."

Selected indicators for infant mortality by socio-economic levels (1978) All India

Infant Morality by sex and Rural/Urban

Area	Males	Females	Persons
Rural	130	142	136
Urban	69	71	70
Total	120	131	125

Infant Morality by Educational level of Women

Educational level of Women	Rural	Urban
Illiterate	132	'81
Literate but below primary	105	59
Primary & above	64	49

Infant Mortality by Mother's age at Marriage

Age of Marriage	Rural	Urban
Below 18 years	141	78
18 – 20 years	112	66
21 years and above	85	46

The data has been taken from a Survey conducted by the office of the Registrar General, India

Reorientation of the approach to family planning

For the purpose of population stabilisation we can broadly divide the population into the following groups:
* The Upper Classes;
* The Median Income Groups; and
* The Under-Privileged Classes

I don't think that at the end of 1984 many people would seriously dispute that the small family message has been driven home as far as the first two groups are concerned and they are consciously limiting the size of their families. Therefore, we must also make a conscious effort to concentrate our resources, especially by way of publicity and creation of new facilities, almost exclusively on the last group, i.e. the under-privileged.

The under-privileged classes that form the bulk of our population and whose response patterns will decide as to where we are headed can again be sub-divided into two different categories:

* The static segment; and
* The mobile element

The static segment generally remains tied to the place of birth. The mobile segment comprises elements that move away to permanent settlement in urban areas or those who leave their native place for varying periods of time due to droughts or as migrant labour.

The first category being the largest are also the ones whose resistivity is the most difficult to penetrate. Their roots are in the soil and they are very tradition bound. Further, their dispersal across the entire country requires vast outlays in field teams and equipment. They are also our most serious challenge because if we can reach these people the family planning programme can never look back.

People who fall into the category called the mobile segment have a commonality in as much as a physical displacement would have subjected them to alien influences and made them more amenable to change in their transplanted state. Secondly, their very concentration in slums or at work sites enables us to effectively monitor these groups and achieve the same results with lesser resources. In fact, we can make a very big dent in population growth, and the resultant improvement in the urban environment, if we can take advantage of the relative accessibility of these people.

There has always been a lot of talk on the appalling conditions prevalent in the slums. The words 'slum living' and 'slum conditions' have been made synonymous with the ultimate in human misery. It is indeed strange that in spite of this we find that migration from the rural areas to the city slums continues unabated. Could it be that the conditions elsewhere are even worse?

We next move to the realm of mass media. We have to infuse a new vitality into the field of family planning propagation – while the publicity division can rightfully boast of some good programmes, their propagation of the theme has an air of sameness about it. Some points for consideration are:

* Link the environment to the problem of population proliferation
* Some themes have universal appeal. They should be complemented by regional ones.
* A different approach for various cultures and groups after studying the patterns of male and female response
* The visual impact of films and posters should be stark and thought-provoking for illiterate men
* Periodic variations to the theme to cut out monotony

Some of our film directors of international repute should be approached to bring out their considerable intellect to bear on documentation carrying the family planning message for the underprivileged classes.

Our family planning machinery must become more dynamic in monitoring the programme in all parts of the country to study the trends, and by extension, the approach must be suited to each region, even sub-region, of this diverse land. For example inter-district variation in Uttar Pradesh in 1971 regarding the percentage of girls married by the age of 15 varies from 30 per cent in Meerut to around 70 per cent in Gorakhpur. These large disparities cannot be ignored. It should not be difficult to establish a link between the age at marriage and the population growth rate for the districts at the two extremes.

No discussion of the demographic problem can be really complete without a look at development strategy for backward areas: a sound proposition of the nineteen fifties may not have remained so in the nineteen eighties. When the strategy was first adopted one of the desired aims must have been the preemption of the drift to the cities. The more idealistic among planners may have even believed in the benefits of civilisation spreading to backward regions. The effects of these benign activities make interesting case studies – from the North East to the remote corners of Bihar, Orissa, Madhya Pradesh, Maharashtra, Andhra Pradesh and elsewhere.

The picture that emerges is not uniformly bleak if viewed statistically – in terms of jobs, death rates (but not birth rates), health centres, trained medical practitioners, literacy and so on. The same if viewed from another angle – destruction of the virgin tracts, soil erosion, pollution of natural streams, tribal exploitation and the like – might appear different.

Whichever view is espoused the time has come for a fresh look. The policy for the eighties and a bit beyond must anticipate the pressures of the nineties and the opening decades of the coming century. If the planning process is to be freed from a conceptual infirmity note must be taken of the reality as it exists on the ground; at the level of implementation of policies.

My rationale in bringing up the subject of development strategies for backward regions is due to the fact that the ecological balance is being seriously jeopardised. If we look at the figures for the entire country disaggregated by state and union territories it becomes instantly clear that remote regions where the population is still low (in comparison), where the ecological devastation has not yet gone beyond the state of irreversibility, we must straightaway reformulate our development strategies. Our immediate endeavor must not be to construct roads and set up industries in these regions but should be towards health, sanitation and female literacy. This should be followed by careful monitoring and assessment of the development needs of each region.

The regional outlook

I would like to end this talk on the population problem in India by placing before you the proposition that I have no doubt that with renewed vigour and a professional approach India will yet stabilise it population at manageable levels, however our neighbours, especially Bangladesh and Pakistan may not be able to do so. For instance, in 1973 these two countries had a crude birth rate of nearly 47, i.e. the same obtained for undivided India at the end of the last century. To put it mildly the governments of these countries do not appear to be unduly alarmed. I foresee a time when the hungry populations of these countries spill over national frontiers under relentless pressure of unchecked growth and faltering economies. The ground work for strife in the years ahead is being laid now. We must avert disaster while it can still be averted.

22

Doomsday Clock Ticks Away

India is not going to explode. It is going to implode. And whenever that happens (in the year 2010, 20 or 30) the tragedy would not simply be the collapse of the nation under the weight of unchecked population growth, it would be that the country allowed itself to suffocate "in spite of" having had the wherewithal to stem the tide.

Everyone sees the doomsday clock of overpopulation ticking away. Yet nobody seems to be able to do anything about it. It can no longer be termed as political inertia or lack of political will. It is nothing short of criminal apathy on everyone's part in the face of the biggest threat to the nation's survival. All external threats, real or imagined, pale into insignificance compared to this threat.

With full realisation of the magnitude of the problem and the Herculean effort that will be involved it is still maintained that in competent hands, the family planning programme could achieve the goals set for 2010, by the turn of the century. As a corollary, it needs to be added that if we do not meet these goals by 2010, the situation would slip out of control.

Our family planning programme suffers not so much from a resistance on the part of the populace to adopt the small family norm, but from an organisational infirmity. On the face of it this seems to be a harsh indictment. Several years ago when a random check on the vast network of primary health centres. main health centres and sub-centres was carried out in Uttar Pradesh (where there were perhaps over 14,000 such centres), it was found that at any one time nearly 50 per cent were without permanent incumbents: either not posted; posted only on paper; posted but not reported for work; not attending regularly; or they would be away at "headquarters" seeking transfers.

The state of affairs in the other most populous states was equally grim. But why only blame junior incumbents and lower level functionaries. They take their cue from their superiors. The latter have gone from bad to worse. One just has to look at the frequent transfers of heads of departments, which are the mainstay of the country's programmes for getting out of the abysmal poverty trap, to realise that unless some of the abominable creatures who masquerade as ministers are first removed from the scene, no progress is really possible.

One would not be far from the truth in saying that with the same outlays results could have been improved 200 or even 500 per cent by putting dedicated professionals to oversee these programmes at all levels, at the Centre and in the states, and by ensuring a modicum of continuity. What is being referred to is an organisational overhaul and better management. Nobody is talking of coercion or sterilisation targets. The people themselves are ready to take the country forward if only the programme is pursued vigorously and imaginatively.

That people are ready for a change is amply corroborated by the National Family Health Survey (NFHS) 1992-93, excerpts from which are reproduced below. The NFHS total fertility rate for India is 3.4 children per woman, slightly lower than the SRS estimate of 3.6 for 1991. According to this measure, fertility in India is lower than in any other South Asian country except Sri Lanka and it is nearly one child lower than the Total Fertility Rate (TFR) for all less developed countries combined (excluding China).

A comparison of completed cohort fertility (5.1 children per woman at ages 45-49) with current fertility (total fertility rate of 3.4 children per woman) demonstrates that fertility levels in India have fallen substantially in the recent past.

In the NFHS, currently married women were asked: "Would you like to have another child or would you prefer not to have any more children?" Women who did not yet have any children were asked whether they wanted to have any children.

If a woman was pregnant at the time of the interview, she was asked whether or not she wanted another child after the one she was expecting. Overall, only one-third of Indian women say they want another child at any time in the future, and 58 per cent of these women say they would like to wait at least two years before having their next birth. Only 13 per cent of women say they would like another child soon (that is, within two years). More than one-quarter of women say they do not want any more children, and 31 per cent of women (or their husbands) are sterilised, so that they cannot have any more children.

Interestingly, the desire for children is very strong for women who have fewer than two children. More than one-third of women with no children say they would like to wait at least two years before having their first child and nearly half of the women have fewer than three living children, the strong desire among these women for spacing children cannot be ignored.

Knowledge of family planning and awareness is nearly universal in India, with 96 percent of women reporting knowledge of at least one contraceptive method.

This level of contraceptive use is comparable to the combined level of 42 per cent for all less developed countries excluding China.

More than half the women in urban areas (51 percent) use contraception compared with 37 per cent in rural areas.

The two-child family is evidently an accepted concept for many couples. More than 80 per cent of females, age six and above are literate in Mizoram (89 per cent) and in Kerala (82 percent). Between 70 and 80 per cent of women in Goa (73 per cent), Nagaland (72 per cent) and the National Capital Territory of Delhi (71 percent) are literate. At the other extreme, more than 50 per cent of females, aged six and over, are illiterate in Rajasthan (75 per cent), Bihar (72 per cent), Uttar Pradesh (68 per cent), Madhya Pradesh(66 per cent), Andhra Pradesh (62 per cent), Orissa (59 per cent), Arunachal Pradesh (58 per cent), and Haryana and Karnataka (54 per cent each).

The survey conducted by the International Institute for Population Sciences (IIPS), Bombay confirms that if the family planning programme is expertly managed, the tide can still be turned before the situation gets totally out of hand. What is now required is a national consensus that population stabilisation is the overriding priority for concerted national action. If those at the helm of affairs are unable to perceive the altered ground realities or are unable to order full-scale mobilisation of national resources to tackle the problem on a war-footing they must step aside and make place for people more competent to meet this challenge.

Aspects which could reinvigorate the programme to meet the desired goals by 2000 are given:

* An unequivocal statement by the government that it is alive to this peril and has the political will to tackle it on a war footing.
* A national consensus (evolved prior to the Lok Sabha elections) that the population stabilisation programme is sacrosanct, and while there would be no coercion in its implementation anyone disrupting the programme by fanning religious hatred would be dealt with severely.
* There has to be continuity in administering the programme at all levels. Even if political parties and legislators keep playing musical chairs the persons

selected to administer the programme should not be moved around frequently. The administrator of the programme should, as far as possible, be the most competent civil servant or any other person selected on merit from any walk of life. A programme which is conceptually sound can be ruined at the execution level if those responsible for administering it cannot empathise with people or are unable to monitor it effectively.

* Adequate funding through channels which are incorruptible.
* Special tax incentives to business houses who undertake to run the programme in entire towns or districts.
* Generous backing for NGOs who have imaginative programmes.
* Use of ex-servicemen and their families as vectors for social change. At any one time there would be five to 10 million such people in various parts of India.

Our leaders have failed to grasp a simple fact which can be discerned by anyone with his ear to the ground, at the ordinary levels of existence. Today, at the grass roots, people are far more aware (than those who govern them) of the need to forge ahead as a nation. All communities are willing to participate unitedly towards building a stronger and more habitable India. It is a very small minority (of misguided politicians and rabble-rousers) who are retarding the progress of the country. Weeding out such elements from the national mainstream is also a national priority.

23

Defusing the Population Bomb

Much has been written about the population explosion since the time India got its independence fifty years ago. In recapitulating the sorry tale it simply needs to be stated that whereas all countries lying to the East were able to stabilise their populations, the subcontinent slid into a nearly irreversible decline. The condition of most of those other countries of South East Asia was far worse than that obtaining in India at the time of independence. A number of them had suffered unspeakable horrors under Japanese occupation; in many cases their misery continued much longer during proxy (Cold War) struggles. Irrespective of the nature of their governing hierarchies nearly all of them managed to get out of the population, poverty and filth traps.

Almost as an exception to the rule, Kerala too achieved dramatic results in the field of population stabilisation. The Kerala model has been quoted extensively as a showcase, in India and abroad. The fact, however, is that the remarkable success story of Kerala could not be replicated in most other parts of India, especially in the BIMARU States. There are several reasons for this, the most important being the status of women in the matrilineal system that was prevalent in the State. There were several other factors of a similar nature which allowed the programme to take off almost exponentially. These conditions did not obtain (and still do not obtain) North of the Vindhyas.

One of the main reasons for India's decline – painfully evident in many other spheres as well – could well be the penchant of the (so-called) educated elite for endless debates and bickering; linked to general inaction. The population of India could easily have been stabilised by the nineteen eighties and at the beginning of the nineties. It can yet be stabilised within the next ten years "without" following the route taken by China.

The "population bomb" has to be defused here and now. For this to happen, independent Population Commission will have to be set up at the Centre and in the States. The model for such a Commission has been lying with the concerned government departments and the Planning Commission since 1980. More recently, Dr. M. S Swaminathan, Chairman of the Expert Group on National Population Policy also recommended the establishment of a Population and Social Development Commission. The commission was to be structured on the "Homi Bhaba principle", that is, it should be vested with the necessary authority to operate a Population and Social Development Fund and at the same time be free from rigid rules and bureaucratic procedures. It needs to be mentioned here that when independent commissions are to be set up on the Homi Bhaba principle, it presupposes that the head of the commission (being given total autonomy and operating freedom) would be an individual with impeccable, credentials for the job. The same criteria would apply to the commission members. The initial mandate of the commission members should be for five years. Renewal, or fresh mandate, would be given by a properly constituted authority, based on results achieved on the ground, and not in the manner of extensions given to compliant bureaucrats and police officials

For a long time, various activist groups have been lobbying against coercion in the family planning programme. We need a clearer perception as to what constitutes coercion. The draconian measures taken by China can be termed as coercion. The forced sterilisations of the Emergency period were coercive. At the stage where India finds itself now other forms of persuasion do "not" fall into the same category. Today, short of the draconian measures mentioned earlier, every method, tactic, strategy and approach available must be used to ensure the success of family planning programmes. In the ultimate analysis the best results would be obtained by an admixture of various approaches provided that the most competent people are allowed to administer these programmes.

Put in another way it means that soft-pedalling and mollycoddling must stop immediately. The lackadaisical, whimsical and woolly approach that appeared to be idealistically right in the nineteen fifties will simply not do for the crisis facing the country at the turn of the century. Such an approach will condemn the nation to a form of slavery far worse than the type witnessed over the last millennium. It artificially enfeebles the nation. There is no justification for it. After fifty years of the family planning campaign it is no longer a case of superstition, backwardness or deprivation. In most strata of society that still breed profusely, it is now often a case of sloth, indifference and plain cussedness.

One can comprehend if people in remote, inaccessible regions produce the third, fourth or fifth child. But how does one describe people in metropolitan cities or in and around mofussil towns who show their contempt by producing a dozen children or more. This latter category are plainly violating the sanctity of the land. They are taking advantage of the benevolence of the government. They are endangering the prosperity or the nation. The government has to step in — infirmity and inaction being indefensible. If one person practices self-restraint and limits his family to one or two children and the other does not exercise any restraint and produces six, ten or twelve children then the latter can be faulted for diminishing the rights and future prosperity of those citizens of the land who exercise forbearance.

There is absolutely no reason for India to wallow in the mire of the unmanageable population growth and population-induced miseries that blight the land. It does not matter as to which approach to family planning is used – cafeteria, target-oriented or any other. Eschewing, for the moment, the Chinese approach the need of the hour is to obtain results before the country is engulfed in an ocean of humanity. There is hardly anybody left who doubts that female literacy, female emancipation, female empowerment and child and maternal health care are the surest ways to achieve the goal of population stabilisation. These themes had been clearly enunciated in the country full ten years before the Cairo conference. The Government of India and the Planning Commission adopted these enlightened norms well before several others did. The results are there for all to see. We come back to the same proposition: There is no dearth of enlightenment or expertise *per se* in the country; what is lacking is effective and enlightened governance.

Unrestrained demographic proliferation could destroy the quality of life and the social cohesion of subcontinental societies more comprehensively than any military threat. For India the threat has internal and external dimensions of almost equal magnitude. India, being the more vibrant democracy and economy, will continue to attract the deprived segments of the populations of Nepal, Bangladesh and Pakistan. The migrations are unidirectional. Reverse migration almost "never" takes place. This problem has to be addressed urgently and by all the governments of the subcontinent and at fora like SAARC.

24

For Operation Population

The earliest population stabilisation infrastructure in the world was set up in India. By the 1980s the infrastructure spanned the length and breadth of the country. By that time the family planning (FP) message had reached the remotest corners of the country; the majority of the people, cutting across caste and communal lines, were not averse to adopting the small family norm. Colossal outlays were made for this programme by the national exchequer. Large sums were made available by international donors.

What happened to the programme and the astronomical sums of money poured in it over the decades? The answer can be provided in one line: "The Bihar model of governance" was applied to the programme in most states in the country.

Many good suggestions made during various national and international meets over the years have already been accepted as the cornerstones of the government's FP strategy, notably MCH, female literacy, women's emancipation and other eminently desirable strategies. The immediate task confronting the administration, especially in the BIMARU states, is the revitalisation of the existing infrastructure. Recommendations in this regard are as under:

In rural areas there are cycles of peak activity when all members of a family are fully engaged with the work at hand, generally conforming to the periods of sowing, transplanting and harvesting. The remainder months are leaner. The intensity of FP activity should conform to the latter.

* Some form of central monitoring must take place at laid down periodicities.

  Clinics providing FP facilities should remain open on all days and attendance of the staff manning the facility should be rigorously monitored.

* Mobile clinics assume greater significance for remote areas. To create favourable conditions for a response that is automatic, the day of visits of mobile clinics for FP & MCH should be fixed and rigidly adhered to.

* One study observed that the unmarried urban women had little understanding of the lives of the rural women they were to motivate. Hence, state governments have to ensure that they encourage outlets that are run by women only so that no diffidence is felt by the rural women in asking for details of all contraceptive facilities at retail outlets.

* Retrenchment and restructuring of staff in districts/ blocks where results over a given period have not been satisfactory.

* The minimum staff at any static FP facility to be laid down for a given size of population and/or geographical extent of the area, related to its accessibility.

* All new staff to be initially hired on a temporary basis. Permanent grade should be given only after performance evaluation which should be counterchecked by special state monitoring teams. Salary increases should not be automatic but would be based on performance indices of each block. Ideally, the lowest level for such an evaluation to commence should be the primary health centre.

* Performance indices need to be carefully spelt out and made broad-based. The emphasis on the number of sterilisations could be shelved and other parameters could be included as supplementary measures for performance evaluation and independent verifications of the statistics provided by local centres.
* The staffing pattern for FP related activities should be commensurate to the output of each block. Where sufficient headway is not being made, it needs to be ensured that: A) approach/strategy being followed is reevaluated, along with attitude/competence of the staff; B) greater assistance to voluntary organisations that have made a breakthrough in the same area; C) induction of fresh blood in the higher echelons in the concerned district/block; D) attachment, for temporary periods, of outsiders could also be considered.

There is need to build an "institutional vigour" into the FP programme at all levels. In the most populous states (BIMARU), the most dynamic, experienced and competent persons should be in charge of the family planning programmes. The concerned ministry should be headed by a legislator who can be trusted to support the programme with imagination irrespective of the political turmoil. It would help if the incumbents were to be assured a full tenure of five years, provided satisfactory work was being carried out.

It is possible for India to pull itself out of the poverty, filth and population traps in meaningful timeframes. The country has both the will and the wherewithal if the programmes are freed from the bureaucratic mindset and handed over to the most competent managers in the land.

Section V
Constitutional Reforms

Introduction

25. Model for the Restoration of Good Government
26. Proliferation of the Bihar Model of Governance
27. Ghettoisation of the Political Elite
28. Revitalisation of Indian Democracy: Transitional Modes
29. Marginalisation of the Indian Voter
30. Appeal to the Paliamentarians of the 13th Lok Sabha

Constitutional Reforms

Introduction

After independence, India has maintained the status of a democracy in a global context where the vast majority of developing countries were unable to do so. This success has, however, been more notional than real for what is unarguably the largest electorate in the world. The implications of this are that the people are asked regularly (and in recent times, annually!) to choose their leaders from a crop of largely undesirable elements and little else. The political and administrative infrastructure that has spread its tentacles far and wide on the Indian soil does not allow this freedom to vote to translate into meaningful democracy. The moral stature of Mahatma Gandhi's India has declined so precipitously that India's ruling class seems as exploitative as the colonial rulers of pre-independence India.

In this section, Vinod Saighal analyses the causes of the terminal degeneracy that has set in within Indian politics. And despite having reservations about the Constitution that was adopted by independent India, he believes that there is sufficient scope for good governance to develop within the current framework.

The author has also put forward a universal model for restoration of good governance that has been widely appreciated around the world and is applicable at all levels of government.

25

Model for Restoration of Good Government

Introduction

The Model for Restoration of Good Government (MRGG) is an universal model which in its local derivative in each country becomes the Movement for Restoration of Good Government (the same acronym). MRGG differs from all other political parties in that, capturing political power per se (to form a government) is not its objective. The Movement aims at establishing a presence in the political mainstream to the extent that it can exercise a benign overwatch. It will ensure that its tenets, which are essentially those enshrined in the Constitution of the country, are not flouted with impunity by politicians in power. With this in mind, the founders of the Movement would have to abide by a blueprint whereby its adherents will eschew political office; and to ensure that they do not ultimately go the way of all flesh and assume the role of king makers for years on end (by their continued presence in the highest decision-making body of the MRGG) they will completely remove themselves from the political scene every five years. Similarly, in a major conceptual departure from the manner in which political parties function the world over, the MRGG will not enrol party members on a permanent basis. It will instead provide a forum for like-minded people, coming together for varying periods of time, for the sole purpose of ensuring that a check is maintained on elected representatives of the people; and that the national interest is not sacrificed for personal or party ends.

The model being presented has an universal applicability. It is amenable to (sensible) modifications to suit local conditions. The guiding principles which govern the model can be stated briefly. These are:
- * The change has to be effected through the ballot box. There need not be a witch hunt. Tainted leaders who wish to fade away gracefully should be allowed to do so.
- * Restoration of institutional vigour in the bodies that constitute the government is the best guarantee against misuse of power.
- * The new force emerging for the restoration of good government should not itself become degenerate over a period of time. Hence, the Trustees of the process of restoration must remain faceless – shunning public office and publicity. By the same token, people who show signs of personal ambition must be allowed to go their own way no matter how worthy their contribution in exposing the bad ways of the present incumbents.

Aims and Objectives

The MRGG aims to restore dignity, decency and decorum to the body politic. It aims to restore the primacy of the rule of law and to revitalise good governance in the country adopting the model by:
(a) Promoting effective governance at all levels by excluding political interference in the day to day work of the civil services and law and order forces.
(b) Upholding the principal of accountability at all levels of governance.

(c) Support of public action litigation by concerned citizens' action groups.

(d) Supporting special legislation for the removal and prosecution of corrupt ministers (the Italian and French models of independent prosecutors could be adopted with suitable modifications).

(e) Strengthening the agencies for effective monitoring and protection of the environment.

(f) Eschewing caste-based politics and communalism in any form and by upholding the spirit of the Constitution.

The MRGG will invite like-minded people to participate in its struggle to restore dignity and decorum to the process of governance. (Mahatma Gandhi has shown the way to India and the world in the earlier decades of this century. Wherever democratic norms are being eroded, the people at the grass roots are ready to carry forward the struggle in the closing decade of the Century).

Charter

The core of the MRGG comprises a Governing Council and its Secretary General. The Convenor (founder) of the Movement will be its (ex-officio) Secretary General. His first order of business will be to set up a framework for the functioning of the MRGG in consonance with its Charter. At the national level, the policies of the MRGG will be laid down by the Governing Council comprising eleven members. The first Governing Council will be selected from a panel of fifty names put before the Eminent Hundred by the Convenor of the MRGG. The Eminent Hundred would be nationally respected figures, who by their pre-eminence in their respective fields and selfless conduct have won the respect of the nation, cutting across party affiliations and all other barriers of race, cast, creed or sex. The Eminent Hundred come into play in the model just once for selecting the first Governing Council.

Thereafter, they have no further role to play as the process becomes self-sustaining and self-cleansing.

Essentially there would not be much difference in the criteria for preparing the panel of fifty names which would be circulated by the Convenor (first Secretary General of the MRGG) to the Eminent Hundred for giving their preference of eleven members for the first Governing Council of the MRGG. The background, eminence and credibility of persons figuring in the panel for the Governing Council (members) would essentially be the same as for the Eminent Hundred. The Eminent Hundred do not have to come together to sit in a conclave. The panel from which the Governing Council is to be selected would be circulated to them individually for indicating their preference. They would be at liberty to reject the entire panel and substitute fresh names, should the person receiving the panel feel that the list prepared by the Convenor was unduly biased or subjective. The Convenor would be bound to maintain all records of the exchange between him and the Eminent Hundred. Transparency in the process of selection of the Eminent Hundred, the panel of fifty names submitted to them for indicating their preference for the Governing Council, as well as the final list of the first Governing Council would be an essential element in maintaining the credibility of the model.

The Eminent Hundred who would be the real initiators of the process of restoration of good governance can themselves be selected in several ways: by polls conducted by all the better known polling agencies in the country in a random survey and by then taking the names which are generally common to all the surveys; by asking all the national daily newspapers to request their readers to send their choice of the Eminent Hundred (or as many names as they can think of and then nominating a team to select the names which are most common, in a transparent process; by asking chancellors of all the regional universities to go through a (somewhat) similar process and by then synthesising the same at the national level by an Academic Council; by establishing a process of this nature under the aegis of respected (retired) justices of the Supreme Court and/or the High Court; or by any other process which will yield the most credible results while ensuring transparency.

The members of the Governing Council and the Secretary General will be changed every five years. After having served out their respective terms, none of these incumbents will seek any political office in the country for at least five years. Nor will they function as appointees of the government in any capacity. The involvement of the core members of the MRGG has to be one of selfless dedication: in deed and in spirit.

The path chosen by the MRGG for restoring the primacy of the rule of law and bringing in accountability will be through the exercise of a moral influence; of a dimension that will ensure that undesirable elements do not enter the political mainstream, either at the Centre or in the Provinces. It will exercise this influence (both by its moral standing as well as through the ballot) in any of the following ways: by supporting independent candidates who in its opinion, best meet its criteria for clean politics; or, where it is not able to exercise the first two options, by backing the candidate coming closest to meeting such criteria, irrespective of party affiliations. Using its considerable prestige the MRGG will ceaselessly endeavour to promote public awareness and public insistence on clean politics and decorum in public life.

Policy guidelines, list of MRGG candidates, or candidates to be supported by the MRGG, will be approved by the Governing Council. The Council will also approve the expenditure estimates, put up to it by the Secretary General and review the balance sheets and auditors reports.

The Governing Council of the MRGG (which will change every five years) will comprise of eleven nationally respected figures from all walks of life, regardless of caste, creed or sex. A panel of fifty names for the first Council, for the years 1996-2000, will be prepared by the Convenor and circulated to 100 respected men and women country-wide to indicate their choice of eleven members, in order of priority. The result of the first selection by the Eminent Hundred will be announced publicly. No politician, past or present, would be eligible for membership of the Governing Council. For replacement Councils (every five years) a similar exercise will be undertaken by the sitting Governing Council six to twelve months before the date of change-over. A sitting Governing Council member would not be eligible for a second term. In the meetings of the Governing Council, each of the members will act as the Chairperson, in rotation, for the Council meetings. The sitting Chairperson will hold the function till the commencement of the subsequent meeting.

The first Secretary General will be the Convenor (founder) of the MRGG. He will hold this function till the year 2002 AD. All subsequent Secretaries General will be appointed by the Governing Council for a five year term. No Secretary General may succeed himself. In case of ill-health or unsatisfactory functioning, the Secretary General may be replaced by a resolution passed by nine of the eleven Council members. The Secretary General will function as Chief Executive of the MRGG on behalf of the Governing Council and would be responsible for coordinating the day to day activities of the MRGG as well as for maintaining the accounts of the MRGG. The audit of MRGG accounts will be carried out annually by auditors appointed by the Governing Council. The audit report would be made available for public scrutiny. The Secretary General, at the time of accepting his mandate, would give a written undertaking to uphold the principles on which the MRGG is founded. He would also be responsible for preparing lists of candidates for election to the Parliament or Provincial Assemblies for approval of the Governing Council. Neither the Secretary General nor the Governing Council members would personally canvass for any candidate for any election or public office. The endorsement of the MRGG Governing Council for a candidate should, over a period of time, become synonymous with eminent suitability of the candidate in the public mind. The Secretary General will not exercise any voting rights in the deliberations of the Council.

Management of Funds

The MRGG will build a corpus by inviting donations from all individuals and bodies who wish to support the aims and objectives of the Movement.

Transparency of accounts will be maintained at all times. As such the accounts will be audited annually by auditors appointed by the Governing Council. The auditor's report would be available for scrutiny to the public.

A Common Platform

The MRGG will initially field candidates for the Lok Sabha election who in the opinion of the Governing Council best fulfill the basic criterion of decency and selfless public service. MRGG members elected to the Lok Sabha, as distinct from independent candidates or candidates of other parties supported by the MRGG, will not aspire to any ministerial post. They will be expected to follow the guidelines laid down by the MRGG parliamentary leader who would be nominated by the MRGG Governing Council.

Should the MRGG be unable to field its own candidate or back a suitable independent candidate, it may elect to back any contender from any party provided that the MRGG Council is satisfied, that even if the candidate does not subscribe fully to the aims and objectives of the MRGG backing, the individual would perhaps defeat a rival candidate whose presence would vitiate the atmosphere of the elected body.

The support provided to the candidates selected for backing by the MRGG could be in the form of financial support or endorsement of the candidate, thereby putting the prestige of the MRGG behind the candidate.

The MRGG will not set up a party machine by enrolling party members in the manner of other political parties. It will set up regional committees for fixed terms in each district comprising volunteers who wish to support the aims and objectives of the MRGG. For the purpose of creating awareness, a massive media campaign will be launched with funds available to it through donations and by inviting citizens groups, environmental groups, NGOs and other like-minded people who wish to usher in an era of clean politics to canvass and work for the candidates selected by the MRGG council in that district.

Silent Majority

Many countries have been kept afloat not by their leaders but by the ordinary voter who has time and again shown maturity and sagacity and pulled the country back from the brink. Unfortunately, for that perspicacious voter his wisdom has not brought the amelioration sought by him due to the tenacious grip of malign elements on party machines and funds, both accounted and unaccounted. Politicians who have been voted out (or thrown out) keep re-emerging, never chastened by the previous debacle but having refined the process of self-aggrandisement. The voter does not really have a choice. He votes out one set of people and votes in the other lot simply as the lesser evil. The MRGG variant in politics could conceivably bring in that element of discrimination and choice.

26
Proliferation of the Bihar Model of Governance

By now quite a few people have arrived at the conclusion that the writ of the government does not run in several parts of the country, unless directly backed by the Indian Army or Central paramilitary forces. Administrative collapse is near total at the grass roots in the most populous states of Uttar Pradesh and Bihar and in insurgency-infested areas. The section of the public still enjoying a semblance of governance in the larger cities is yet not able to comprehend the magnitude of the problem.

Blows to democratic order that would not be tolerated by any self-respecting government are multiplying. Several instances can be cited to show that unless something is done about it law and order could soon become words only to be found (for academic reference) in the statute books. A group of farmers led by a populist leader just break into the Taj Mahal *en masse* and go on a mini rampage without anyone being able to stop them. Who was there to interfere had they proceeded thereafter to defecate on the Mausoleum or start ripping open the floral designs after the fashion of the officers of the East India Company who prised out the precious stones when they first beheld the marvel. The second case, though not in the same category, should be equally worrisome. A police officer booked for taking bribe by the Central Bureau of

Investigation (CBI) brings along a gang of ruffians to the courtroom. The ruffians prevent the press and the photographers from covering the case. The incident was not reported from some mofussil town. It pertained to the capital of India.

Elsewhere, ministers including chief ministers and erstwhile prime ministers, have used their goon squads to intimidate and rough up opponents. That is not all. They even used law and order forces to intimidate the judiciary. A religious leader who has a history of holding governments to ransom proceeds to carry out illegal construction adjacent to one of the grandest monuments in the country. At first, the authorities appeared to be helpless in the face of the grave provocation. They were perhaps afraid that the worthy individual might whistle up a thousand strong mob in the twinkling of an eye and then invite the world media to witness the restoration of order. Not too long ago a right wing party tore down an historic monument. The leaders of the outrage still move around with impunity. They even talk of ruling the country, not realising that the outrage humiliated the very community whose interests they sought to represent.

These are not stray incidents. This is the new pattern of governance evolving in the land. It is not accommodative politics. It is the breakdown of societal order. It is dereliction of duty. It is, in a manner of speaking, the "beginning of the end" of governance. It is pertinent to ask as to why the concerned authorities failed to discharge their duty. The answers are simple. The politicians are themselves responsible for this descent into anarchy. They are unable to control the situation when it gets out of hand – their presence exacerbates it. This only leaves the civil administration, whose moral fibre has been completely destroyed and who have moreover been politicised, victimised and "de-professionalised".

The state today is diverting a disproportionate amount of its energies, mental capacities and resources in protecting and shielding individuals who are responsible, in the first instance, for the existing state of affairs. Their removal from the scene can only do good to the country. As things stand, however, this category is multiplying exponentially. People do not seem to be aware, or do not seem to care, as to what is happening before their eyes. Some of the names being proposed for chief ministership are ones that should cause dismay and horror. What is being ushered in is not, by any stretch of imagination, empowerment of the downtrodden. It is an headlong rush into political anarchy.

Unless the people in the country "unitedly" take steps to face the menace that looms, the Bihar model of governance could rapidly spread across the face of India, if it is not already the case. Ironically, it will be the downtrodden, in whose name the change is sought to be brought about, who will bear the brunt. The damage caused by mob violence cripples the have-nots, the daily wage earners, those who do not have insurance cover, or any other viable alternatives to fall back on. The ordinary folk would not willingly support chief ministers whose only claim to fame is the use of choice words that would make a journeyman blush. Should such leaders again aspire to chief ministership, it is only because the ground is being ceded to local cabals by people who should know better. Instead of bestirring themselves by reaching out to the people, the "rotten political elite" who have made the Capital their home (whether in or out of power) are busy trying to square up the rigging power.

While the politicians fiddle, there are a number of remedial measures which need to be considered by citizens more concerned with what is happening. These can be summarised as under:

> * The civil servants, especially those inducted by fair competition, must realise that more than anybody else, they are the cornerstones of the country's administrative edifice. Politicians who come and go may or may not have a stake in the system. The

administrators, on the other hand, will be a vital pivot of government for the best part of their lives. They have to now "stand up and be counted". They must eschew sensationalism and quietly go about putting their house in order.

* Police officers have to discharge their duties fearlessly. When things go wrong and politicians pass the buck to them, as is usually their wont, they must not wilt under the stress of frequent transfers. They should draw strength from the fact that the public instinctively recognises and respects upright public servants, when they act in good faith. They must not become mere instruments of state oppression.

* The country is fast degenerating into administrative chaos due to frequent transfers and (on the other extreme) extensions. In this way public funds are not only wasted but literally poured down the drain due to administrative lapses; many of them on account of straightforward corruption and perhaps an equal number due to "lack of continuity". The recent scams in Bihar and elsewhere are not the exception. They are the rule. After presenting the budget one of the priorities of the new government for reducing the country's fiscal deficit should have been to bring in continuity and in-built independent monitoring into programmes administered through central government releases. Should the Finance minister be able to bring in, and ruthlessly implement this reform, the fiscal deficit could be considerably reduced by the turn of the century. In its absence all additional revenues generated will continue to disappear into this gaping hole. And yet, there is talk of divesting the Centre of responsibility that it must continue to discharge through professional monitoring. If such bodies have been found wanting in the past then the answer would be to streamline their

functioning. Should partial dismantling become necessary it should be done after a thorough examination by professionally constituted committees of outside experts and not on sudden whims and fancies of individuals who may not have had the time to go into all the ramifications of their *ad hoc* pronouncements.

* The misery visited upon the poorest of the poor due to the siphoning of thousands of crores of rupees is several orders of magnitude higher than the ravages caused by all the wars fought by the nation after independence, or on account of insurgencies. The monies pocketed by the rulers (many of whom still have the temerity to sport Gandhian garb when not on foreign jaunts) came in part from taxes paid by soldiers on the frontline. Instead of recoiling in horror, a large segment of the political leadership continues to shield comrades (the word is perhaps apt). The inference is obvious. The harshest action that the laws of the land allow would be insufficient punishment for this breed of people who have artificially induced misery on millions upon millions of their most destitute countrymen. "Professionalising" the investigative agencies and "restoring institutional vigour" should have been a high priority for the new government or, for that matter, any government. Those, at the helm of affairs, who routinely tamper with the professionalism of these agencies "should be deemed to be deliberately undermining the security of the nation" and like in the armed forces, their actions should face the extreme penalty.

As early as 1988, a French weekly quoting a criminal lawyer from Bihar stated: "This state is not the poorest state of the country, nor the most backward, nor even one in which violence is the most widespread, but it is the only one where all these elements are concentrated at a point. Hence, it is an underdeveloped state on the political plane, completely neglected by the central authorities as well as the local administrations."

It is sad, amazing and inexplicable that none of the political parties have given priority to population stabilisation in Bihar and the other most populous states of India. Almost every citizen of the country is now alive to the crushing burden being borne by every under-privileged person due to unabated population growth. If there is one segment that appears to be singularly oblivious to the horrendous implications of this unchecked proliferation, it is the political leadership of the country. The problem cannot be simply wished away. It has to be tackled urgently here and now before the whole discussion of good governance becomes an academic exercise.

27

Ghettoisation of the Political Elite

By definition an elite would be the best or choice part of a large body; or a select group or class. Hence, when one refers to the polity it would be the elected members of the legislatures and their leaders who would be deemed to be the elite of that polity.

It should follow that the elite of a democracy if not revered should at least be respected. Such was the case at independence. It is not the case now. It would hardly be an exaggeration to state that a fair share of the political elite today are perhaps the most despised lot in the country. How did this come about?

From reverence to ridicule was not something that came about overnight. The decline had started to set in before the end of the Nehru era. The intelligentsia had begun to feel uneasy. It was, however, willing to suspend judgement. The public veneration for the leaders had not diminished visibly. It required a leader of the stature (and nature) of Indira Gandhi to really erode the institutional vigour of organisations that had withstood the buffeting of time.

The dark days of the Emergency need not be recalled here. Enough has been written about that period. The electoral humiliation that followed did not chasten Indira Gandhi or her supporters. The short stint in the wilderness merely hardened their hearts. Unfortunately the pattern established then is being repeated.

Notwithstanding the jolts received during the Emergency the scaffolding of the democratic edifice still held. The political elite could interact with the people and felt free to move about with relative ease. Except in a few insurgency-infected areas the writ of the government generally ran. The bureaucracy and law and order forces in well-administered states like Maharashtra still commanded respect.

It required a Sanjay Gandhi to hand-pick satraps who finally demolished, in a trice, the residual vigour of a hundred years of (governance) stability. Surprisingly, and regardless of the high handedness of the three Gandhi's (mother and sons), the aura of the Prime Ministerial office remained largely intact: till the eruption of the Bofors scandal.

At about the same time the flare-ups in Punjab, Sri Lanka and Kashmir established the gun culture in many parts of the country. The turmoil on the other side of the subcontinental divide added fuel to fire. Inexorably, the cycles of violence, and the harsh repression which followed, engendered feelings of insecurity not known in the country at large since the days of *thuggee*. The concomitant decline in the quality of elected representatives brought the country to the brink of terminal degeneracy.

At the stage where the country is now there are two distinct tendencies which have come to the fore; both streams pulling in opposite directions with almost equal force: the peoples of India versus the governing elite.

The first category, comprising the vast majority of deprived population and ordinary law abiding citizens has moral force and the strength of numbers; the second category derives it strength from the stranglehold on party and government machinery and money and muscle power. Any advance made by the mainstream revitalises democracy; any (further) gain by the ruling elite, will drive one more nail in democracy's coffin.At this point of time the ruling elite, realising that it is not on the same wavelength as the people, has developed a siege mentality. Sensing that it is despised by the public at large it is no longer able to go out and mix freely with the people. This leads to further alienation.

The distancing that has taken place between the governors and the governed now includes the majority of the civil servants as well. Most magistrates and police officials dare not move about without large parties. Where, just ten or twenty years ago, an SHO with a constable could boldly sally forth and get his man it now requires a posse of policemen to do the same.The compulsive need for 'armed escort' cult has mushroomed to envelop the majority of politicians, senior policemen and bureaucrats. It is difficult to predict as to where and when this vicious cycle will end. Most of the ruling elite and the moneyed classes have not even tried to come to grips with the problem. They are content to remain in their affluent ghettos and to move about in a semi-cocooned fashion. The class apparently feels no estrangement from the vast majority of citizens in the country. They are more comfortable rubbing shoulders with ordinary people in other climes. The irreality of the situation is lost on them. The ghettoisation of the elite comprising the upper reaches of the politico-criminal nexus as well as the portion of the civil servants who have been subverted – has had many deleterious effects; whose true import has yet to be realised.

The estrangement between the rulers and the ruled has become pronounced. It has led to a breakdown of meaningful dialogue between the two. Additionally, for the segment of the elite that has managed to "stick" to Delhi almost continuously for several decades, the perception of the ground reality (from its ghettoised perch) is far removed from the actual conditions obtaining at the ordinary levels of existence. Obviously, if this state of affairs continues much longer it could bring about a total collapse of the democratic order. If a semblance of order still obtains in larger cities and towns part of the credit must go to the vigilance of the press. Judicial intervention, which the tainted variety of politicians and bureaucrats view with such consternation, has actually saved them from a far worse fate. In most societies, where terminal degeneracy sets in, justice is dispensed through more rough and ready means. It is because of the intervention of the judiciary that they have been saved from frontier justice. Judicial activism has allowed the anointed to linger on well beyond the appointed hour. It has been the safety valve that has kept public anger in check. People who wish to tinker with the safety valve must realise that at this juncture such a step would be tantamount to suicide political as well as physical. Since the country is passing through a turbulent phase in its quest for meaningful democracy some tough measures will have to be taken to right matters in spheres where terminal degeneracy has set in. When cancer becomes widespread it is either rooted out completely or it destroys the body. Where firmness is called for half-hearted measures engender a false sense of well-being. Nobody would want the judiciary to exceed its mandate if other alternatives were available. It is because softer options seem to be unavailable that the public wholeheartedly and overwhelmingly supports what is being referred to, for want of a more appropriate term, as "judicial activism".

A simple analogy will illustrate the point. In the high seas if a boat springs a leak and starts listing the weight has to be redistributed to prevent the boat from capsizing; till the leak has been plugged. In like fashion, when the body politic demonstrates its ability to steer a steady course judicial activism will wane and will automatically revert to the benign over-watch mode. The judiciary aside, it is time to start the process of de-ghettoisation of the elite. Only a small percentage of the rulers really require a full-fledged security apparatus due to reasons of state or on account of the office they hold; while they hold that office.

The rest must make a conscious effort to get back into the mainstream. This cannot come about by clever posturing. The people see through the sham. Soon even the tried and tested back door entry through rigged elections or the Rajya Sabha route – will cease to be available. *One party rule is over. In fact, the party is over.*

The press is becoming more vigilant. The judiciary which has the full support of the public in its attempt to clean the Augean stables is not going to succumb to the blandishments of rogue politicians or well-heeled criminals. The Election Commission has found its feet. It has re-established its ascendancy. It will go from strength to strength. The peoples of India are behind it. They too will go from strength to strength. They have begun to throw off their yoke.

The regenerative phase of Indian democracy has well and truly begun. The caste-based politicians is an interim condition. The winds of change are blowing over the entire subcontinent. Those who come in the way will be swept aside. The party is indeed over, especially for the Grand Old Party. Unless, that is, they get out of their ghettos mend their ways, shed their sloth, and get back into the mainstream.

28

Revitalisation of Indian Democracy: Transitional Modes

Democracy in India is in a state of flux. Although conditions in many parts of the country are tending towards the anarchic, one would still hesitate to call it a state of chaos. If, in spite of constant buffetting, the edifice of democracy still holds, it is only because some of the pillars that provide it foundational stability continue to be reliable. Henceforth, whatever the means adopted to stem the rot in the body politic, it has to be ensured that the pillars that provide it a modicum of stability are not allowed to be weakened any further.

In initiating the revitalisation process one has to proceed on the basis that the worst fears relating to terminal degeneracy in the body politic have not been groundless. Almost the entire process of governance at the political apex today seems to be concentrated solely upon devising stratagems to subvert the law and order apparatus of the state; to put a veil over misdeeds of the governing hierarchy of yesteryear. What a swan song for the party that comprised towering personalities of India's freedom struggle, among whom could be counted some of the most illustrious figures of the twentieth century. In the confusion thus created newer misdeeds are being piled on at a pace faster than the country's ability to deal with them.

Intractable national problems crying out for immediate attention are glossed over in two line inanities in party manifestos just before elections. Hardly any political party seems to have any real idea as to how to address these problems. Whatever governance that is taking place is by default.

For several years, the process of governance, has been terminally subverted. Many key appointments, including ambassadorial appointments, have been made with an eye to safeguarding the personal interests of one or two families. Had these appointees displayed the same zeal in safeguarding the national interest as they displayed in looking after the interests of individuals who have long ceased to be respected by the nation – many of them are actively despised – the country would not be in such dire straits today. These patterns too are being repeated, and condoned, in power centres developing elsewhere.

Stark as it may seem, the worst case scenarios flowing from such assumptions have the following connotation:

* The report by a Committee headed by an erstwhile Home Secretary on the political – criminal nexus was only able to look at the fringes of the problem; the nexus in actual fact has penetrated so deeply and extensively into the system that it would be "prudent" to assume that in many cases elements inimical to the state have assumed actual control of the levers of power. With such control they would be in a position to systematically thwart, at every stage, all attempts at reform.

* The principal organs of state security and governance stability have ceased to be accountable to any institution, body or process that "guarantee" the primacy of the national interest.

* A majority of the police departments and protection agencies of the government have reached such a state of terminal degeneracy that the normal remedies available in functional democracies to right the situation would no longer be efficacious.

The sums of money available to the interests that threaten India's cohesion and governance stability are so large that an accurate analysis of their net worth could still send shock waves in a public innured to such revelations. For a long time to come it may never be known whether a deliberate process of sabotage is under way when weak or clumsy chargesheets against suspected individuals are filed in the courts after months and years of preparation. "Is it a systematic sabotage of the Rule of Law?" These people are managing to kill two birds with one stone. On the one hand the public is informed that the law "will" take its own course. The high and mighty will "not" be spared. The high and mighty are named. Very few of them, in spite of the fanfare, are actually brought to book. Here an analogy from another part of the subcontinent may not be inappropriate. Kabul and some other Afghan cities fell without fighting. Money power tells. To what extent is it "telling" in New Delhi?

Unless one is "fully" alive to the seriousness of the situation all attempts at redressal are bound to fail. The crux of the dilemma can be stated simply: "barring the instrumentality of last resort (the Indian Army) almost all the instruments available to tackle terminal malignancies have either been blunted or are in the process of being blunted." The grimness of the situation gets magnified with the realisation that, in many cases, the instruments "themselves" have become the biggest threat to the security of the state and well-being of the peoples. Should the present decline continue it could only be a matter of time before the penultimate stage of structural collapse comes about. Put even more succinctly, that stage can be described as the State (in its partially commandeered form) versus the people of India. "The resolution of the problem then lies in the ability of the revitalisation process to eject the undesirable elements who have commandeered (or crept into) key positions without irretrievably damaging the basic structure of the Constitution."

Ideally, the situation could be remedied overnight by flooding the *sub rosa* domain of influence-peddling in the

Capital with the light of total judicial exposure. By its nature this process is slow, conservative and cautious. The process has already started. It is irreversible. It is being hastened by the complete disregard of the national interest by the dying remnants of the ancient regime. The reprieve is temporary. The rout, when it takes place, will be absolute. The electorate had already indicated its desire for change. The process will be completed well before the century is out. What has now to be ensured is that in the interim, elements as degenerate as those being replaced do not move in to fill the vacuum. Change is inevitable; constant vigilance will ensure that the change is for the better. In order to prevent the "Bihar model of governance" from occupying the central space in India's polity anticipatory proposals that can be implemented without major constitutional changes should be considered at the earliest.

The title of the article suggests that Indian democracy could be in a transitional phase. The pertinent issue here is whether the transition is towards a more degenerate state or is it the churning process that will usher in a just order. It is the latter process that will assert itself, if the enormous residual strengths of the nation are harnessed for strengthening democracy. The old order is dying before one's very own eyes. It is yielding place to the new. Hence no tears need be shed for that which must wither away. One could go astray, however, in "rivetting" one's attention on the rotting corpse; thereby, failing to discern the long term trends – both degenerative and regenerative – which are manifesting themselves on the horizon. Briefly, the trends which can be clearly discerned are:

* A tendency towards "warlordism ". This is a direct result of fragmentation of polity on caste and communal lines. In the most populous states the established law and order machinery is being deliberately destroyed by the political parties and subverted along parochial lines. Elsewhere, the formation of local *"senas"* is going unchallenged. The tendency must be nipped in the bud, without

further ado, before the instrumentalities that can deal with them, "effectively and constitutionally", are weakened; as was attempted during the Emergency.

* A strange reversal in the pattern of instability appears to be taking shape. For several decades after independence the rays of stability radiated from the heartland – the great Indo-Gangetic plain – to the periphery. Today instability is increasing at the core while stability might start returning at the periphery. The prime role of the Indian Army in restoring stability at the periphery, against overwhelming odds, must be taken note of; and this instrumentality of last resort strengthened as a high priority. Strengthening refers to an entire gamut of steps that must be taken urgently to restore the self respect and self confidence of the personnel of this magnificent, globally-respected fighting force; and not merely an increase in defence budget.

* The "body" of the Constitution is being savaged at the hands of its prime custodians. The "spirit" of the Constitution is still alive. It is being kept alive by millions upon millions of ordinary law abiding citizens, conscientious civil servants, uniformed men, the press, the judiciary and countless others who greatly outnumber the handful of people in the first category. The spirit will prevail. The body will, thereafter, be restored to health.

* The term "judicial activism" is a misnomer. The judiciary, media hype notwithstanding, has not been active. If the judiciary had really been active the daily charade being witnessed in this regard would not be taking place. This pillar of the Constitution too was sought to be emasculated during the Emergency and the decade which followed. The judiciary did not cover itself with glory in the intervening period. It was relatively

inactive and pliable. It is only now becoming conscious of the enormous responsibility it shoulders for saving the Constitution from a polity which has gone berserk. Now that it is alive to the expectations of the people, and confident of the confidence they repose in it, it is beginning to find its feet. Judicial activism has to begin now to restore the enormous damage to the collective national psyche.

* Meritocracy is being systematically destroyed in the country, mostly by people who should never have been anywhere near the process of governance, if democracy had found its moorings earlier. Excellence is being killed in academia, scientific bodies and almost every government department. Should a concerted effort not be made (by people who should know better) to halt and then reverse the trend, the situation could become irretrievable within a decade. A conscious decision will have to be taken by all concerned to resist unwarranted political interference. Two other measures will have to be adopted urgently to halt the drift to mediocrity; followed, thereafter, to imbecility. The measures relate to a decision by the Parliament, and if that body fails the judiciary, that with effect from I January 2000 the process of "dereservation" will be set in motion. Progressively, all reservations under the existing criteria should be phased out by the year 2010. The polity, however, sees things differently. It seems to be bent upon creating further divisions in society. The vast majority of the classes who are supposed to be the beneficiaries never really benefit from ill-conceived reservation policies; which merely set in motion more vicious forms of sub-casteism and create new power centres for those who know how to manipulate the system. It is the ultimate in lack of accountability. Governance, as well as the management of the higher institutions in the country, besides being

extremely complex require considerable experience, skill and specialised knowledge. It mandates that the most talented people in the land manage such organisations. Elevating mediocre or semi-literate individuals on caste basis can never raise the standards of these castes. What will surely happen is that the national standards will go into an irreversible decline. Public Service Commissions, the Election Commission, Vice Chancellors of central Universities, Heads of certain Public Sector Undertakings and all important agencies of the Government of India should be made by impartial bodies, guided solely by the national interest and the ineluctable need for preventing further deterioration in standards. The President, or the highest Judicial body, should *suo motu* appoint such an impartial body, headed by a retired Chief Justice of the Supreme Court. The other members would comprise the leaders of opposition parties having not less than fifty elected members in the Lok Sabha, the Deputy Chairman of the Rajya Sabha, the Speaker of the Lok Sabha, the Home Minister, the Cabinet Secretary and the Secretary, Department of Personnel. Similar interim measures, limited to a period of ten years, could be adopted for the states.

* The criminalisation of politics has been extensively covered in the media in recent years. Nevertheless, almost every political party unabashedly continues to field candidates with criminal backgrounds for election in greater numbers. Since the political parties are unable, or unwilling, to check this grave threat to the democratic process the judiciary might have to impose an across the board injunction against such people to prevent them from standing for elections, with effect from the next general election. This could be an interim injunction for a period of ten years, or until such time when the Parliament is in a position to enact suitable legislation.

* More and more political leaders are threatening to plunge their states in a bloodbath whenever their criminality stands exposed, or when their warlordism is checked; and while the law takes its lengthy course their henchmen play havoc with the lives and properties of their opponents. It behoves the nation to take up their challenge at the first utterance. The ordinary citizens are being killed, maimed and harassed in increasing numbers. An immediate stop must be put to this, by whatever means available.

* Condemnation of the political class as a whole should cease. While the majority of the earlier lot, who dragged the country into the mire, are beyond redemption there is a glimmer of hope. Many politicians are themselves realising that it can no longer be business as usual. They are trying to wrest control from the existing political hierarchies. Similarly, the bureaucracy too is doing some soul searching. The conscientious variety are gradually standing up to be counted, not necessarily by parading their virtues, but quietly and purposefully. The time may have come to start making lists of the most honest, rather than the most corrupt, officials. The regenerative process to be lasting needs the active participation of the politician and the bureaucrat.

Before suggesting any remedies it needs to be reiterated that the Constitution of India, in its essentials, is intrinsically viable. It is, all things considered, a workable Constitution. Where the framers of the Constitution made a gross error of judgement was in not being able to fathom the depths of venality to which the politicians who would follow the first batch of Gandhian leaders would be capable of sinking. Even in their wildest dreams the founding fathers could not have imagined the distancing that would take place between the Gandhian values of yesteryear and those of latter day politicians. It was an error of judgment that was to cost the country dear. Essential safeguards were left out in the belief that these would be incorporated as the wisdom of the polity, improved over the years. These safeguards have to be incorporated now.

A clamour is often generated for re-casting the Constitution or for a new Constituent Assembly. What many of the proponents of these demands do not seem to realise is that the members of the Constituent Assembly at the time of independence possessed a sagacity, maturity, stature and selflessness that can seldom be replicated in this day and age; in this country, or elsewhere. It would be worth remembering that were a new Constituent Assembly to take shape today its members might not measure up to the eminence, respectability and universal acceptability of the members of the first Constituent Assembly. Further, it becomes a moot point as to who exactly would nominate these members. Should a new Constitution be considered for India at some future date, the most appropriate time would be when the literacy level across the country embraces at least seventy five per cent of the electorate.

Transparency, Decentralisation and Recentralisation

There is a persistent demand all over the country for greater transparency and decentralisation. Justifiably so. There is no denying the fact that democracy will be strengthened by more direct involvement of people in all parts of the country. This process is under way. It needs to be speeded up. Again, it has to be kept in mind that greater participation at the periphery does not necessarily mean the dismantling of agencies which, if well-handled, could actually strengthen participative democracy. Decision-making today is not as simple an affair as it was only a few decades ago. Sitting under the *banyan* tree around a *"hookah"* might not always lead to wise decisions. At best, the village elders (if they have not been politicised along caste lines) can decide the priorities of development and help in ensuring that the funds reaching them are not mismanaged. The optimum utilisation of resources, however, requires skills, (and inputs) which at this stage of India's literacy and social development would neither be available at the village level nor fully grasped without benevolent expert advice. Hence, there has to be a drastic change in the mind-set of officialdom at higher levels.

It is in everyone's interest to decentralise – but imaginatively – in a manner where the ills that have overwhelmed society at the upper political and administrative levels are not visited upon the levels which have yet to be empowered. The present situation, practically everywhere in the country, does not lead one to believe that the process which reins supreme at the apex is not being replicated at the grass roots. Doubters can visit almost any backward area to verify for themselves the actual state of affairs where responsible social workers are not present or the press is not vigilant (some of the "innovative experiments" in decentralisation now being tried-out in Kerala and elsewhere are a step in the right direction).

Development processes everywhere in the world are becoming more interactive and complex, often due to reasons beyond the control of local inhabitants. Conversely, their activities, if not monitored from a larger perspective could, over varying periods of time, have deleterious effects beyond their horizons – of geography, perspective and development. Global environmental strains, hereafter, will require far more drastic supervision (and centralisation) than ever before. This is true both at the country and global planes.

India is blessed with a Constitution that gives sufficient powers to governance centrality, to tackle the almost insurmountable problems of tomorrow looming over the global horizon of every nation, and mankind as a whole. It has taken nearly half a century of painstaking negotiations for the nations of Europe to centralise "some" of the powers considered essential for an United Europe to meet the challenges of the next century. These powers have been ceded, often in bruising national referenda, by countries having some of the highest living standards and educational levels in the world. The leaders of the states that form the Union of India would be well advised not to clamour for weakening the powers vested with the central government, simply because these have been misused in the past, or for the sake of populism, or short-term gains. The remedy lies elsewhere — in fielding better people for the Parliament and by appointing the right people to man central agencies and organisations, especially the autonomous ones. In any case, with the end of one party rule the sins of the past may not be visited again on the country, at least not to the same extent if the public, press and judiciary remain vigilant and do not allow any diminishment in their independent functioning.

The Process of Revitalisation

The provisions governing the use of Article 356 have been gone into by the Sarkaria Commission which made several recommendations to check the blatant misuse of the Article. It is not as if the provisions of the Article were not clear. In most cases, where it was used merely to safeguard the interests of the ruling party or to quell opposition, the implied extra-constitutionality was fully comprehended by everyone. In almost every case public and press condemnation followed swiftly. That it made no difference to the rulers of the day is a separate issue. Its misuse started with the leaders of near absolute power (and lack of accountability) under the one party dispensation continued over several decades. Their opponents, when they came to power, shed their earlier inhibitions and, in turn, became equally blatant in its misuse. That is hardly surprising. It is the reason why the public tars all politicians with the same brush.

Coming to matters of immediate concern it would be universally conceded that the state of Bihar, if not already in its death throes, would soon reach that stage the way things are going. Administration, wherever it existed, is in a state of collapse. Law and order has deteriorated. Even if guilty politicians and officials are brought to book speedily there will hardly be any amelioration in the actual living conditions of the people. Terminal degeneracy has set in. No matter which lot of politicians replaces the previous lot governance is not going to improve perceptibly. It is here that the strength of the Constitution comes in. It is here where the peoples of India can "collectively" come to the rescue of their brethren in Bihar – a state where the people, under the guise of democracy, are suffering a tyranny far worse than any suffered in the turbulent centuries that preceded British rule. Article 356 was tailor-made for the situation obtaining in Bihar today. At this point of time the "amelioration" of the unsupportable plight of the peoples of the state must take precedence over all other considerations.

President's rule should be imposed in Bihar under Article 356 without further ado with or without an all-party consensus. Should the parties demur the Government bolstered by a perception, shared by almost everyone, that the situation in Bihar has indeed deteriorated to an unacceptable degree, should order the imposition of President's rule in its own right. This time the President's rule can be a model which people would respect for all times to come. The model should remove the general fear from the minds of political parties that the ruling coalition, or any component thereof, would stand to gain from the imposition of President's rule due to any biased conduct on the part of the interim administrators. An outline of a "Model President's Rule" are spelled out below:

* A new Governor (no aspersion is intended on the present incumbent), respected by all segments of society, to be nominated along with the imposition of President's rule. The personal conduct of the Governor should harmonise with the ethos of the land. During the period of the President's rule the new Governor would function in a manner analogous to the functioning of the President of

India i.e. under normal circumstances he would be bound by the advice of an Administrative Council nominated for the duration of the President's rule by the Centre.

* The Administrative Council (hereinafter referred to simply as the Council), comprising nine members would be nominated along with the new Governor. Where the incumbent is not required to be changed the Council would still be nominated at the time of proclamation of President's Rule. This Council, whose panel would be prepared by the Home Minister, would also have to be approved by an interim committee comprising the Prime Minister, Home Minister, Speaker of the Lok Sabha and the Leader of the Opposition. The main criterion for selecting the members of the Council would be that the appointees should be persons of integrity possessing a "well-founded" reputation for impartiality, dedication and competence. The members could be from the administrative services, retired armed forces officers, technocrats, legal luminaries and the like. The private sector need not be excluded. For the duration of their tenure the members of the Council would be given all privileges and emoluments obtaining for secretaries to the Government of India. The Council would "automatically" stand dissolved on the restoration of popular rule and their emoluments and privileges cease, within thirty days of the swearing in of the new ministry.

* The Governor and the Council would be required to concentrate primarily on restoration of administrative vigour and the rule of law, pending the return of elected representatives. In the process the Council would enjoy all powers vested in the Governor during the President's rule as well as additional powers specifically conferred upon it by the Centre. Concomitantly, special efforts would be directed towards restoring competence, credibility

and excellence in the departments of health, education and all aspects related to poverty alleviation, women's emancipation ecological restoration and population stabilisation. Anti-social elements would be weeded out ruthlessly during this period. The Centre would provide all assistance to post competent officers of high integrity from any department or organisation during the period of revitalisation of the democratic process and restoration of good governance under President's rule. Major policy decisions, which could be construed as falling within the domain of political decision-making, would be avoided.

Only the bare outline of the Model for President's Rule under Article 356 of the Constitution, restricted to cases of terminal degeneracy with a single point programme of restoring the rule of law, has been spelled out in this article. Sensible refinements can be made at any stage. The model can be extended to other areas of administrative concern. It would be seen that the model does not visualise a radical departure from any of the constitutional provisions in vogue.

Transitional Modes

Irrespective of the present turbulence fundamental changes in the people's perception of politicians and the political process is taking place all around. Barring the really tainted variety of political leaders of the old school, many politicians themselves are coming around to the point of view that "sacrificing the national interest for the sake of yesterday's power brokers" might not turn out to be a sound proposition in the long run. A few politicians have even started demanding that their party hierarchies loosen their tenacious hold on party machines. However tentative, these are welcome signs. Therefore, whilst the country deliberates upon long term political reforms several interim measures that can be implemented through an informed dialogue amongst all the concerned segments are spelled out in the ensuing paragraphs.

The most important of these relates to extensions and the need to abide by service rules. In a country the size of India nobody should be indispensable, at least not in the field of administration. Therefore extensions must not be given to anybody. Since it would be extremely difficult to enforce this rule with immediate effect it should be possible to arrive at a consensus amongst the political parties, in the Parliament, amongst the Chief Ministers and in the bureaucracy itself that with effect from 1 January 2000 no extensions would be given to any incumbent on any count.

It is not fully appreciated that extensions are killing excellence and leading to unhealthy and undemocratic practices. The trend is not confined to the administrative services and law and order agencies. Scientific bodies, think tanks, other government-funded bodies and public sector enterprises have all fallen prey to this disease. The armed forces have remained professional largely because the government did not allow this pernicious practice to take root in the forces. Recent attempts to make inroads must be vehemently opposed.

Organisations and bodies which have been terminally degraded cannot be easily turned around to accountability and transparent functioning. In some cases the rot is too deep. For all such terminally sick bodies the surest way to set things right would be to wipe the slate clean and start afresh.

In as far as it relates to good order and good governance – even elementary governance – serious thought has to be given to the imposition of a form of "judicial restraint" on tainted politicians and bureaucrats against whom prima facie cases have been established. In all such cases the concerned persons should be deemed to be restrained from holding any public office from the time of framing of the charge sheet till the finalisation of the case. Concomitantly, procedures can be established for the speedy disposal of such cases. Judicial restraint would be in keeping with the highest democratic traditions.

And finally, overriding national priority must now be given to population stabilisation and ecological restoration. No more ground can be yielded on these counts if any semblance of democratic order is to be retained in the country. In ecologically fragile areas the cause for disquiet is so great that the full force of an enhanced Terrorist Apprehension and Detention Act (TADA) should be brought into immediate effect under a core group functioning directly under the Prime Minister with an independent, specially equipped, special protection group for endangered species. The mystery and mystique of India throughout the ages has related to its forest, flora and fauna. Destroy these and you destroy India's real heritage – and its soul.

A Ray of Hope

The people of India are awakening. Nine hundred and fifty million citizens are not going to allow a few hundred self-serving politicians and misguided civil servants to stand between them and the country's destiny any longer. Destiny still beckons. At long last the citizens themselves have heard the clarion call. In the coming millennium India has a role to play in the comity of nations. It will contribute to the global fraternity by providing alternative models for the cultural and spiritual well-being as well as the economic betterment of mankind, not by pontificating as has been its wont in the past but by quietly demonstrating these strengths in the subcontinent as a whole. It has to indicate more harmonious (and humane) pathways to replace the destructive models ascendant today. Before embarking on its global mission, however, India must "first" cleanse and strengthen itself. The process is under way.

29

Marginalisation of the Indian voter

Whereas the Constitution confers sovereignty on the people of India, in real terms this sovereignty is becoming notional with each passing decade. The voter in India has been expressing his dismay, disgust and dissatisfaction at almost every election since the Emergency. Apparently it has made no difference to the quality of governance in the country. As a matter of fact it keeps deteriorating and if the current state is anything to go by governance seems to have entered a phase of terminal decline in several parts of the country.

In view of the overwhelming – across the board – revulsion against corruption in the body politic serious thought needs to be given as to how a few hundred or, at most a few thousand criminally-inclined elements are able to hold ninety-five crore people to ransom. Those in the forefront of the reform movements to rid the governance process of degenerate elements will not achieve very much unless they radically change their strategy to combat the malaise.

While politics and politicians may have become dirty words, cleansing of the body politic cannot be brought about by mere intellectualisation. Good people will have to shed their inhibitions and jump into the hurly-burly of politics. They will have to dirty their hands. What is more, they should be prepared to take flak when it comes their way.

Recently an eminent jurist expressed extreme pessimism while recounting his own experience in persuading a well known business tycoon to stand for the last Lok Sabha election from a constituency close to Delhi. The philanthropist not only did not win but possibly lost his deposit as well. This was followed by pervasive gloom. The sentiment was misplaced. Why should the public have placed their faith in an individual who was not prepared to "muck in" in the real sense of the word. If one is not prepared to lose and soldier on in adversity one can never really win great victories.

This case needs to be contrasted with another individual who decided to carry the fight to the heart of the badlands – perhaps the worst crime affected district in Uttar Pradesh where one of the *supremos* who is a minister in the Union Cabinet holds sway. It is also a stronghold of a right wing political party. The new entrant, who can be referred to as Mr. X for recounting the episode, besides an utter novice in ways of electioneering could hardly muster enough resources to fight the election. As opposed to two vehicles and a handful of supporters that he could gather his opponents could muster literally hundreds of vehicles and any number of faithfuls. Mr. X survived one or two attempts to eliminate him. He lost the election. His courage and tenacity, however, won him many admirers. He managed to garner a few tens of thousands of votes. He has chosen to sit out the present Lok Sabha election which came too soon after the last one in which he had exhausted his meagre resources. Mr. X remains undaunted. He spends more time in the area and has started social work. After five years he will fight again, determined to win. Mr. X is not a loser. He never expected victory on a platter. He has the guts and grit to stay the course.

There is no doubt that caste considerations have started affecting the outcome of elections in a big way in many parts of the country. The causes for such coalescence along caste lines need to be gone into more thoroughly. Possibly the most important factor for the rise of this phenomenon can be put down as "insecurity". Plain and simple fear, in areas where law and order has collapsed; where justice is not rendered impartially; and where the state is unable or unwilling to provide security. In these circumstances ghettoisation along caste lines invariably takes place; mostly for seeking solace and security amongst one's own kind. It is here that one man's criminal becomes another's Robin Hood.

The other important factor which leads to voting along caste lines is the lack of clear alternatives. In spite of their caste based predilections voters have been routinely throwing out corrupt and inefficient leaders. The fact is that after a few years in the wilderness they resurface on account of their stranglehold on party funds and machinery; added to the fact that their successors did not turn out to be any better than them. Where strong new faces with adequate resources to fight the election have emerged voters have been showing their preference for the latter. This trend needs to be encouraged.

30

Appeal to the Parliamentarians of the Thirteenth Lok Sabha

The din of elections is behind you. You are about to enter the portals of the most hallowed institution of Indian democracy. You have now become the repositories of the aspirations of India's teeming millions, the vast majority steeped in grinding poverty. What do they expect from you?

Your foremost duty, before all else, is to apply salve to the wounds inflicted during the elctions. Forget the past. Look to the future.

You have been sent to the capital city to address the larger national concerns; even if you happen to be a person of the most humble origins, from an area so remote that not many people would have heard of it. In taking your seat in the national parliament you automatically become endowed with a majesty that can be diminished only by your own conduct. Be ever mindful of the fact that if you allow your stature to be diminished, by conduct unbecoming of a national parliamentarian, it is not only you who are diminished. You will thereby be diminishing, in some small measure, the self-respect of every citizen of the country. Therfore, affect simplicity and conduct yourself with decorum. Ostentation and waste are not the culture of this land. They are the culture of lands that threaten our freedom and dignity.

While you cannot turn your face from the winds of change sweeping the globe you must not be unmindful of the appalling misery in which the majority of your countrymen find themselves. In finding a mean between the pull towards greater prosperity of some segments and the drag of deprivation of others it has to be remembered that progress does not necessarily lie in bringing down the former. It lies in raising the level of the latter. The best way of achieving this is to empower the downtrodden, at the grass roots by giving them greater opportunity. In doing so, do not drive away the talented from your shores; to seek their fortunes in other climes. It is not possible to mass produce excellence. Talent and merit, therefore, must be given their due.

You should not be unheedful of the anxiety expressed everywhere at the prospect of what was being referred to as 'hung' parliament or unstable coalitions. Remember, the country is vast enough, amorphous enough, and resilient enough, to democratically manage any change that is necessitated by the threat to its cohesion and integrity. You are the vectors of the change. The mental association formed by the words unstable coalitions in relation to the type of politicians that people have become used to could have one meaning. It could have an entirely different connotation for a new set of representatives who just might have a changed concept of national security and parliamentary decorum. Many of you, not carrying any dead-wood from the past, could decide to first supply a vital dose of oxygen for reviving democracy before starting to bicker about the spoils of office.

Should you still get sucked into the guagmire of unprincipled politics it would be worth keeping the larger national interest in mind; in areas that for all national-minded citizens should be forever beyond petty trade-offs. If these larger concerns, relating to national security, education, women's emancipation, alleviation of poverty, environment, population stabilisation and law and order are addressed by all of you jointly, the nation need never look back.

If you are conscious of the dangers confronting your country the composition of the new Lok Sabha need not be cause for disquiet. It could be a time for introspection; a time for renewal. The intrinsic strengths of the country are still greater than its weaknesses. The honest citizens still vastly outnumber the dishonest elements. Indian democracy has come to an historic turning point. It is for you to prove the cynics wrong. You have to show the world that the spirit of tolerance is as strong as ever in this land, home to the largest and most varied democracy in the world. The public at large, from the very humble to the very able, are sick of divisive politics. The silent majority that sent you to the Lok Sabha is ready to launch a strong India into the next millennium. It is for you to take up the challenge and not disappoint, yet again, your long-suffering countrymen who have reposed their faith in you.

There are many things wrong with our country. It has, however, hidden strengths which are not perhaps to be found elsewhere in the world. If you have the patience you too can tap those eternal reservoirs of India's timeless wisdom. If you can learn to drink from these well-springs the riches that will be yours would be far greater than those provided by the coin of the realm. The choice is yours. Choose well.

Section-VI
Trauma and Critical Care

Introduction

31. Global Perspectives of Trauma and Disaster – 21st Century
32. Understanding the Nature of the New Societal Traumas
33. Traffic Accidents: Driven to Disaster

Trauma & Critical Care

Introduction

In its confused rush towards modernisation, the Indian project has moved forward haphazardly in many a field – on the one hand it is now able to develop sophisticated technologies for satellites, but on the other, it has been spectacularly unsuccessful in the sectors of education and healthcare. As a country, currently India spends less than 3 per cent of its national budget towards health. This reflects in the quality of health care that is available to the vast majority of its population, excluding, of course, the elite – the so-called VIPs and the very Indian coinage of "VVIPs".

In this section, Vinod Saighal points out that, despite fifty years of post-independence development, "trauma and critical care" in India is at best rudimentary in the cities, and virtually non-existent for the rest. Moreover, the country is completely unprepared to handle the modern onslaught of "trauma" caused by traffic accidents. Any visitor to India, would hardly be surprised by the chaotic nature of traffic movement as it is common to large parts of the Third World. However, he would be quite astonished by the complete lack of discipline and disregard for rules that the so-called educated classes show behind the wheel. It is, therefore, hardly surprising that India ranks among the top few nations in terms of number of road accidents and traffic casualties. With the introduction of new higher speed vehicles, the statistics will only get worse.

The author addresses the issue by listing a number of steps that need to be taken to ameliorate the situation with regard to trauma management at all levels.

31

Global Perspectives of Trauma and Disaster – Twenty First Century

Today it is my pleasure and privilege to talk to you on the "Trauma and Disaster Perspectives of the Twenty First Century". Since there is an apparent gap between the scope of the subject and the time allotted for the talk I shall endeavour to straightaway come to the heart of the dilemma facing medical practitioners, who in essence are the business end of trauma management; and the disaster relief agencies, on whose anticipation, understanding and competence will depend the management of traumas at societal levels when disasters of higher magnitudes strike any region.

The dilemma can be simply defined in the following manner:

* The "resultant" of the daily traumas afflicting ordinary people in their everyday work, on any given day, is generally, larger than the sum total of (individual) traumas resulting from most of the low and mid-intensity natural disasters visiting the globe.
* That, in spite of technological and scientific advances, "trauma care" in developing countries, for the large majority of the population living below

the poverty line, is actually declining; and could continue to decline "unless the development models being implanted on these societies are planned and executed more imaginatively".

* That, by the turn of the century, media globalisation would have brought about such a degree of insensitivity to human suffering that the "disaster relief quotient" would stand revised upward to an extent where only mega disasters will evoke humanitarian response on a global scale.

I shall elaborate further on these three statements.

At the beginning of the 1980s decade the World Health Organisation, in one of its releases, had judged the gap between needs and available services for the disabled to be 98.9 per cent, that is, of all persons needing particular services at a particular time, only 1.1 per cent in fact received them. If we take the example of India, the population of India at that point in time was approximately 640 million. The population of the country today is racing towards the billion mark, in just fifteen years. Since the infrastructure, to cater to this very substantial growth, has not increased proportionally it would not be wrong to assume that the gap between needs and available services in the same context could have gone beyond 99 per cent, that is, of all persons needing particular services at a particular time, less than one per cent would, in fact, receive them. Should present trends continue, or to put it differently, should we extend the graph along the same curve, based on existing (and growing) needs, and the "availability differential", then we will soon reach a point whereby, at the dawn of the twenty first century, the whole exercise could become academic, literally so.

Considering the globe as a whole we can say that, on a daily basis, the highest number of casualties, or traumas to individuals, are directly attributable to automobiles, explosives (including mines), and firearms. Taking the case of Delhi, the number of traffic related accidents annually could now well be beyond the hundred thousand mark. Of these, between fifteen and twenty per cent of the accident cases become fatal. On an all India basis (seeing that many accidents go unreported) the annual figure for casualties on account of road accidents could well run into millions. At the rate at which induction of automobiles is taking place these figures could show a sharp increase. Hence, without our realising the magnitude of the disaster, death on a daily basis has started stalking our roads on an unprecedented scale. Because of the numbers involved general concern for individual suffering (except on the part of close family members) is fast descending towards zero; and since human suffering these days can only be comprehended as an (inhuman) statistic, response to distress, at levels where international relief agencies respond, is elicited only when sufficient zeros are added to the base numbers 10, 100, 1000 and so on. The point that is sought to be highlighted is that mitigation of unmitigated daily suffering (brought on by rapid modernisation of underdeveloped societies) must become an important component of trauma care and disaster relief. This, to my way of thinking, is the most urgent task before us in the ensuing decades.

Where trauma care is unavailable, or non-existent (as is the case in most parts of the country) those who are killed on the spot may be the lucky ones. The plight of the seriously wounded who land up (if and when they land up) at hospitals has to be seen to be believed. Facilities are inadequate. The attitude of the hospital staff borders on indifference. The terms trauma management or critical care hardly apply. Most of these casualties are turned into disabled persons due to lack of proper attention and, what is more, timely attention. The list which follows gives an indication of the potential of certain kinds of injuries to result in disablement if timely care is not given:

* If open injuries with compound fractures are not attended to within 6-8 hours, a permanent disability may result;

* If damaged limbs become infected, they may have to be severed;
* If a hematoma in the brain is not attended to in a hospital, mental disability for life may result;
* If bleeding occurs at knee level and a tourniquet at the thigh remains in place for 3-4 hours, the person may lose his leg;
* If a severe head fracture occurs and is not attended to immediately in a hospital, blindness may ensue due to a severed optic nerve;
* If aseptic bodies in cornea of the eye are not removed skilfully and rapidly, loss of sight or permanent cornea damage will result-,
* If blood exudes from the ear, the base of the skull is fractured: if this is not diagnosed correctly, the patient will become deaf;
* If blood exudes from under the eyelids, immediate specialised treatment of the eyes is required to avoid blindness;
* If the spinal cord is damaged, and the person is being moved about more than absolutely necessary, the patient will be permanently paralysed;
* If simple fractures are not set quickly and skilfully, permanent damage and disability will almost certainly occur.

Although this list is by no means exhaustive, it provides striking examples of how injuries can become life-long disabilities, with all their implications for the individuals concerned, and their families. It underlines the need for medical and para-medical personnel, especially in rural areas, to receive special instructions regarding the prevention of disabilities.

Away from the metropolitan cities the subcontinent of India lives on a different plane. The ground realities in the hinterland are also different. The vast majority of the inhabitants of this troubled land have no chance, whatsoever, of receiving timely care. Unless we start ministering to the needs of those segments of society who constitute the real India the twenty first century will not be the harbinger of the change that we are all so fervently hoping for. The spectacular advances of science and medicine will remain a chimera for the majority of the peoples of the world.

The First International Conference on Trauma and Critical Care is taking place at an opportune moment. If real progress has to be made towards the amelioration of human suffering through medical intervention then the processes whereby a far greater number of people can be made the beneficiaries of the great advances in the medical field must be identified before we usher in the third millennium.

32

Understanding the Nature of the New Societal Traumas

Many years ago a Parisian director had made a film on India. The film concerned a young person who, disillusioned with life in a materialistic society, comes to India to seek answers to the doubts that beset him. With the film's haunting music providing a backdrop a friend coming in search of the young person, who seemed to have vanished into the depths of India's spiritual vastness, visits the sites where his friend might have been. At one stage the film lingers for a long time on the general ward of a government hospital in Bombay. It is midnight. The ward and the corridors are littered with people lying on the floor at all angles. They include the old and infirm and women and children. There is hardly any place to move between the beds. An obviously overworked Dr. Pinto explains to the young visitor, moving about in search of his friend, that "everything is bursting at the seams."

Amongst the crowd coming out of a Paris cinema after seeing this film some people were heard to remark on the depressing squalor of the Indian hospitals and the lack of trauma management. A woman in the same group who had been to India put a different construction on it. She related her experiences in India. In spite of the grinding poverty she had found that families seldom abandoned their sick people. They would go hungry and trudge for miles to administer to the needs of their near and dear ones, although they happened to be lying and dying in far away hospitals. Nobody who had a family passed into the next world unloved and uncared for.

May be the Frenchwoman had a romantic vision of India based on what she had seen when she visited the country a long time ago; when the population had not yet reached unmanageable proportions and before the degradation in public life had reached its nadir. Nevertheless, her spontaneous outburst did bring out an essential difference between the approach to the problem in the materially advanced societies and the subcontinent.

The ground reality in this part of the world is, however, quite different. There is no trauma care worth the name except for a pampered few who monopolise the scarce resources through either money power or political clout. The meagre facilities are further stretched by the personal staff, relations and political supporters of VIPs and VVIPS. The telephone calls and summons from the powers that be stifle the dedicated work of many good doctors who still remain impervious to the temptation to make the transition to greener pastures.

The description given earlier, of the vast majority of people dying like flies, is closer to reality than the romanticised version that makes the rounds every now and then. A person subjected to trauma requires expert attention and care at the earliest. The word "earliest" has lost its relevance. Perhaps it never had any relevance in the fictionalised "cities of joy" mushrooming and multiplying at a rate faster than the statisticians ability to keep up with them. At the beginning of this century when there was only one "City of Joy" (Calcutta) at least one good samaritan would emerge from every house. After a century of path-breaking scientific progress and "development" one would be hard put to find one good samaritan in an entire locality of any city in India.

The nature of trauma suffered by individuals too has undergone change in the last hundred years. Slow death has been replaced, to quite an extent, by sudden death. In the time of our grandfathers many of the people who passed away did so after wasting away from an incurable disease. Periodic famines too took a devastating toll. The dead were reckoned in millions and not in tens or hundreds, as is the case now when crops fail. To that extent the misery brought about by malnutrition and hunger has been considerably reduced. In the old days a million people dying made news after months and years when the true extent of the tragedy became known. In these days even a few dozen starvation deaths get highlighted within days of their occurrence.

Of course, slow, lingering death on a very large scale has again manifested itself due to the AIDS virus. Other more virulent forms of viruses, unbeknownst to humanity, may be in the pipeline for the coming generations; on account of the lack of "effective global regulatory mechanisms that should have first been established" before genetic mutations were experimented with. "Potentially, this form of unregulated experimental proliferation could turn out to be far more hazardous than nuclear proliferation". Given the will global regulatory mechanisms could (in reality) reverse nuclear proliferation. However, that may not be possible (even in principle) with the forms that emerge from genetic tampering.

The nature of traumas that have come to the fore in most modern societies, at the turn of the century, relates largely to the culture of the automobile and the drugs culture. The latter, in turn, has spawned a culture of savage beatings, knifings and gunshot wounds. The pattern of traumas suffered by individuals in developing countries had a different nature. The Western model is now almost globally in the ascendant. Western societies, however, having gauged the nature of their afflictions, have attempted to put in place facilities to cope with these traumas. They had the wherewithal to do so. On the other hand neither the exporters of the development model of the advanced countries nor the leaders effecting the change in the developing countries have grasped, or even attempted to comprehend, the mismatch between what is being exported and the ability of the recipients to manage the change; a change which is not taking place in phase with the country's capacity to absorb and harmonise it, but at the pace dictated by the exporters of the new economic model. A single example will serve to illustrate the point, especially in as far as it relates to the management of trauma.

The Capital city of India is a good example. Economic liberalisation linked to the export push of the global giants has led to an exponential increase in the number of vehicles on Delhi's roads. There is no way that the infrastructure of the Capital city and its environs can keep pace with this increase. In fact, with each passing year, the gap between what needs to be done and what is actually being done on the ground continues to increase. The pet theories of the best and the brightest economists from the leading universities of the West, based on the statistical models of growth of Singapore, South Korea, Taiwan, Hong Kong and Japan cannot be applied to India at the macro level. There is a false glow of surface prosperity. It is masking the sub-surface dislocation (and pain) engendered by the change; in which the vast majority of the population cannot participate. The manner in which the change is being legislated and the speed with which it is sought to be imposed is wreaking havoc across large swathes of subcontinental society. Should timely corrections not be applied, devastation and disorientation will result for the vast majority of the people.

Coming back to Delhi - where the new economic model is being synthesised, neuralised and regurgitated to the rest of the country. The latest cars coming on the roads of the Capital of India are faster, sleeker and costlier. The condition of the roads on which they ply has generally remained the same. The traffic patterns have not changed very much. They cannot change overnight. The traffic, for the foreseeable future, will remain multi-faceted and multidimensional. Even if they push out the pushcarts and rickshaw-pullers there is no way that the authorities can prevent pedestrians from swarming all over the roads; because the pavements have come under encroachment of one type or the other.

Nobody is sure as to how many migrants, from far away places, pour into Delhi every day. They continue to squat on pavements and wherever they can find a place. The little children, used to village life, will keep running on to the roads without warning. The older people, used to the speed of bullock carts, cannot suddenly muster the reflex to cross the road fast enough between one speeding pulse of traffic and the next. They are bewildered. They cannot read the traffic signs. They cannot comprehend that in the new world order coming into this ancient land their priority as road users is hardly a notch above zero; at least in the minds of the inheritors of the new dispensation who are buying cars which have sudden acceleration from zero to ninety kilometers per hour in just a few seconds. Nobody had warned them. Nobody in their native place had taught them the art of survival in the face of the steel monsters hurtling across the arteries of the new concrete jungles that the once gracious cities have yielded place to. So they keep paying the price for their ignorance. The accidents keep multiplying; and they keep dying. The new model of economic growth stipulates that flyovers (for speeding up traffic) take precedence over pedestrian subways (that prevent people from being run over).

The next category of road users who cannot be banned from the Delhi roads are the cyclists. They too are traumatised at every turning and roundabout. The cars and buses, the former in their super accelerated mode, will knock down the cyclists, even after having duly warned them to make way, with the blaring of horns. In this day and age how can the impatient city driver realise that it is not possible for the cyclist to inject a spurt of fuel-induced horse power into his tired old leg-muscles. This category of road user too must pay a daily toll (in death and disability) to the priority road users of the new era.

Before coming on to mechanical transport a thought has to be given to the animals who share the roads in a land where till as recently as a few decades ago man lived in harmony with animalkind. It is simply not possible, in a trice, to push the cows, camels, donkeys, monkeys and the occasional elephant completely off the roads. They too must face their traumas.

When talking of the biggest category of road users we refer to the fossil fuel burners comprising buses, cars, three wheelers and two wheelers. Each one of these have different speeds, different approaches to road use; often incompatible with the other users. Any number of inexplicable anomalies remain. For instance, it is mandatory for the scooterist to wear an helmet. The pillion rider is not obliged to wear one. Injuries to both take place with the same frequency.

It is pointless commenting on the quality of trauma management in Delhi hospitals when the number of road accidents has multiplied with the sudden increase in the number of automobiles. Even before the rapid growth in the city, of both population and automobiles, the medical facilities were considered inadequate. With the increase they can be deemed to be non-existent in the Western sense of the words "trauma management" – right from the site where the accident occurs, to the speed and method of evacuation (if indeed evacuation takes place), to the reception and post-hospitalisation trauma care. It is not even a question of lack of resources. If a thorough investigation is carried out the mismanagement of funds in hospitals will, in all probability, turn out to be at par with the siphoning that has taken place in the other scams that have come to light so far.

While no end seems to be in sight for the amelioration of the traumatic conditions obtaining for the under-privileged in India's Capital (where funds are seldom lacking) there seems, nevertheless, to be an inane desire to spread the rapid transport growth model of Delhi to other Indian cities, where conditions in many respects are already far worse.

"India is not yet ready for the automobile revolution of the West". Indian society will remain less traumatised, and more civilised, if we allow China and the rest of the world to surge ahead in automobile production. India is not geared to adopt the automobile route to super abundance, in the manner in which it is being implemented now. The country is not required to emulate this pattern, at the rate at which it is being presently imposed. It is time to take stock, and progress in a manner more suited to the genius of the people. Before we bring in more automobiles we have to professionally manage the pain (of transition) caused by road accidents to thousands of families every day all over the country. Concomitantly, hospital administration will have to be first thoroughly overhauled in all government-funded hospitals. Casualty evacuation will have to be streamlined before the hydrocarbonised variety of road users proliferate any further. In the interim the troubled multitudes of this vast country will have to share each others pain in the traditional way; and learn to manage on their own the new traumas imported from far off lands.

33

Traffic Accidents:
Driven to Disaster

Traffic of the mechanical variety is wheel based. It is when the wheels get out of control that most traffic related accidents take place. The first essential then is to "ensure" that the man behind the wheel is competent to drive. It is the single most important factor affecting road safety. All advanced countries enforce this rule stringently. It is a tenet of faith. There is no compromise on this score. In India as well, there can be no compromise on this count.

India and most of the developing countries have given the go by to this basic rule of road safety. The resultant chaos is there for all to see. Recently an official of the Government in the Capital was provided a civil hired transport to enable him to go around while his office car was at the garage. The Ambassador car was hired from a registered agency. On the very first day the official had to ask for a change of driver after three narrow misses. The driver pleaded to be given another chance citing his poverty as the reason for a reprieve. He confessed to having obtained a driving license after having paid Rs 1700 to the touts at the licensing office. He admitted that he was "learning on the job"; a devastating admission which, translated literally, meant gaining experience by knocking down a few pedestrians and cyclists.

The story is neither apocryphal nor rare. It is the norm. Any Blueline (or the earlier Redline) driver would confirm it off the record, as would countless other drivers falling in this category – potential killers all. Who is to blame for this state of affairs. The blame lies squarely on the bureaucracy and its political masters. They are the real killers. As in the case of law and order aspects of good governance road safety too is a contract between the government and the citizenry. When a pedestrian steps off the kerb onto the pedestrian crossing or when a motorist exercises his right of way when the traffic light turns green they move forward with the quiet confidence that the societal contract between them and the other road users remains valid; thereby protecting them from all kinds of sudden traumas, because they expect the others to abide by the rules of the road. By granting licenses to people who are unfit to drive the licensing authority is not only involved in a breach of contract but indulging in the worst form of criminality. It connotes a breakdown of the social contract.

Therefore, when one talks of amelioration of the chaotic traffic conditions on the roads of the Capital the very first corrective action has to be the immediate rectification of the basic flaw of faulty licensing. The delay in implementing fundamental reforms in driving license procedures is unpardonable. No amount of seminars or high profile committees will be able to bring lasting relief unless the people responsible for governance get their basics right. One has to begin with first causes. Remedial measures which could be considered in this regard are tabulated below:

* Immediate supersession of all (driving) licensing authorities in the Capital (as a first step) and their replacement by an independent licensing authority functioning under the government (itself) or under a mandate from the Delhi High Court.
* The mode of functioning of the Independent Licensing Authority (for driving licenses) should be

worked out by a committee nominated for the purpose. This Committee could be nominated by the Delhi High Court, the Lieutenant Governor of Delhi, the Ministry of Home Affairs or the Government of the National Capital Region. In actual fact there needs to be coordination between the various government agencies and departments. The constant bickering between them for the flimsiest of reasons denies good government to the citizens.

* Introduction of the principle of criminal liability, individually and severally, against the Chief Licensing Officer and the concerned department personnel in cases where a motor accident results in death and where investigations after the accident conclusively prove that licensing authority had connived in issuing the driving license without proper checks, for pecuniary or other considerations. Such investigations should become mandatory in all cases of death. To be able to pinpoint blame, documents will have to be maintained giving details (in each case) of testing officers, medical officers (for eye sight) and the supervisors endorsing the new license.

* Immediate clearance of the premises of the licensing authorities of touts and other undesirable elements.

* Streamlining of the entire procedure for issue and renewal of driving licenses to free the ordinary law abiding citizen from harassment and interminable delays.

* The giving of letters of recommendation by high government officials or elected representatives of the people for grant of a driving license without proper tests to be made a cognisable offence. Where such nefarious influence is still brought to bear liability for damages sought by accident victims against persons making such

recommendations (should this fact come to light during investigations) should be entertained by the Courts.

* Encouraging bodies like the Chambers of Commerce and concerned NGOs (after due vetting) to establish modern driving training facilities. Certificates of excellence to be awarded to establishments maintaining international standards by a designated authority.

The recommendations listed above are amenable to sensible modification and mid-term corrections as the new procedures come into force. Allied measures which can be immediately implemented without much ado are as follows:

* Proprietors and heads of transport agencies, whether private or public, to be made responsible for ensuring, in the first instance, that they do not hire drivers without the requisite driving skills. The holding of a valid driving license should not become an excuse for not establishing the competence of the person hired, as per the procedures followed all over the world by most reputable companies and departments, irrespective of the licenses and certificates produced by the applicant. Where elementary care has not been exercised, the law courts to entertain Public Interest Litigation (PIL) cases for personal liability of the managers. Concomitantly, where extreme negligence of the employer stands established in this regard the company or agency concerned to be debarred from all government contracts for a given period of time.

* Immediate and automatic departmental action against drivers of vehicles belonging to the government, including defence, police and other such departments, where the driver of the vehicle

is found flouting the rules of the road simply because of an assumed immunity. Officers using such vehicles should be the first to check their drivers for over-speeding and violating traffic rules. Their duty to the citizens of city that allows them to live in the style that they do should come before they start enjoying the perks of their high office.

One can continue in this vein to highlight the point that while the high functionaries of the government deliberate unendingly on macro level plans that seldom seem to fructify there is enough that can be done at the elementary levels to bring in a modicum of order into a situation which seems to be getting totally out of control of the present incumbents. People in high positions who are unable, or unwilling, to bring in a measure of good governance must demit office and make place for Citizens Committees functioning directly under the Courts till the time the bureaucracy and the elected representatives are able to abide by their contract with society.

Index

ABM Weapons, 42
AIDS, 145, 189
AIDS Virus, 286
ASEAN, 17, 50, 66, 112, 114, 123, 169
Abu Dhabi, 45
Academic Council, 239
Afghanistan, 47, 48, 55, 111
Africa, 37, 189
Ahmed Shah Masood, 47
Air Defence, 120
Aksai Chin, 162
Al Bukhoosh Oil Fields, 45
Aliwal Escape, 180
America, 21, 22
American Asia-Pacific Security Strategy, 128
American Economic Growth Model, 51
Amoco and Texaco, 65
Anglo-Saxon, 48, 53, 54
Anglo-Saxon World, 43
Anti-Chinese Bureaucracy, 62
Anti-Social Elements, 268
Arabian Sea, 47, 166
Armed Forces, 107, 120
Arms Race, 25, 32, 33, 42, 131
Asia and Australia, 60
Asian Co-prosperity Sphere, 70
Asian Tigers, 17
Asia-Pacific Region, 60, 136
Asoka, 58
Atlantic, 32, 33
Atlantic and Pacific Oceans, 54
Aurangzeb, 17
Aurobindo, 195
Australia, 17, 48, 70
Avi Fauna, 181
Aviation Industry, 50

BIMARU States, 227, 231, 233
Balcans, 162
Baluchistan, 47
Baluchistan and Sind, 130
Bangladesh, 48, 133
Bangladesh-Pakistan, 221
Bartolomeu Dias, 104
Baltistan, 162
Bay of Bengal, 63, 64, 127, 133, 156, 166
Belgium, 32
Berlin Wall, 33
Bhutan, 113, 199
Bihar Model of Governance, 244, 258, 287
Brahmputra, 133, 166
British Empire, 72

CBI, 244, 245
CTBT, 18, 20, 23, 24, 28, 35, 97, 122, 123
Cairo Conference, 205, 230
Canberra Commission, 128
Capitalism, 194
Cardinal Principles of India's Foreign Policy, 144
Central Asia, 134, 135
Central Asian Region, 47, 161
Central Asian Republics, 161, 168
Central Paramilitary Forces, 244
Chambers of Commerce, 294
Charar-e-Sharief, 82, 83
Chechnya, 31
China, 16, 17, 18, 40, 51, 80, 89, 90, 94, 108, 109, 110, 112-115, 117-120, 124, 131-133, 136, 137, 139, 162, 164, 165, 167, 168, 169, 173, 176, 199, 201, 205, 228, 229, 290, 291
China and India, 58, 73, 74, 75, 76, 77
China and Japan, 256
China, Japan, Taiwan, Malaysia, 44

Chinese, 16
    Policy, 16
Chinese Game Plan, 52
Chumbi Valley, 119
Civil Services, 237
Civilization, 57
Cohen, William S., 128
Cold War, 37, 53, 71, 82, 94, 99, 103, 114, 135, 150, 227
Cold War Era, 33
Communism, 135
Communist Bloc, 32
Conference on Disarmament, 26
Constituent Assembly, 263
Constitution, 235, 236
Continental Europe, 53, 54
Counter Insurgency and Mountain Warfare School (CI&MWS), 160
Criminalisation of Politics, 261
Crony Capitalism, 139
Crown Colony, 62

Dalai Lama, 66, 165, 173
Danube River, 162
Darwinism, 194
David and Goliath, 102
Defence and Strategic Studies, Institute of, 128
Defence Planners, 17, 60, 64, 73
Defence Planning, 158
Defence Technologies, 131
Defence, Ministry of, 140
De-forestation, 166
Delhi High Court, 292, 293
De-militarisation of Himalaya, 199
De-militarization, 163
Demographic Terms, 207-208
Demographic Threat, 113
Deng Xiaoping, 61
Deng, 16
De-nuclearisation, 203
Dereservation, 260
    Process of -, 260
Developing Societies, 147, 151
Diego Garcia, 47

Disarmament, 21
    Nuclear, 21
Disarmament Conference, 25
East Asian Oil, 44
Eco-Management Institute, 167
Eco-Monitors Society, 162, 166
Economic Growth, 46
Economic Liberalization, 73, 139, 287
Economic Superpower, 17
Economic Warfare, 62
Eco-Patch, 180
Eco-Restoration of Himalayas, 192
Eco-Restoration Zone, 203
Eco-Revival Plan, 200
Eco-Revival Scheme, 189
Eco-Revival Summit, 184
Eco-System, 199
Eco-Tone Restoration Measures, 182, 183
Eco-Tone Restoration, 197
Eco-Violence, 194
Election(s), 19
Election Commission, 254, 261
Electro-Magnetic Interferences(EMI), 97
Electronic Counter Measures(ECM), 96
Emergency, 250, 251, 259, 271
Energy Sector, 46, 47
Ethical and Moral Decline, 41
Euphrates, 58
Europe and Canada, 53
European Community, 31
European Consortia, 47
European Languages, 55
European Union, 30, 31, 61, 64, 69
Exports, 49
    Indonesia, 49
    Malaysia, 49
    Philippines, 49
    Singapore, 49

FDI, 148
Falun Gung, 173
Falun Gung Sect, 167

Index

Family Planning, 206, 215, 219, 220, 222, 224, 229, 231, 232, 233
   Propogation, 219
   Reorientation, 217
Family Planning Programmes, 205, 212, 222, 225, 229, 233
Famine, 210
Female Literacy, 216
Fiscal Deficit, 247
Five Year Plans, 140
Flora and Fauna, 270
Formusa Straights, 61
France, 32
Freedom, 17

G-15, 35, 138, 139
G-77, 35, 56
GDP, 157
Gandhi, Indira, 250
Gandhi, Mahatama, 193, 195, 235, 238
Gandhian Leaders, 262
Gandhian Pacifism, 58
Gandhian Values, 262
Ganga Action Plan, 196-198
Gazprom and ONGC, 168
Gazprom, 46, 47
Gendum Choeki Nyima, 66
Geneva, 22-25, 122, 123
Genocide, 119
Germany, 32
Germany and Japan, 36
   Economies of -, 36
Global Inferno, 74
Global Media, 137
Global Military Competitors, 21
Global Technology, 95
Globalization, 73-75, 144, 147, 150
Gorbachev, Mikhail, 61
Great War, 94
Gulf War, 16, 96, 99, 117, 142

Himalayan Ecology, 162
Himalayan Glaciers, 166
Himalayan Military Deployment, 164

Hindukush, 124, 160
Hitech Paralysis, 96, 117, 118
Hitech Warfare, 96, 97
Homi Bhaba Principle, 228
Hydro-Carbon Reserve, 135

IMDF, 142
IMF, 49, 50, 66, 69, 137, 138
Independent Licensing Authority, 292
India, 17, 18, 20, 22, 34-36, 41, 44, 46, 50, 51, 52, 55, 57, 58, 60, 63, 66, 71, 72, 73, 77, 81-84, 89-92, 103, 104, 105, 107-110, 113-115, 118, 123-126, 127, 129, 130, 132, 134, 135, 136, 137, 139, 140, 141, 143, 144, 146, 151, 155, 157, 158, 161, 165-169, 173, 174, 176, 180, 187, 188, 190, 192, 199, 201, 205, 207, 213, 214, 221, 222, 224, 227, 229, 230, 235, 238, 245, 246, 249, 255, 257, 258, 265, 266, 270, 271, 278, 280-285, 287, 290
   Cultural and Spiritual Heritage, 192
   Defence, 104, 124
   Defence Planners, 131
   Economic and Cultural Relations, 136
   Economic Dominance, 57
   Foreign Policy, 104, 125, 134
      Cardinal Principles, 126
   Literacy, 264
   Media, 164
   Run Away Population Growth, 209
   Security Planning, 103, 105
   Spiritual Vastness, 284
   Wild Life, 177
India and China, 80, 164
India and Pak War, 81
Indian Army, 48, 115, 116, 158, 159, 160, 244, 257, 259
Indian Coast Guards, 141
Indian Defence Planners, 60

Indian Democracy, 255
Indian Industry, 95
Indian Navy, 141
Indian Ocean Region, 141, 156
Indian Ocean Rim, 123, 124, 141
Indian Ocean, 63, 157
Indian Polity, 146, 187
Indo-Gangetic Plain, 259
Indonesia, 50, 55, 61, 151
    Military Strength, 151
Indonesia, Malaysia and Singapore, 17
Indonesia, Thailand, Malaysia, 137
Indus, 58, 166
Industrial Pollution, 75
Industrial Revolution (Europe), 194
Infant Mortality, 214, 215
    Census, 214-215
    Indicators, 217
Insurgency, 244, 257
Inter Services Intelligence (ISI), 83
International Court of Justice, 163, 201-203
International Institute for Population Science (IIPS), 225
Intra-Regional Trade, 50
Iran and Turkey, 168
Iran Sirri Oil Fields, 45
Iran, 55, 134
Iran, Russia and China, 47
Iraq, 48, 96, 131
Iraqi Weapon System, 96
Islamic Bomb, 108

J&K, 160, 200
Japan, 17, 35, 36, 39, 45, 52, 53, 54, 56, 66, 67, 68, 70, 112, 169
Japan Indonesia Petroleum Company, 45
Jiang Zemin, 61
Joint Ecological Reserves, 167

Kabul, 83, 135, 257
Kanyakumari, 183
Karachi, 83

Kargil, 154, 155, 158, 159, 160, 161, 170, 172, 173, 200
Kashmir, 48, 127, 132, 183
Kashmir Issue, 161
Kerala Model, 227
Khomeini Revolution, 131
Kosovo and Kargil, 154
Kuwait and Saudi Arabia, 44-46
Kuwait Oil Company, 46

Ladakh, 162
Latin America, 54
Law and Order, 255, 266, 269
Law and Order Force, 237, 245, 251
Leaders, 58, 61, 82, 83, 88, 94, 161
    Baluchistan and Sind, 161
    Chinese, 58
    Indian, 58, 61, 83, 198
    Indian and Pakistanis, 82
    Military, 82, 94
    Western, 82
Lee Kuan Yew, 19, 118, 119
Lhasa, 19, 167
Libya and Saudi Arabia, 108
Limcolnesque, 21
Lok Sabha, 242, 261, 267, 272, 274, 276
Lok Sabha Elections, 225, 272
Low Intensity Conflict (LIC), 108

MAD (Modified Disarmament Treaty), 20, 24, 27, 28
Malabar Coast, 104
Malaysian Petronas, 45
Male Child Syndromes, 206
Malthusian, 145, 189
Manekshaw, Sam, 88
Mao, 61
Mason, Edward and Asher, Robert, 138
Matrilineal System, 227
Media Globalization, 280
Mediterranean and Balcan States, 54
Mekong, 166
Mi Zhenyu, 64

Index

Migrations, 113
    Reverse, 113
Military Blocs, 32
Military Commission, 170
Military Disparity, 17
Military Hierarchies, 31, 32
Military Industrial Infrastructure, 130
Military Leadership, 85
Military Planners, 63
Military Security, 150
Military Technology, 95, 100, 151
Ministries of -, 56
    Defence, 56
    Finance, 56
    Foreign Affairs, 56
Missiles and Nuclear Technology, 23
Model for Restoration of Good Government (MRGG), 236, 238, 239, 240, 241, 242, 243
    Aims and Objectives, 237
    Charter, 238
Model President's Rule, 266, 267
Models, 59, 60, 61, 62
    Explosive Expansion, 59, 61
    Implosion, 59, 62
    Study Expansion, 59, 60
Modernization, 74, 278
Moming Refinery, 46
Mortality Rates, 210
Mother Earth, 190
Mynamar, 64
Mynamar and Combodia, 65

NAM, 35
NATO, 30, 31, 33, 36, 69, 77, 94, 97
    Military Alliance, 31
NCC, 191
NGO, 25, 177, 185, 189, 191, 226, 294
NPT, 35
NRPs, 164
Napolean Bonaparte, 31
National Capital Region, 293
National Defence Academy, 188

National Defence Review Panel, 140-142
National Family Health Survey (NFHS), 223-225
National Income, 83
National Parks, 179
National Population Policy, 228
National Resources, 225
National Security, 22, 36, 37, 39, 40, 89, 92, 93, 109, 133, 160, 275
    Cold War -, 36
National Security Council (NSC), 18, 55, 116, 140, 141, 170
National Task Force (NTF), 196-198
Nehru Era, 119, 251
Nepal, 167, 199, 203
Nepal and Mynamar, 113
Netherlands, 32
New Societal Traumas, 284
New World Order, 76
Nile, 58
Non-Alligned Bloc, 32
Non-Asian Power, 17
Non-military Joint Commission, 201
Non-Nuclear Weapon States, 28
North and South America, 60
North and South Korea, 60
Northern Alliance, 47, 135
Nuclear Blackmail, 54
Nuclear Club, 35
Nuclear Disarmament, 24, 28, 123, 167
Nuclear Explosions, 35
Nuclear Holocaust, 74
Nuclear Missiles, 109
Nuclear Powers, 151
Nuclear Technology, 18
    China to Pakistan, 18
Nuclear Terrorism, 127
Nuclear War, 82
Nuclear Wastes, 166
Nuclear Weapons, 22, 31, 35, 54, 123, 127, 133, 158, 158
    Trading of -, 54
Nuclear Weapon States (NWS), 18, 24, 25, 27, 28

Nuclear Weapons Technology, 28
OPEC, 48
Oil route, 47
Oman and Qatar, 45, 46
Oman's Bhkha Oil Fields, 45

POK(Pakistan Occupied Kashmir), 127
Pacific Rim Nations, 17
Pakistan, 40, 47, 53, 54, 81-84, 101, 103-105, 107-112, 129, 130, 132, 133, 135, 156, 159, 160, 161, 163, 164, 173, 176, 200
    Army, 131
    Army Chief, 131
    Indian Policy towards -, 160
    Missiles and Nuclear Weapons, 54
    Shariat Bill, 164
    Society, 111
    Troops, 47
Panchen Lama, 66
Paris Cinema, 285
Parliamentary Committee, 141
Persian Gulf, 44
Petronet LNG Venture, 46
Planet Earth, 25
Planning Commission, 197, 228, 230
Police-Politician-Criminal Nexus, 178
Policy Studies, Institute for, 148
Political Anarchy, 246
Political Parties, 236, 249
Politico-Criminal Nexus, 252, 256
Population, 145, 146, 190, 205-208, 210-214, 217, 218, 220, 221, 225, 227, 231, 249, 276, 278, 279, 280
    Nepal, Bangladeah, Pak, 230
    Stablization, 213, 214, 225, 227, 249, 276
Population and Social Development Commission, 228
Population Commission, 228
Population Explosion, 227

Populations of -, 113
    Bangladesh, Nepal, Pakistan, 113
Portugal, 104
Post Cold War, 132
Post-Deng Xiaoping, 73
Poverty Line, 200
Private Sector, 146, 187
Programmed Democracy, 91
Project Manhattan, 44
Proxy War, 53, 82, 227
Public Interest Litigation (PIL), 294
Public Service Commission, 261
Punjab and Rajasthan, 108
Punjab Srilanka and Kashmir, 251

Qingdao, 45

Rajya Sabha, 254
Rapid Action Force, 151
Rasgas Project, 46
Regional Powers, 156
Reke, Lars, 109
Reservation Policies, 260
Revolution in Military Affairs (RMA), 150, 151
River Ganges (Ganga), 192, 196
River Systems, 165, 181
Robin Hood, 273
Roosevelt, 21
Royal Society for the Protection of Birds, 180
Rule of Law, 237, 257, 268

SAARC, 64, 113, 130, 131, 132, 138, 230
Saddam Hussain, 131
Salween, 166
Sansar Chand Poacher, 177
Sarkaria Commission, 265
Satluj, 166
Saudi Arabia, 47, 135
Scams, 139
    Bofors, 139
    Fertilizers, 139
    HDW, 139

Index

Scandal, 52, 251
  Bofors, 251
  Campaign Funds, 52
  Sexual, 52
Science and Technology, 134
Second Great War, 76
Second World War, 58, 94
Secret Laboratories, 21
Sector, 200, 201
  India, China, 201
  India, Pakistan, 200
  Ladakh, 200
  Pakistan, Afghanistan, 200
Security, 24, 36, 37, 44, 89, 91, 92, 108, 109, 112, 114, 116, 124, 132, 133, 150, 155, 156, 160, 171, 178, 256, 257, 273
  India, 91, 110, 116, 118
  Internal, 91, 92
  Military, 36
  Planning, 89
  Policy, 156, 160
Security Council, 18, 19, 23, 26, 35, 39, 71, 76, 89, 92, 118, 201
Security Options, 18
Siachin, 200, 201
Singapore, 90, 118
Skardu and Gilgit, 163
Socialism, 128
Societal Violence, 194
Solar System, 208
Somalia, 97
South Asia, 145
South China Sea, 68, 166
South East Asia 60, 64, 66, 70, 108, 113, 114, 124, 136-139, 156, 165, 169, 227
  Societies, 133
South East Asian Countries, 49-51
South Korea, 45, 137, 139
Soviet Empire, 72
Soviet Union, 31
Space Ventures, 134
Stalin, 31
Standstill Agreement, 27

Statistical Models of Growth, 287
  Hongkong, 287
  Singapore, 287
  South Korea, 287
  Taiwan, 287
Status of Forces Act (SOFA), 48
Studies in, 150
  Geo Economics, 150
  Geo Environmental, 150
  Geo Political, 150
Sun Tzu, 64
Supreme Court, 170, 196, 240, 261
Swaminathan, M.S., 228
Sweden, 109

TADA (Terrorist Apprehension and Detention Act), 270
Taiwan, 16, 67, 68, 69, 124, 136, 137, 173
Taiwan Straits, 16, 18, 19
Taj Mahal, 244
Taliban, 47, 48, 111, 135
Taliban Bogey, 48
Talibanization of Pak Society, 164
Technological and Military Security, 144, 150
Technology Transfer, 65, 131
Terrorism, 130
Terrorism, 157, 161
Thailand, 49
Third World, 35
Tibet, 58, 66, 73, 80, 113, 118, 199, 164-167, 173, 203
Tibet to China, 119
Tibetan Monks, 66
Tibetan Plateau, 165, 166
Timber Mafia, 177
Total Fertility Rate (TFR), 223
Trans-Himalayan Region, 203
Trans-National Corporation (TNC), 149
Transparency and Decentralization, 263
Trauma and Critical Care, International Conference, 283

UN, 26, 27, 48, 53, 76, 126,151, 154, 157, 162, 193
    Agencies, 157, 178
    General Assembly, 26, 122, 123, 127
    Member States, 26
    Secretary General, 162, 193
    Security Council, 26, 27, 48, 76, 126
    System, 39, 57, 126, 150, 152, 155, 215
UNCTAD, 148, 149
UNDP, 163
UNICEF, 215
Urals, 33
USA, 16, 18, 21, 36, 40, 41, 42, 43, 45, 46-49, 51-54, 60, 65, 67, 69, 70, 71, 74, 75, 90, 108, 110, 114, 128, 131, 134, 135, 146, 148, 149, 168, 173, 186
    Agencies, 34
    Arms Sale, 42
    Continental -, 67
    Declaration-Power, 41
    Demographic Changes in -, 42
    Justice Department, 52
    Military Establishment, 42
    Military Umbrella, 17
    Policy, 116
US Japan Defence Treaty, 136

Veto Right, 118
Vietnam War, 96
Vietnam, 94, 137
Vindhyas, 228
Violence, 248, 251
Vivekananda, 195

WNC (World Nuclear Council), 26, 27, 28
    Charter, 27
    Composition, 26

Warsaw Pact, 94
Washington, 20
Water Management Institute, 168
West Asia, 46, 54, 55
West Asian Oil Sector, 45
West Asian Oil, 44
Western Bloc, 32
Western Democracies Model, 74
Western Europe, 31, 32
Western Powers, 139
Western World, 33, 34, 35
    Powers, 34
Wild Life Habitat, 179
Women's Emancipation, 216, 268, 275
World Bank, 50, 69, 137, 138, 163, 178, 203
World Health Organization, 280
World War, 30, 31, 33, 34, 36
    First, 33
World Wild Life Fund, 163
WTO, 69

Xin Jing, 54

Yahya (Khan), 81
Yangtse, 58, 166
Year of Oceans, 193
Yellow River, 166
Youth Ecological Revival Party of India, 190
Youth Ecological Revival Fund, 188, 189
Yunnan Province, 64

Zojila, 162
Zones of -, 201
    Absolute Tranquility, 201
    Continuous Tranquility, 201
    Hostility, 201